Globalization, Communications and Caribbean Identity

Edited by
HOPETON S. DUNN

St. Martin's Press
New York

Printed in the U.S.A.
Text–cover design and production by
Prodesign Ltd., Kingston, Jamaica

ISBN 0-312-12764-2

Library of Congress Cataloging-in-Publication Data applied for

*The front cover incorporates a painting by the acclaimed Haitian
artist Valcin II, depicting the meeting of cultures on the arrival of
Christopher Columbus to the New World and the global challenges
which have since ensued. The work, commissioned by Christian
Aid, marks the quincentenary of the encounter, and is used with
permission, and thanks to the artist.*

First Edition 1995

CONTENTS

LIST OF ABBREVIATIONS

AM	Amplitude Modulation
AT&T	American Telephone & Telegraph Company
BARTEL	Barbados Telephone Company
BBC	British Broadcasting Corporation
BCS	Bar Code System
BET	Barbados External Telecommunications
C&W	Cable and Wireless
CACR	Caribbean Association for Communications Research
CANA	Caribbean News Agency
CARICOM	Caribbean Community and Common Market
CARIMAC	Caribbean Institute of Mass Communications
CBC	(1) Caribbean Broadcasting Corporation (Barbados)
	(2) Canadian Broadcasting Corporation
CBU	Caribbean Broadcasting Union
CIM	Computer Integrated Manufacturing
COMSAT	Communication Satellite Corporation
CRTC	Canadian Radio and Television Commission
CSN	Caribbean Satellite Network
CTU	Caribbean Telecommunications Union
CUSO	Canadian University Services Overseas
DAT	Digital Audio Tape
DBS	Direct Broadcast by Satellite
DECFS	Digital Eastern Caribbean Fibre System
DECMS	Digital Eastern Caribbean Microwave System
EMPROTEL	Empresa de Proyectos de Commucaciones (Cuba)
EXIS	Exporters of Information Services
FCC	Federal Communications Commission (USA)
FDI	Foreign Direct Investment
FM	Frequency Modulation
FMS	Flexible Manufacturing System
FSA	Firm-Specific Advantages
FTC	Fair Trading Commission (Jamaica)

GATT	General Agreement on Tariffs and Trade
HDTV	High Definition Television
IDT	International Discount Telecommunications
INTELSAT	International Telecommunications Satellite Organization
ISDN	Integrated Services Digital Network
ITU	International Telecommunications Union
JAMINTEL	Jamaica International Telecommunications Ltd.
JBC	Jamaica Broadcasting Corporation
JIE	Jamaica Institution of Engineers
JIT	Just-in-Time (Production)
KBPS	Kilo bits per second
Ku Band	Transmission frequencies between 12.5 and 18 GHz
LEDS	Light Emitting Diodes
LSA	Location Specific Advantages
MBPS	Mega bits per second
NAFTA	North American Free Trade Association
NASA	National Aeronautics and Space Administration (USA)
NATPE	National Association of Television Programme Executives
NGO	Non-governmental Organization
NTSC	National Television Standards Committee
OECD	Organization for Economic Co-operation and Development
OLR	Optical Line Reader
OLTP	On-line Transaction Processing
PAL	[Scheme for TV signals employed in Western Europe and many former colonies]
PBS	Public Broadcasting System (USA)
RAM	Random Access Memory
ROM	Read Only Memory
SECAM	[Scheme for TV signals (used in France and Eastern Europe)]
STV	Subscription Television (Subscriber TV service in Barbados)
TCI	Tele-communications Incorporated
TCS-1	Trans-Caribbean Cable System
TOJ	Telecommunications of Jamaica
TTT	Trinidad & Tobago Television
TVRO	Television Receive-only Installations
UHF	Ultra High Frequency
UNCTAD	United Nations Committee on Trade and Development
UNESCO	United Nations Educational, Scientific and Cultural Organization
USAID	United States Agency for International Development
UWI	University of the West Indies
UWIDITE	University of the West Indies Distance Teaching Enterprise
VHF	Very High Frequency

ACKNOWLEDGEMENTS

My first expression of thanks goes to the contributors of the various chapters in this edited volume. Without exception, they responded positively and enthusiastically to the invitation to present the results of on-going research and to contribute the fruits of their critical analyses towards the creation of this book. Both the contributors from within the region and those who work in institutions outside of the Caribbean, made special efforts to keep the flow of dialogue, diskettes and manuscripts going, and for this we are indebted to them.

This book is the development of a long-standing shared interest in communications technology and global communication policies. The preliminary outline was developed while teaching on the MA Communications Policy Programme at City University, London. I wish to thank Professor Jill Hills for her invaluable support and for recommending many of the critical readings which have helped to develop my thinking in this area. Planning for the publication was advanced further on my return to Jamaica. The catalyst was a regional workshop on Globalization, to which I was invited as a speaker by CUSO. The issue of globalization and Non-Governmental Organizations (NGOs) was the central theme and the event provided an opportunity to explore further my ideas on the issue. I am indebted to CUSO's former Caribbean Regional Field Officer, Selena Tapper for placing the issue of globalization so urgently on the regional agenda of action and for her encouragement and practical support in the production of this book.

My profound thanks also to the Director of CARIMAC, Prof. Aggrey Brown, and to the academic staff and students of the Institute for the supportive and collegial environment within which to pursue this project.

My wife Leith, a Sociologist and Project Development Consultant, was a constant sounding-board, supporter and critic who made very valuable inputs at various stages in the process. Beverly Pereira, Mark Figueroa, Dorothy Hollingsworth, Sonia Gill and Marcia Forbes all provided much needed feedback, practical support and encouragement, for which I am grateful. To colleague members of the Caribbean Association for Communication Research (CACR), I also express appreciation for their critical academic support and friendship.

Finally to my children, Jessica and Jamani and members of my extended family, I say thanks for your constant help and understanding.

Hopeton S. Dunn, Ph.D.
University of the West Indies, Mona.

FOREWORD

The rapid and profound technological changes which have occurred in recent years, have ushered in a new era in world economy, which is distinguished by a comprehensive globalization of all spheres of economic activity. Advances in electronic data interchange, establishment of systems for the computer controlled trans-shipment and clearance of goods, improved voice and data communication networks, automated banking and international telemarketing have defined the character of economic activity. Global society and international politics have been transformed by developments in telecommunications technology, which have revolutionized the speed and conduct of all aspects of global interaction — economic, social and political. The instant global availability of information via satellite, computers and telecommunications technology has the potential to change, irrevocably, all aspects of human life.

It is culture which binds societies together and ensures that social interaction is practised on the basis of commonly accepted norms and behaviour patterns. Accompanying homogenization of ideas and behaviour patterns reduce cultural diversity. This is particularly evident in young people who are the most exposed to global media, the least immune, and who consequently exhibit a remarkable similarity in taste and consumption patterns. Modern societies cannot be insulated against the media and further integration into a global society, but do not have to succumb to an homogenous global culture, which is functionally integrated with global production and consumption.

In political relations, the integrity of the nation-state, the notions of sovereignty and national identity all require re-examination, given these global changes. Global media have aggravated tensions between developed and developing countries, as they reveal for all to see the vast gap in standards between rich and poor, exacerbating social contradiction and international tension. At the same time, global communications media have also established world public opinion as a potent force in international relations and a significant factor in the internal politics of countries, as evidenced in the liberation of South Africa and the implosion of communism.

At the same time that economic forces and the availability of information have become global, there has been a countervailing movement towards smaller social units. This is evident in a major resurgence in nationalism and ethnicity. Even as the nation-state yields to the amalgamation of the national economies into transnational blocs, there is an accompanying psychological impact, characterized by a feeling of being overwhelmed and disoriented. Individuals seek, but often can no longer find a secure sense of identity in the political and social formation of the nation-state. Inevitably, identity begins to be located in culture, race, language and ethnicity, which both transcend and fragment the society and the nation-state. The individual's attachment to smaller groups, threatens traditional societal identity.

Caribbean countries have been continuously exposed to international media in the form of books, magazines, periodicals, radio broadcasts (including shortwave), and more recently a bombardment of TV channels, particularly those originating in North America, transmitted by satellite technology. This has had a profound impact on Caribbean lifestyles, consumer habits and patterns of behaviour. To the extent that exposure has escalated, there is corresponding erosion of Caribbean identity, as by osmosis, external influences begin to permeate all aspects of life and begin to change, or at least threaten, the uniqueness of Caribbean identity.

These issues raise profound political, economic and ethical policy questions for Caribbean societies. How resistant Caribbean cultures are to these global influences, the policy approaches to the region's use of technologies and the Caribbean's own contribution to global culture are among the central issues raised by this very valuable book. Its focus on globalization is both pertinent and timely, as the volume correctly links change in telecommunications technology with rapid globalization of economic processes, information and cultural patterns, while analysing their impact on Caribbean society and identity.

The book, edited by Hopeton Dunn, sounds a timely warning that the Caribbean, in common with many other regions of the world, could become a society which is even more fragmented by externally acquired behaviour patterns and cultures. It points us in the direction of a more thoughtful and selective approach to policy-planning in an era of globalization.

Richard L. Bernal
Jamaican Ambassador to the United States

INTRODUCTION

This book explores the social and cultural implications of the most recent phase in the on-going, combined development of communications and information technologies and the policy and regulatory issues spawned by their emergence. It does so against the background of increasing global, as distinct from national, patterns of economic and cultural interaction. In this emergent globalized process, the boundaries of political, economic, military and cultural activities are becoming de-linked from national borders. The technologies have brought once remote regions of the world into on-going daily contact, in effect, dramatically contracting old conceptions of time and distance.

Satellite, microwave and fibre-optic cable transmission systems have combined with digital switching and advanced computer techniques to enable constant distribution of cultural products and information across national borders in real time. Variations and combinations of these technologies have led to a wide range of global applications. So-called multi-media systems, High Definition Television (HDTV), satellite-based transborder communications technologies, high-volume fibre-optic transmission systems, large-scale electronic publishing and sophisticated data storage and retrieval systems are all among the innovations which are either in advanced stages of development or are already being marketed as part of the tool-kit of a process described as Globalization.

Increasingly, we now expect live and immediate coverage of major world events, regardless of where they are occurring. In the aftermath of the historic 1994 South African elections, for example, millions of people around the world looked forward to sharing in the graphic presentation of Nelson Mandela's inauguration, as they did in the epic moment of his release from prison three years earlier. Equally, the crowd-stopping drama of the final few minutes in Brian Lara's record-breaking Test cricket innings in Antigua was as much a spectacle for cricket enthusiasts in the Caribbean as it was for their counterparts in Britain or Pakistan.

The enabling technological innovations have had both positive and negative effects globally. They result in intended and un-intended consequences for the political sovereignty and cultural identity of recipient societies and peoples. The same technologies which enable the live transmission of the happy events are also the ones being used in the deployment of deadly new weapons systems around the world. Indeed, many of the technologies had their origin in military research and development (R&D). Armed conflicts, such as the Gulf War, graphically demonstrate the enlarged and refined destructive capabilities inherent in technologies of even conventional warfare. Not only were the military strategists able to claim use of the new weapons systems with computer-aided precision, but the world media systems were also able, by satellite, to 'bring the war into people's homes'. Selected aspects of the warfront action, involving techniques of ballistic interception, laser-guided precision missiles and weapons mounted with infra-red night-sights were among the staple television output of the conflict. And we find that events in distant locations are often more available on television in the Caribbean than information originating in our own rural areas or in neighbouring regional capitals.

In industry and commerce, similar developments have made it easier to procure raw materials and supplies from far-flung global locations. Contract Electronic Manufacturing (CEM), for example, now enables the establishment of large or small world market factories for specialised global distributors, each requiring rapid completion times, premium quality and the flexibility to respond to sudden changes in market trends and individual customer specifications.

The Commonwealth Caribbean region in common with most under-developed territories of the world, is on the receiving end of much of this technological innovation, designed mainly to meet the requirements of the industrialised north. But, some of these technologies, global by their very nature and their social impact, can offer important opportunities to address productivity, developmental and communications needs of our people. Technological applications in the delivery of such services as health care, in the provision of distance education and the availability of interactive self-teaching facilities can enhance the quality of life in our societies. The re-generation of traditional agriculture through advances in bio-technology, improved customer services in the banking and the financial sector, the creation of new and more productive means of employment, and the possibility of systems-reform in the administration of both the governmental and non-governmental (NGO) sectors are also among the potential or actual benefits of the on-going techno-scientific revolution. At the same time, other aspects of the technologies can place our region at a disadvantage, particularly when, as recipients, we become uncritical hosts or fail to ensure our own independent understanding of the social and policy implications of these innovations.

In acknowledging the scale and potential of the changes underway, the Director of the United Nation Research Institute for Social Development (UNRISD), Dharam Ghai, has observed that 'the dominant economic and political paradigms will need radical re-thinking to come to terms with the new reality.' Globalization, he notes, 'is certain to exercise an increasing influence on the pace and pattern of growth of the world economy.... . Its implications for national political and social processes and international governance are far-reaching and startling.' [Ghai 1992 : i].

The process of globalization has been boosted over the last decade by a shift in favour of market forces, as well as in the wide-spread adoption of policies of de-regulation and economic liberalization. International cross-border flows of people, data, capital, technology and services are already so extensive as to give rise to real concerns that the political sovereignty of countries is being undermined. The state is increasingly unable to monitor the flow of assets and of encoded information across its borders into computer-based international markets. And the inward flow of television news and entertainment programming are transmitted and received at will, without regard to any national communications policies in force in 'recipient' societies. Faster and cheaper air travel facilitates tourism, while more attractive pay and living conditions provide a magnet for enhanced out-migration of both skilled and unskilled labour.

International diplomacy, too, has had to adjust to the implications of these changes. The traditional information-providing and negotiating roles of an ambassador are being re-defined in an era when direct tele-conferencing among heads of government and foreign ministers are commonplace, and where satellite communications allow for trans-border intelligence-gathering and information flows beyond the capacity of embassies. In the Caribbean, as in many other parts of the world, multi-lateral financial agencies exercise transborder jurisdiction over important national economic decision-making. And the global character of such issues as the illegal trade in drugs and the degradation of the environment all defy solutions by any single national entity.

Even while we witness challenges to the nation state by supra-national processes and powerful concentrations of economic and military power, countervailing patterns of global diversity and fragmentation have also emerged to defy the existing order from below. In some instances, long existing ethnic or religious identities have arisen internally to confront the concept of geographical jurisdiction or of a unified country. Anglo-French tensions in Canada, Irish, Scottish and Welsh nationalism in United Kingdom politics, muslim militancy in Trinidad and Tobago and the ethnic de-construction in the former Soviet empire all provide ample evidence of this process. Nietschmann identifies '5000 distinct communities in the contemporary world [that] might claim that they are national peoples on grounds that they share common ancestry, institutions, beliefs, language and territory.' [Neitschmann in Boulding: 1993: 229]. Yet the modern world is divided up into 168 nation states, many subsuming diverse ethnicities.

In the Caribbean, historical patterns of out-migration to Latin America, Britain, the United States and Canada are now creating new cultural entities which interact positively and negatively, with their host societies as well as with their societies of origin. As from the global north in a previous era, such migrants from the south, arrive with already existing cultural and social lifestyles, which they have continued to practice. This trend, on a wider scale, represents both a source of cultural globalization as well as contributing to the fragmentation of pre-existing norms in the host society. 'Modernization theory', says Boulding, 'assumes that ethnic groups will be assimilated into modern nation-states. Yet, supposedly extinct ethnicities are reappearing at a rapid rate, and new ones are created as migrant streams from the Third World settle in First World societies and create new hybrid cultural identities, distinct from those of the society in which they have settled.' [Boulding 1993: 213].

It is often argued that the very existence of this ethnic and cultural diversity is threatened by the homogenizing, centrifugal force of the emergent global systems, which convey transcultural values via the new communications technologies. This approach sees the diverse lifestyles, work ethic and cultural expressions of recipient societies being reached at source, within homes and communities, by way of global satellite television, among other media. Assimilation of such target populations into the cultural milieu of the transmitting society would then become routine. But important questions are raised by other analysts: Are societies such as the Caribbean passive recipients of the output of the global North or are they engaged both in contributing to global culture as well as in the re-interpretation and selective assimilation of received information or entertainment? It is precisely this issue which forms one of the central concerns of this book.

This volume seeks to make a contribution to a better understanding of both the advantages as well as the deficiencies of technical innovations in the sphere of global communications. The implication of these developments for cultural identity and for political sovereignty are explored. While the focus is primarily on the communications sector of the global technological panorama, the technologies do have an extensive reach into all sectors in the global economy and society. Accordingly, the approach in this book is inter-disciplinary, examining by way of a varied range of specialists, the different elements which have a bearing on the issues.

Part 1 provides an overview of the central themes: Globalization, Communications Technologies and Cultural Identity. In the opening chapter, Dorith Grant-Wisdom begins the discussion with a detailed examination of the concept of globalization. She discusses the prevailing 'techno-paradigm shift from material capital and physical labour to intellectual capital and intellectual labour.' Grant-Wisdom argues that services are not becoming a substitute for manufacturing. The real impact of the technologies 'lies in the erosion of the boundaries between manufacturing and services, and the concomitant spread of production on a global scale.' The chapter provides the economic framework and analytical context for later discussions of the prevailing trends in technology policy both in the Caribbean region and globally.

Chapter 2 takes as its point of departure the numerous innovations which have transformed the manner in which information is generated, stored and transmitted globally. Among the issues examined by Hopeton Dunn are the increasing convergence between broadcasting and telecommunications, the use of the radio spectrum and the economic and social cost of inadequate advance assessments and adaptation of the global technologies, whose development is motivated by the transnational corporate quest for greater profits. In Chapter 3, Aggrey Brown argues that present conceptions of cultural imperialism are misconceived, and that 'the very concept of cultural imperialism itself is a misdiagnosis.' Presented against the background of over a decade of satellite exposure of Caribbean audiences to large scale foreign television programme content, the chapter argues controversially that the people of the region are 'willing consumers' and that 'cultural ennui is the price we pay for passive consumption.'

Part 2 of the book presents case studies and analyses on the issue of audiences and imported media content. Studies are presented from Jamaica, Trinidad and Tobago, Barbados and Canada. Reporting in Chapter 4 the results of original research, Hilary Brown hypothesises that 'the underlying, unobserved concept of cultural dependency has multiple observed causes and multiple observed indicators.' She uses survey data and the Multiple Indicators, Multiple Causes (MIMIC) variety of structural equation modelling to evaluate 'American Media Impact on Jamaican Youth'. The comparative study of three locales, explores the connection between such variables as international travel, exposure to foreign media and rural/urban residency as factors contributing to pro-American attitudes, high knowledge levels about the U.S., negative attitudes to Jamaican culture and high levels of consumerism among Jamaican youth.

In another empirical study, Lynette Lashley reports in Chapter 5, the result of survey research conducted among students of four secondary level schools in Trinidad and Tobago. Her findings indicate a strong influence of foreign programming on youth attitudes to attire, speech, entertainment preferences and preferred country of residence.

Chapter 6 presents an analysis of television programming policy in Barbados by Cheryl Renee Gooch. The case study systematically examines factors which mitigate against the development of coherent policies governing media systems in Barbados. Many of the findings and arguments are equally applicable elsewhere in the region and in many other developing countries. The study benefits from interviews with a wide cross section of key informants, including ministers responsible for broadcasting, statutory board chairmen, media managers, journalists, advertising executives and educators. The final contribution in Part 2 provides a reflective overview by Robert Martin on Canada's experience in wrestling with similar issues of American cultural influence on its northern neighbour. Professor Martin pointedly observes that 'the central lesson to be drawn from the Canadian experience is that the most effective means of challenging foreign programming is the creation of national programming.' He argues that 'producing local programmes is ferociously expensive' partly because 'we have all come to expect the 'production values' of U.S. network programming.'

Part 3 of the book focuses on telecommunications and globalization. Chapter 8, by Hopeton Dunn highlights issues in the on-going debate of tele-communications policies in Jamaica and other countries in the English-speaking Caribbean. It discusses why, in divesting their telecommunications services, governments in the region have also divested regulatory control. The role of the International Monetary Fund is presented as part of an analysis which argues that economic dependence on the global system, severe indebtedness as well as failures in domestic and regional policy-making have mediated on the side of strengthening the monopoly transnational service provider, Cable and Wireless.

In Chapter 9, Beverley Mullings discusses telecommunications re-structuring and the development of export processing services. Based on her 1994 study, Mullings reports that 'Instead of becoming an industry which provides foreign exchange earnings, jobs and technical skills, export information processing in Jamaica remains at the low end of the information processing industry.' She argues that the monopoly position held by Telecommunications of Jamaica, a subsidiary of Cable and Wireless, has restricted the growth of the country's export processing industry. In addition, a lack of government support, poor marketing and inadequate training have stunted the potential of the sector.

Chapter 10 goes beyond the English speaking Caribbean with an analysis of the technical and policy development in the Cuban telecommunications industry. An analysis by Hopeton Dunn and Felipe Noguera argues that policy changes both in the U.S. and in Cuba regarding telecom access to Cuba, resulted from economic pressures within both Cuba and the United States itself. The American transnational telephone lobby has been demanding greater liberalization by the US State department in the face of potential competition by European companies for the gradually re-opening Cuban telecommunications market. These requirements, as well as acute economic and social pressures in Cuba itself, are converging to pry open the hitherto highly restricted Cuban telecom environment.

The concluding section of the book, Part 4, addresses the important regulatory and ethical issues in the debate on communications and globalization. Using as a case study the deficiencies in the regulatory environment for broadcasting and telecommunications in Jamaica, Martin Mordecai argues, in Chapter 11, for an informed refurbishment of existing laws and institutions in the region's communications sector. 'Telecommunications and broadcasting are still being governed by legislation written in the 1920s and 1940s respectively. The regulatory agencies reflect, in their structure, the realities of those times, while the resources available to them are derisory by any measure. 'Combining both historical and contemporary analyses, Mordecai assesses the regulatory implications of the already evident convergence between broadcasting and telecommunications: 'Before tomorrow's putative regulators ask themselves the question: How do I regulate?, they must ask the question: What am I seeking to regulate?'

Pradip Thomas provides a thought-provoking, concluding analysis on ethics in the new era of globalization. He advocates a strategy of diffusing the power and dehumanizing influences of global systems by building alliances and strengthening ethical demands from below. 'An exercise in ethics-building that evolves from the bottom up, will be able to contest the power of information as "surveillance", the invasion of privacy, and the dominance of corporate entities or governments over resources.'

Overall, then, the book provides valuable insights into the implications for the South of the on-going globalization of economics, politics, culture and communications. It does so from the perspective of a region, which maybe more than any other, has experienced the multiple and diverse consequences of this process. The fundamental issue of how combinations of exogenously-generated innovations have affected audiences, policies, cultural identity and ethical values, forms the central motif of this volume. Original research and comparative policy analyses are presented by an inter-disciplinary team of academics, analysts and researchers in communications, economics, law and international relations. The exploration of relevant policy issues, the critical perspectives as well as discussions on the technologies themselves form, part of the wider global debate on coping as human beings, with dramatic transformations in our conception of time, space and distance.

Hopeton S. Dunn

References

Boulding, Elise — Ethnicity and New Constitutive Orders in Jeremy Brecher, John Brown Childs and Jill Cutler — Global Visions: Beyond the New World Order, South End Press, Boston, 1993 pp 213-231.

Ghai Dharam — Preface — in Keith Griffin and Azizur Rahman Khan -Globalization and the Developing World: An Essay on the International Dimensions of Development in the Post-Cold War Era, United Nations Research Institute for Social Development, Geneva, 1992 p v-vi.

PART ONE

Exploring the Central Issues

1

THE ECONOMICS OF GLOBALIZATION:
IMPLICATIONS FOR COMMUNICATIONS AND THE SERVICE SECTOR

Dorith Grant-Wisdom

INTRODUCTION

If one should look at a map, there are clearly defined boundaries that separate the various countries of the world, reinforcing a sense of territoriality, identity and nationality. In reality these boundaries are becoming less important, because the economic logic which made them useful lines in the first place is being undermined by the phenomenon called globalization. The world is increasingly being confronted with changes that affect humankind as a whole. These issues present challenges, ranging from the economic requirements for human development to the critical issues of communications, energy and ecology, health, education, food and employment, genetics, and bio-technology.

This chapter seeks to decode the inner logic of the new economic environment, looking at communications in relation to other broad changes that are occurring worldwide. This treatment is meant to provide a conceptual understanding of the issue of globalization, using the Caribbean as a frame of reference. The expanding nature of services is discussed in relation to the restructuring of methods of production. Trade in services is then examined, highlighting the change in the pattern and volume of world trade, especially within the financial sector. The catalytic and integrating role of information technology and telecommunications are also considered especially in relation to territoriality.

Before giving a working definition for globalization, it is important to quickly look at some other terms in order to provide more clarity. Terms which are in everyday use, like 'domestic,' 'international,' and 'multinational' now have to be re-examined for their more precise application within the new environment. They are words which we frequently employ in describing economies, firms, products and services. In our usage here, 'domestic' refers to the domain of a single economy. It implies that area which is presided over by the government, and falls within specific geographical limits. 'International' is the term used for activities or relations that take place between nations. It assumes the presence of nations with territories and domestic jurisdiction. 'Multinational' means that there are activities taking place in more than one nation and again implies that sovereign borders are maintained.

The term 'global' is then, a combination of elements of 'international' and 'multinational,' but with a strong degree of integration between the different national parts. It is therefore used in reference to activities within an integral whole. Whenever nations interact, if the national distinction is still important, then the term international is used. If there is integration of interconnections that blur the national borders, then global is regarded as the more appropriate term.

Globalization is therefore, a process that refers to operations within the whole globe. It speaks to the intensification of political, economic and social interconnectedness between states and people, thus blurring geographical boundaries. In addition, despite the fact that all aspects of people's lives seem to be becoming more and more linked to others in other countries, it is the economy that tends to be the driving force towards globalization.

It is important to emphasize that globalization is a historical process which is taking a different form in its contemporary emergence. The process is a dynamic one, whose ultimate logic lies in the axiom that 'a truly global services knows no internal boundaries.' The reality is that nation-states are still significant in the present era and are likely to be around for some time to come. There is no denying, however, the pulling force of global tendencies towards the end of the twentieth century.

THE EXPANSION OF SERVICES AND GLOBALIZATION
THE INTEGRATING ROLE OF COMMUNICATIONS

Restructuring of Industry and Expansion of Services

A major feature of the historical development of capitalism is the growth of the division of labour and specialization. Influenced by technological revolutions, this advancing division of labour was first characteristic of industry itself and later developed in agriculture. The more advanced the division of labour and specialization, the greater was the importance of intermediate functions and the transport system. This importance increased at a rapid pace with the diffusion of advanced technology throughout the industrial, agricultural and service sectors. The division of labour now acquires a new dimension with the erosion of traditional boundaries that separated the sectors of economic activities. Automation now pervades all sectors with the increasing application of technology to services.

The emergence of 'high technology' has ushered in a new era characterized by a techno-paradigm shift manifested in: the redefinition of the manufacturing company from being a place for production to being a place for thinking; the business dynamics; the innovation pattern and technology diffusion. The new reality is that the corporations that are most profitable no longer engage in mass (high-volume) production. They have restructured and shifted to high-value production in which services are playing an integral role. Unlike mass production which derives benefits from economies of scale, higher profits now accrue from high-value production through economies of scope. The most important difference between the two lies in the nature of the technology of production. The capability of high-value production rests on various forms of automation such as flexible specialization. Flexibility lies in the fact that machinery is now reprogrammed rather than replaced when there is a switch to a new product. In addition, there is now a diversified range of products with product lives fundamentally reduced through machine technology such as Computer Integrated Manufacturing (CIM) and Just-In-Time (JIT) production. According to Kodama:

> The technological capability level of FMS (Flexible Manufacturing System) should be higher than that of mass production by a factor of one or two, in every aspect from process accuracy, quality control, reliability, maintenance, through worker skill requirements....FMS can exist only when both machines and men are capable of a very much higher technical level than in mere mass production system... Thus, it has become possible for manufacturing companies to increase R&D (Research and Development) which is related to the future.

The application of the new technology of production results in an increased specialization of services. For instance, the complexity of high-value production requires that producer services be rendered throughout production. An UNCTAD study has identified the service inputs required at the following stages in the production process:

1. Up-stream: pre-production service inputs, such as pre-feasibility and feasibility studies, venture capital, product design and market research.

2. On-stream: service inputs incorporated into production, such as quality control, equipment leasing, maintenance and repair.

3. On-stream parallel: supportive service inputs required for the operation of a firm, such as accounting, human resource management, legal services, telecommunications and information networks, insurance, finance, real estate, security and cleaning.

4. Downstream: post-production service inputs, such as after-sales services and maintenance, advertising, shipping and distribution.

Producer services are therefore critical in raising the profit margins of the manufacturing industry by holding on to the value added that they generate. It is in light of the pursuit of 'total quality' that companies such as Boeing, Xerox and Apple are integrating services into R&D and product development, increasing the relative contribution of knowledge.

A central aspect of the techno-paradigm shift is the increasing importance of knowledge in the production of wealth. There is a rapid decrease in the value of raw materials relative to the information and technology in the selling price of finished products. Wherein mass production harnessed human and mechanical energy relative to the knowledge input,

> the fundamental product of the information age, the microchip, the key component of all modern communications and computer technology, consists almost entirely of information. Raw materials represent about one percent of its costs; labor of the traditional sort accounts for another five percent. A majority of the cost — and value — comes from the information incorporated into the design of the chip itself and into the design and development of the highly specialized equipment used to manufacture it.

Accelerating scientific knowledge has increased in value as products and processes consist more of the power of the mind than of matter. This means that capital and technology are more focused on knowledge and service worker productivity, indicating the shift in importance from material capital and physical labour to intellectual capital and intellectual labour.

Grasping the new reality of this techno-paradigm shift negates the thesis of the arrival of a 'post-industrial' service economy, where the central role played by manufacturing is steadily being replaced by new service industries and service jobs. Services are not becoming a substitute for manufacturing. The process of development amidst technological changes, 'is not one of sectoral succession but instead it is one of increased sectoral interdependence driven by an ever extended and complex division of labor...we are not entering a post-industrial economy, we are shifting from one kind of industrial economy to another.' The real impact therefore lies in the erosion of the boundaries between manufacturing and services, and the concomitant spread of production on a global scale.

Globalization of Production and Services

Globalization has to be seen in relation to two fundamental changes in the process and structure of production. First, flexible specialization allows for product differentiation tailored to more discriminating consumer tastes and needs. The technology of production is such that firms can now produce more and different commodities beyond the capacity of national markets, so the realization of surplus profit in part, can no longer be maintained within the framework of the nation-state. The changing environment for gaining profit has ushered in a new era of intense competition. There is the pressure for constant innovation so that each new cycle of production will proceed with an increase of value over the previous one. Competition becomes more vital as a result of the pressure of emerging tendencies toward full automation. The innovative pattern not only allows for product differentiation but shorter product cycles and lives to the extent that new products or processes are introduced before the learning process is complete on the previous innovation. This creates for each enterprise the risk of being left behind in the competitive struggle. There is therefore no choice but to invest to ride the wave of innovation, or be left behind by competitors.

The real consequences of all this is a shift in the emphasis of the activity of capital. The critical factor in terms of profit lies in the selection and not in the running of production processes. The decision now rests on what, where and how production will take place, which in turn is increasingly global in scale. This globalization of production is reflective of the second fundamental change in the technology of production. Flexible specialization enables the production process to be broken down into various subprocesses and subassemblies of parts and components. This facilitates interfirm linkages with each firm specializing in one or a few subprocesses or subassemblies.

In the face of falling profits and increased competition, the structural pressure exerted by technological innovation puts the cost of many research projects beyond the financial means of individual firms. The new organization of production allows for the coordination of efforts. Competitive advantage is attained through strategic partnerships and contractual arrangements making production fragmented and dispersed in many geographical locations.

In addition, the range and complexity of the services that are now required are becoming more and more demanding for single firms resulting in the externalization of service functions formerly performed in-house. Many firms are finding it more cost-effective and easier to de-integrate and purchase these services from outside specialist suppliers. For example, it is more economical to out-source with an independent firm for research and development than to commit substantial resources to procuring the technology or licensing.

The range of services to facilitate these changes have expanded with rapid technological diffusion. The horizontal spread of production beyond and across borders has increased the growth of services to support trade and the management of dispersed corporate activities. It therefore means that globalization of services is the inevitable corollary to the globalization of production, especially in the realm of communications. The critical importance of communications in particular comes to the fore; for the coordination and linkage of the various service inputs within and outside of the firm, could not be maintained without advanced telecommunications systems and information networks.

The Integrating Role of Telecommunications

To enter the world of high-value production based on flexible automation, a telecommunications network must be established. It is now possible to build a different kind of organizational structure of flatter networks in various geographical areas, with the availability of technology to provide access to the information required for functioning and collaborating. The higher levels of information exchange are the resulting effects of advances in electronics and telecommunications. Prior to the 1950s, computer and communications technologies were two distinct worlds, with improvements in each sphere occurring separately. There was the provision of communication pathways for analogue voice transmission on the one hand, with stand-alone large computers on the other. By the 1970s, the mechatronics revolution (combining mechanics and electronics) and the optoelectronics revolution (combining electronics and optics) engendered a new era of technology fusion.

The merge between communications and computing (now termed information technology) results in two things. Firstly, there is the provision of enhanced communications through voice, data, video and facsimile using computer technology; the change being dependent on the digitization of information. Transmission of data is more effective in the digital rather than analogue form because switching, i.e., connecting one subscriber to another, can be done electronically. Secondly, computers have moved towards networks of geographically separate computers interconnected through communications pathways for data transmissions. On top of this, the traditional mode of transmission via the copper wire is now challenged by microwaves, fiber optics, cellular mobile radio, coaxial cables, and communication satellites. The proliferation of innovative transmission and distributed switching technologies that have ensued, have tremendously altered production and services and changed the nature of competition.

The new technology has facilitated the shift to a 'new organizational paradigm' with the rise of the open, networked enterprise. According to Tapscott and Caston, there are three fundamental shifts in the application of information technology, with each affecting a different level of business opportunity. The first shift is from personal to work-group computing which enables enterprises to have a high-performance team structure. This enhances productivity and improves responsiveness. Shift number two is from system islands to integrated systems, making it possible to generate an entire enterprise architecture for the new open networked enterprise. The latter can function cohesively, providing corporate-wide information for decision-making and new competitive enterprise applications through electronic means. The third shift from internal to inter-enterprise computing enables enterprises to reach out and develop new relationships with external organizations; allowing for outward links to suppliers, distribution channels, and consumers. With information being the strategic new resource, technologically advanced telecommunications are the threads linking organizations and people in a combination of skills and ideas across states. These technologies play a crucial role in establishing a symbiotic linkage between manufacturing and services. The problem of geography is reduced even for service enterprises for:

> The advent of more efficient logistics and telecommunications systems combined with the introduction of information technology in the value chain and into many physical products has meant that some service functions can be performed at a location remote from the buyer. Diagnostic programs run over the telephone, can check and sometimes repair products. Enhanced communications make remote data processing, telemarketing, and answering services possible.

The economies of scale has traditionally been modest in most services because they had to be performed on buyers' location and was labour intensive. Telecommunications technology has allowed expansion of service enterprises outside their national boundaries, and at the same time increased the potential for competition within domestic markets (of course, mostly within the advanced economies). This partly explains why capital, since the 1980s, has become diversified to embrace services as new opportunities for creating value arise. Competition in the application of telecommunications technology and in the provision of telecommunications services create the atmosphere for a more dynamic industry. The drive for profit comes from producing the new systems and delivering the myriad of new services the technology makes possible. The unlimited opportunities for innovation in the new communications technologies enable the application of more information, the configuration of networks to unique requirements, and the ever decreasing cost of communications relative to transportation. Being a cause and effect of changes in industry structure, the technology is a major force driving the evolution of global production and marketing.

TRADE IN SERVICES AND TELECOMMUNICATIONS

The Changing Nature of Trade

Trade in services is a more difficult subject to conceptualize than trade in goods when viewed in conventional terms. For one thing, it is perceived differently in different national fiscal systems. In addition, trade accounting systems grossly under-represent the economic importance of services as a whole, and that of telecommunications in particular. Despite the fact that statistics show a massive increase in world trade, trade in services (the most rapidly growing sector) has not been factored in. The huge flow of capital that far exceeds world trade has also been left out. The reality is, the techno-paradigm shift is:

> Making obsolete the policy arguments of science and technology which have hitherto been common sense in theories of business administration and international relations. Because of the lack of full appreciation of the paradigm shift in science and technology these phenomena, and malfunctions such as mismatch in management practices, the paradox in economic policy and international disputes are occurring.

Knowledge intensive production on a global scale along with telecommunications technology have brought trade to a new level. There is the fragmentation of former mass markets with a fundamental shift in the geographic flows in finished goods, semi-finished goods and raw materials. In turn, there are increasing flows of services, capital and technology. Foreign Direct Investment (FDI) is a key measure of these flows relative to the globalization of production. Since the 1980s there has been growth in FDI away from raw materials and primary products to services such as finance insurance, real estate advertising, communications, and media; as well as an increased flow between the developed economies and away from developing countries. In fact, at the end of the 1980s, 'foreign direct investment in services accounted for 40 percent (about $400 billion) of the world stock and more than 50 percent (about $600 billion) of annual flows of FDI.' The complexity of trade patterns is heightened by the fact that services are exported through FDI, yet the locally produced sales in an overseas market do not count as trade. The motivation behind FDI is to ensure flexibility in production and distribution; to take advantage of the opportunities provided by technological change; and to penetrate foreign markets. The global spread through outsourcing and the need to avoid tariffs and quotas have encouraged the flow of FDIs.

Growing consumer demands for quality products and services, and the constant need for product differentiation through innovation, have raised the level of competition for controlling market shares and/or securing new markets. Competition can arise from anywhere: from traditional markets which are changing dramatically; from entirely new markets; from new entrants to a specific industry or economic sector; from the disintegration of barriers that separated market sectors; and from the erosion of barriers to protected and insulated markets.

Innovation and continued productivity necessitate the free flow of knowledge and information. The new dynamics is one in which the competitive edge is based on obtaining instant information. The ability to manage information flows has become a prerequisite for participating in the global market. In turn, there is an increase in the swift and widespread dissemination of information of all sorts. The quality of the communications infrastructure in this scenario, is vital to enabling all kinds of information to be exchanged in 'real time.' Telecommunications technology therefore lies at the heart of trade in services. For one thing, a major and growing element of global merchandise trade is the sale of information technology, which by 1989 had approached U.S. $500 billion per year. Beyond this, the potential scope for trade in services is defined by the tradeability of such services. Global telecommunications networks influence the tradeability of services through the ability to incorporate innovative telecommunications equipment services in intra-corporate network, and to facilitate advanced communication links with customers and suppliers. Products are easier and more profitable to trade, as information becomes the dominant source of value-added.

One of the single most powerful developments in global communications has been the satellite. Enabling instant communications, satellites and fibre optics link the world in an electronic infrastructure carrying news, data and money, making borders porous to information. The technology has revolutionized the quantity and types of information which can be handled using electronic methods. Networks can involve more players and more information. In fact, the volume of telecommunications traffic has expanded to the point where the market can easily support competitive systems. Added to this is the declining cost of transmitting information, especially with respect to satellite-based long distance communications.

In short, improved communications make for further expansion in the global exchange of services. There are new services for markets and new markets for services. The new technology has altered the dimensions of markets, the relative importance of location and the organization of firms. It has been destroying those barriers around markets that have been synonymous with specific geographical areas especially in the financial sector.

Financial Integration and Telecommunications Networks

Revolutionary changes have been taking place in the speed, quality and depth of communications, influencing all aspects of economic life. However, these dimensional changes have had a dramatic effect in finance. Telecommunications has impacted on all areas of the financial sector in a number of profound ways. First, the technology has afforded a greater mobility and flexibility in capital and financial flows and services. It is so much an integral part of operations that financial institutions are ranked among the largest purchasers and users of telecommunications services and data-processing equipment within domestic economies. They are devoting increasing resources to enhancing the ability to monitor and exchange information on a continuous basis. The nature of competition presents the added pressure to constantly invest in the state of the art telecommunications technology.

As established earlier, information is a prime determining factor in creating competitive advantage. Financial institutions are pivotal in this respect. The central issue is, they are engaging in the 'marketing' of that special commodity called money. The latter is unique in that it can exist in a number of forms — from being a physical piece of matter, or an entry in a ledger to an item of information which is essentially invisible. The new communications technology has now brought out the 'invisible' qualities of money by 'having a powerful impact on the role of money in the world economy... Its existence as an information item also gives money its flexibility and its "fungibility," the ability to be transferred from place to place, to move from purpose to purpose.' Because of the ability to codify money as an information product, it can be moved around the globe at tremendous speed and invisible ways.

Telecommunications has therefore provided the means of overcoming barriers that previously existed. The velocity of the circulation of money has been massive. Integration in finance has been progressing at a much faster pace than in other areas. In fact, the amount of money does not correspond to the increases in the proportion of commodities produced. The quantity of money has rapidly outpaced the volume of physical production to the extent that there is a delinking — growing independence — of the financial sector from the real economy. The increasing flows enabled by technology have been and continue to be a powerful force behind the globalization of finance and the interconnection between economies and economic policy. For instance, it is these flows that are the main determinant of exchange rates. All currencies are involved to a greater or lesser degree. Technology has now afforded the opportunity for currencies to be traded in a global foreign exchange market. In addition, all international financial transactions and transfers pass through this market. All these transactions and trading are carried out through computerized networks and over the telephone, on a 24-hour basis regardless of the limitations of different time zones.

A second major impact is that telecommunications has engendered the creation of innovative financial instruments. The shift towards securitization of finance during the 1980s was a main driving force in the changing financial service industry. Securitization makes an open market for financial assets, a feature that encourages and is in turn enhanced by globalization. Propelled by telecommunications technology, both securitization and globalization offer more opportunities, deeper markets, more choice of borrowers and more market liquidity. The trend towards securitization has assisted in eroding the separation between sectors. Along with deregulation and liberalization, it has influenced the growing interrelationship in the financial services, thus the merging of banking, insurance and brokerage. In addition, there is the development and wider usage of other new financial products. In the wholesale market, besides securities, there are derivatives, options, futures, and swaps. The retail sector is seeing the widening use of plastic credit and the electronic provision of financial services such as Automatic Teller Machines. All of this is dependent on the new communications structure. As a whole, the introduction of telecommunications to financial trading has resulted in a shift in market behavior, manifested in the move away from trading floors to computer-based and telephone trading. The traditional means of trading on stock-exchange floors are giving way to computer screens. This, in addition to other changes in the financial service industry are posing really acute territorial questions for regulatory authorities.

Trade and Territoriality

Governments have traditionally needed and relied on a definition of trade that is based on territory. Any activity inside a country's borders is seen as domestic, and sales to anyone living and working in another country's territory is therefore treated as trade. The control of territory in this sense, is a major element of sovereignty. The nature and significance of this is however, changing in a number of ways. Globalization of production and markets along with restructuring have been transforming the system of national economies linked by government-regulated trade. An increasingly integrated global economy is pushing this system beyond the reach of much national regulation.

There is the difficulty of asserting sovereignty over the flow of information. Satellites are the principal force diverting power over information away from the state to the individual - be it the firm or a person. Information products, telecommunications expertise, computer hardware and software are not geographically dictated in the same way that raw materials are. They are not inherited natural factors of production; they are portable and temporary — dependent on ever expanding technological innovation that is not bound by geography.

Governments are good at regulating things that are tangible and measurable. This has now been altered. The crossing of borders to provide or to receive a service is now mostly in the form of persons or transactions which present serious problems for national regulation. The likelihood of tracing transactions has been reduced by information technology. It is difficult for an official agency to record transactions outside of the country of origin. For one thing, the information may be invisible or the knowledge may only be found in people's heads. This kind of capital is difficult to measure and is extremely mobile. It goes where it is wanted and where it is most attracted. Tantamount to this, with the globalization of production, how does one define the country of origin of a product that is made up of parts and service inputs from all over the globe?

In relation to the financial system, where exchange rates are determined by observable flows of goods and services, the world money traders exercise greater power than do governments. No central bank can control money flows — despite attempts to influence flows through raising or lowering interest rates. Capital accounts are determining the state of current accounts rather than the other way around. Attempts to control capital movements and foreign exchange are met with cutbacks in investment, flight of capital and in turn, a foreign exchange crisis. The transformation of the financial system by the global electronic market driven by private traders have made the survival of national currencies, national credit policies, and national budgets and taxes more and more problematic, especially for those of the Caribbean.

All this calls into question the appeal to nationalism in an open global economy with networks that link peoples towards a 'consumer culture.' Satellites have dramatically expanded television reportage, and increased the reach of broadcasts, making it difficult for governments to regulate programming. The main point here, is that information capital in an inherently global environment, will be intolerant of nationalist restrictions. Sovereignty as developed in the sixteenth century did not assume the control of information, obviously because there was not much of it and the state of technological know-how did not warrant this. Now, transnational flows of information in its various forms are nullifying national policies and undermining national and cultural identification.

The extent of the problem at least in regards to trade, is reflected in the inclusion of trade in services on the agenda for the Uruguay Round of negotiations for GATT. In fact this round of talks concluded in December, 1993 did address some problems such as removing barriers in the areas of banking, brokerage and insurance. However, a lot of the results were inconclusive, leaving untouched inadequacies in supervisory structures and competitive and regulatory frameworks. A promising feature is the creation of a World Trade Organization as a means to addressing the problems that pervade the new economic environment.

SOME POLICY IMPLICATIONS FOR THE CARIBBEAN

To understand the new emerging economic, political and social arrangements affecting the global system of production, exchange and distribution, the Caribbean governments and people have to bear in mind the following:

1. These new arrangements/changes are not divinely ordained, nor are they products of blind chance such as the 'invisible hand' of markets. They are the result of human decisions and must be seen in relation to man-made institutions, rules and customs.

2. We need to understand who has power. What is the source of this power, and how this power has been used to distribute costs and benefits, risks and opportunities to nations, groups, organizations, etc.

3. The recent splurge in globalization is part of an ongoing process with a long history. The way economies are organized in a free enterprise system is subject to change. In the past, (as in the present) competition and the need to control raw material sources have spurred business enterprises (corporations) to reach beyond their national boundaries. This expansion has varied over time, influenced by changes in political and economic conditions, and the available technology for transporting goods and communicating. It is just that this new phase of restructuring has new qualities and result in 'spatial' shifts.

With the onset of these changes, a major issue facing the Caribbean countries is the locational significance of trade in services. The Caribbean as a whole, derives positive returns from trade in services that involve travel: the movement of persons into the Caribbean as tourists, and the movement of persons out as providers of services in other countries. However, most of the world receipts and world payments from the global trade in services in relation to high-value production, involve the developed (OECD) countries. This of course, translates into the fact that countries which have the most appropriate communications infrastructure for the delivery of services globally, will have a larger share in service trade flows. For the Caribbean, this is a barrier to gaining access to trade.

Constraints in both demand and supply retards the development of producer services as a whole throughout the Caribbean. The demand is constrained by the low level of development of technologically sophisticated manufacturing which requires a whole range of producer services. In terms of supply, there is a deficiency in the telecommunications infrastructure and the educational and technological base that are essential to providing producer services. This therefore, highlights problems in relation to policies geared towards developing a favourable environment for higher quality services and building competitiveness in the global marketplace.

One thing is certain, and that is no one policy can address the problems facing the Caribbean today. The new paradigm is one that brings to the fore the basis on which countries adopt policies geared towards competitiveness; because it comes with a major impact on the labour force. Innovations in both manufacturing and service industries require greater knowledge inputs and so result in an increase in white collar occupations. The displacement and marginalization that comes with this, especially in light of structural adjustment programs have serious concerns for social policy. Debt-ridden economies thus face the conflicts that arise in pursuing export-led growth to achieve competitiveness.

Decisive in the mix of all this is telecommunications policy, for the latter is integrally related to the nature, structure and direction of Caribbean economies. A central question that governments must deal with is, whether a deregulated marketplace should decide how and when telecommunications will occur. The private use and acquisition of telecommunications mean reduced control over revenues and the setting of uniform standards of quality and compatibility. Standards are not neutral and when introduced usually reflect the values, norms and interests of the provider. With private control, comes other questions related to who will have access and how can the public interest be realized. Finally, telecommunications policy also affects trade and vice versa. Opening barriers to value-added telecommunications services, direct broadcasts of advertisements and news raise questions of preserving social and cultural patterns of behavior.

In short, given the new dynamics of the global economy, the Caribbean governments need to take stock of the widening gap between the advanced countries and those of the Caribbean. They need to seriously examine the wide range of policy issues and the potential for collaboration to compensate for national deficiencies especially in the area of telecommunications.

BIBLIOGRAPHY

Aharoni, Yair (1993). 'Globalization of Professional Business Services,' in Yar Aharoni, (Ed.), *Coalitions and Competition - The Globalization of Professional Business Services* (New York: Routledge).

Bell, Daniel (1973). *The Coming of the Post-Industrial Society: A Venture in Social Forecasting* (New York: Basic Books).

Daniels, P.W., Ed., (1991). *Services and Metropolitan Development: International Perspectives* (London: Routledge).

Eliasson, Gunnar, S. Folstek, T. Lindberg, T. Pousette and E. Taymaz (1990). *The Knowledge Based Information Economy* (Stockholm: The Industrial Institute for Economic and Social Research).

Gershuny, J.I. and I. Miles (1983). *The New Service Economy: the transformation of Employment in Industrial Societies* (New York: Praeger Publishers).

Giarini, Orio and Walter Stahel (1993). *The Limits of Certainty: Facing Risks in the New Service Economy,* 2nd Revised Ed., (Dordrecht: Kluwer Academic Publishers).

Jussawalla, Meheroo, Tadayuki Okuma and Toshihiro Araki, Eds., (1989). *Information Technology and Global Interdependence* (Westport: Greenwood Press).

Lanvin, Bruno, Ed. (1993). *Trading in a New World Order: The Impact of Telecommunications and Data Services on International Trade in Services*, The Atwater Series on the World Information Economy, (Boulder: Westview Press).

Mandel, Ernest (1978). *Late Capitalism* (London: Verso).

O'Brien, Richard (1992). *Global Financial Integration: The End of Geography* (London: The Royal Institute of International Affairs, Pinter Publishers).

Porter, Michael E. (1990). *The Competitive Advantage of Nations*(New York: The Free Press).

Putterman, Joshua Adam (1992). 'Transnational Production in Services as a Form of International Trade, *World Competition*, Vol. 16, No. 2, Dec.

Reich, Robert (1991). *The Work of Nations: Preparing Ourselves 21st Century Capitalism* (New York: Vintage Books).

Review of the Month (1992). 'Globalization - To What End? Part1,' *Monthly Review* (February) Vol. 43, No. 9.

Tapscott, Don and Art Caston (1993). *Paradigm Shift: The New Promise of Information Technology* (New York: McGraw-Hill, Inc.).

Tussie, Diana and David Glover, Eds. (1993). *The Developing Countries in World Trade: Policies and Bargaining Strategies* (Boulder: Lynne Rienner Publishers).

Price, D.G. and A.M. Blair (1989). *The Changing Geography of the Service Sector* (London: Bellhaven Press).

Riddle, Dorothy (1986). *Service-Led Growth — The Role of the Service Sector in World Development* (New York: Praeger Publishers).

Wriston, Walter B. (1992). *The Twilight of Sovereignty: How the Information Technology is Transforming Our World* (New York: Charles Scribner's Sons).

NOTES

1. O'Brien (1992:5).
2. Ibid.
3. Kodama (1991: Chapter 1).
4. Reich (1991: 81-86).
5. Kodama, op. cit.
6. Industry and Development Global Report (1992/1993: 141).
7. Wriston (1992: p.5).
8. Ibid., p. 6.
9. Bell (1973).
10. Cohen and Zysman (1987: 49-50).
11. Kodama, op. cit., p. 8.
12. Ibid., Chapter 5.
13.Tapscott and Caston (1993: 13).
14. Ibid., pp. 14-18.
15. Porter (1990: 246).
16. Wriston, op. cit., p. 79 and Riddle (1986: 108-109).
17. Kodama, op. cit., p. 1.
18. Review of the Month (1992). Monthly Review, Volume 43, No. 9, p. 2.
19. Aharoni, Yair (1993: 1-2).
20. Putterman, Joshua Adam (1992: 124).
21. O'Brien, op. cit., p. 8.
22. Ibid., p. 7.

23. Ibid. Also see Lanvin (1993: 114-122 & 202-206).
24. O'Brien, op. cit., p. 40.
25. Wriston, op. cit., pp. 37-38.
26. Wriston, op. cit., pp. 37-38.

2

POLICY ISSUES IN COMMUNICATIONS TECHNOLOGY USE:
CHALLENGES AND OPTIONS

Hopeton S. Dunn

INTRODUCTION

Within Caribbean and other under-developing societies, the last ten years have seen an unprecedented strengthening of the power of transnational companies and a considerable weakening of the authority of the nation state in industrial and communications policy-making. The transition from a state-led to a private sector led industrial policy in Jamaica and elsewhere provides an excellent framework for observing the interplay and underlying tensions between the centrifugal forces of global capital represented by the transnational corporation and the forces for national and regional development, often poorly represented by governments. This is occurring at a time when governments are increasingly subject to demands not just for the provision of shelter, jobs, education and health services, but also for access to the most advanced technological means for improved service delivery and increased agricultural and industrial productivity.

Unable themselves to meet these demands and unwilling to face the political consequences of a failure to provide these services, governments have turned to the corporate global providers. In doing so, the state authorities in these societies often find themselves unable to regulate these companies or even to articulate the technical and policy requirements for the protection of local service users and the wider society. The central problem which emerges from such a situation is how to reconcile the global scope and legitimate profit-generating objectives of the transnational interests on the one hand, with the requirement for regulation and informed national-level planning to fulfill the perceived needs of people at all levels in societies on the global periphery.

It is to this dilemma that this chapter addresses itself. Using an analysis of the emerging technologies as a point of departure, it argues that a central issue for social and industrial policy-making is how to select, adapt and introduce global technologies in ways which are beneficial to the cultural and economic development of large sections of the population. Selection and adaptation imply the need for informed, on-going assessments not only of the inherent capabilities of the innovations but also of the relevance and future impact of some of the technologies being marketed by transnational corporate interests.

In the following section we present as a conceptual framework, a brief discussion of (A) the transnational corporation in an era of rapid technical innovation and globalization and (B) Policy-making and Implementation in a regional context of economic underdevelopment.

CONCEPTUAL FRAMEWORK

Transnational Corporations, Technology and Globalization

Like other forms of business enterprise, the transnational corporation exists to maximize its economic advantages. In most cases it seeks higher profits by effecting economies from its global scale and comprehensive scope and through the application of technology for increased productivity. The established capacity of the TNC to adapt and grow contributes to its pre-eminence as an institutional form of capital accumulation and an efficient carrier of technology in the present era of enhanced globalization. According to Saskia Sassen 'The central role played by transnational corporations...can be seen in the fact that they accounted for 80% of international trade in the United States in the late 1980s. Furthermore than a third of the US "international trade" was actually intra-firm trade. Almost all foreign direct investment (FDI) and a large share of technology transfers were undertaken by TNCs.' [Sassen 1993: 63-64].

The capacity to process, store and transmit information is now of central importance because it is access to information that is increasingly creating the basis for wealth. The growth or formation of new super-companies reflects the search by the information transnationals for profit sources which cut across traditional industrial sectors. Because the scope of these companies is often so large, many establish subsidiaries to provide products or services in a particular niche market. To do this on a global scale multimedia companies aim to secure flexible working contracts with employees in whose knowledge level they are prepared to invest.

Despite the multiple subsidiaries, policy remains under the control of the corporate headquarters, where each entity forms part of a carefully designed global strategy honed by knowledge of the competition. These conglomerates are constantly seeking alliances with or takeover of other companies in an on-going process of industrial concentration. In the mid 1980s, for example, the top eleven publishing firms controlled 62% of the total book market and the top nine firms together held 95% of the paperback market. The film producing company Paramount controls such book companies as Simon and Schuster, Allyn and Bacon and Prentice Hall. And the publisher of Time magazine is the movie company Warner Brothers, which also operates Atlantic, Electra and Chapell records as well as Warner Home Videos and Cable companies.

These conglomerates use forward and backward linkages into such other industries as music, movie production and television programmes to take maximum advantage of multimedia environment. After all, a bestseller is never far away from the screen version, and the theme songs commissioned for these movies would already be on the music charts shortly after the movie itself opens. Within months a television version is out, thus extending the process of product diversity. It is a process of corporate and technological convergence based on the integration of the technologies. This process is ensuring that the number of large traditional operators is contracting with a few hi-tech companies dominating the market.

The aim of the transnational enterprise is to be indispensable. To do this, particularly in competition with other transnationals or with local interests, the global TNC traditionally seeks to gain what Enderwink describes as 'location specific advantages'(LSAs) and 'firm specific advantages'(FSAs). LSAs are achieved by consolidating a base in the host country or from acquiring multiple sites or service locations in a national or regional market. In the context of existing production and operational norms, the flexibility to relocate is now more of an advantage than locational stability or permanence. In contrast to location specific advantages, firm specific advantages are distinctive corporate qualities, such as expertise and reputation which are transferable among subsidiaries. FSAs provide a basis for product or service differentiation derived from company history, policy, technology or business practices. Corporate teleconnectivity on a global scale has enhanced the capacity of the TNC to refine and purvey its specific service, product and market practices and maintain or vary its locational advantages in ways that help to outstrip local competition and preserve market dominance.

As conceptual tools, both FSA and LSA allow us to better understand internal corporate practices which can be manipulated to the benefit of the transnational corporation. Global information and communication technologies have made the pursuit of these practices both less expensive and more effective as weapons in the battle to gain or retain global, regional or national markets.

At the economic level Caribbean countries are particularly vulnerable to the financial strength and private decision-making machinery of increasingly large transnational corporations (TNCs) whose global budgets often dwarf the national budgets of many of these micro-states. While pointing out that TNCs can make an important contribution to small states in providing much needed capital, technology and market outlets, a landmark study by a Commonwealth Consultative Group also drew special attention to the potential inequality in firm/country relationships.

> In general, Third World states tend to be in a disadvantageous position in relations with transnational corporations through inadequacies in negotiating skills and access to information; and with their slender human resources, small states are in an even weaker position than other developing countries. In many cases, the agreements transnational corporations draw up may be said to resemble those 'unequal treaties' that imperialist powers used to impose in earlier centuries upon weaker nations. The crucial issue for small states is to avoid inequitable contractual arrangements and political interference. [1985:56]

This concern is among those at the heart of the issue of communications technology use in the Caribbean and the wider global south. According to Norman Girvan, the controllers of the global technologies exert enormous bargaining power. 'In contractual arrangements for manufacturing industry, this power is used to impose a large number of restrictive and monopolistic practices on the buyers, which often have the effect of ensuring that the technology is not effectively transferred, but only that the right to use the technology is leased for a specific period of time.' [Girvan 1983:23].

Addressing the need for an 'active technology strategy' in countries of the global south, Girvan argues that this will require an appropriate partnership between the State and producing enterprises. [Girvan in Lewis (ed) 1994: 193]. He describes technology as 'the knowledge, skills, methods and procedures associated with the production of socially useful goods and services from products of the natural environment.' The definition underlines the need, in the present era for local software production which is the critical locus for indigenous valued-added features. In a study of Technology Policies for Small Developing Economies, Girvan further observed that 'the importation of developed country technology, especially in unmodified form, does not necessarily lead to self sustaining development and can exacerbate the social, economic and environmental problems of poor countries rather than attenuate them.'

Policy making and Implementation. In considering the issues of corporate power and governmental deficiencies in policy-planning, it is necessary to clarify our understanding of the policy-making and regulatory processes and their application to the telecom sector in the Caribbean and other societies of the global south.

In many approaches to public policy, the distinction is made between policy planning, policy implementation and the evaluation of policy outcomes. The handling of each of these aspects can either be broadbased and inclusive or bureaucratic and confined to corporate and political elites. The latter — top down model — facilitates speedier, but sometimes more costly decision-making. More democratic approaches, including public dialogue and consultations with affected actors, provide the basis for more sustainable policy planning. A second useful set of distinctions can be made between formal and informal policies. Doing nothing to change existing arrangements is as much a policy as a proactive approach in developing new, appropriate regimes and regulations.

According to Herbert Simon, the process leading up to the making of policy decisions involves the identification of goals. Simon emphasises that the stage of setting clear objectives is fundamental in giving purpose to administrative behaviour. The policy process itself is concerned with the selection from among a range of alternatives the course of action best suited towards achieving the stated goals [1945:5]. Simon's early approach to policy-making was founded on the concept of rationality, in which options and consequences are comprehensively evaluated before action or implementation takes place. Other theorists, notably Lindblom, regard this purist, linear conception of the policy process as unrealistic. While it is prescriptive of an ideal course of action, implementation in the prescribed form is often impractical. Instead, decision-making typically proceeds through successive limited comparisons, in which both facts and values, as well as the means and consequences are considered. [Lindblom 1964:157].

Lindblom discusses his approach in terms of an on-going deliberative process of 'remediality'. 'Policy-making is typically a never-ending process of successive steps in which continual nibbling is a substitute for a good bite.' This incremental system, he argues, is better adapted to the diversity of situations in which policy problems may arise, because it takes more into account human deficiencies, inadequacy of information, cost limitation and other constraining factors. It allows for mid-stream correction of errors based on-going monitoring and learning. This approach recognises, however, that the policy design process has to begin somewhere. Particularly in post-colonial societies such as ours, some holistic conception or re-conceptualization of the overall strategies and goals have to be planned in line with certain commonly agreed values.

Frequently in our societies, policy-making and implementation are confronted by disjunctures arising from transitions in party political leadership. Even where the ideological basis for such shifts has been disappearing, they occur out of the propensity of leaders to seek to make their own mark. In addition, there is significant institutional fragmentation in the policy environment. Rist [1985:32] notes that goal identification, like policy implementation itself, can be fraught with difficulties derived from 'the sectorization of policy-making', in which 'each policy area develops into a semi-watertight compartment, ruled by its own policy elite.' Traditional bureaucratic and legislative separations in the administration of telecommunications and broadcasting and in the management of other users of the radio spectrum have created these compartments. In Jamaica, broadcasting is handled by the Office of the Prime Minister, telecommunications by the Ministry of Public Utilities and movie production by the Ministry of Industry. This 'sectorization' requires time-consuming inter-organizational bargaining between ministries or even among departments within single ministries. Such policy fragmentation and shifts militate against rational or even incremental policy-making.

Despite the existence of many variations (Lasswell 1951, Dror 1964, Etzioni 1967 etc), the contrasting policy approaches presented by Simon and Lindblom provide a useful set of options from which to consider the policy-making scenario in the Caribbean. While both place primacy on pre-definition of policy objectives, Lindblom's incremental approach allows for revision and re-definition of these objectives. That approach, rather than a linear, rational one, is what appears to inform the work of established regulatory institutions which need constantly to be learning and adjusting to the multiple permutations of a dynamic global communications environment.

COMMUNICATION AND TECHNOLOGY

The distinction between communication — the process, and communications — the technologies, is important in the formulation of policy. Basic communication is here being regarded as the interchange of meaning. Whether the means of communication have been the primordial drum-beat of the Ewe people of Africa or the early Chinese pictographs and Egyptian hieroglyphics; whether they are printed words or the modern technologies of satellite transmission and electronic mailboxes, the basic process itself has not changed over time. Encoding and sending messages as well as receiving, interpreting and responding, are essential transactions which have always been part of human existence and civilization, regardless of the available means or channel for transmission of these messages.

The proliferation of new methods of communication doubtless represents an important transformation. But if we confuse the prevailing technologies of communication with the basic process itself, we run the risk of ascribing more importance to the technologies than they objectively merit. The elementary process of one-to-one communication within families or peer groups, for example, is still widely regarded as the most powerful means of achieving behavioural change. This is despite the absence of modern technological intermediaries in this basic process. The technologies often used in these circumstances are a combination of the human voice, language, non-verbal expressions and the context. Effective communication is nevertheless taking place, demonstrating the centrality of the process itself and that only in specific contexts are the advanced technologies appropriate and useful.

HISTORICAL ANTECEDENTS

Equally, it is important to recognize that the present-day innovations in the means of communication are based on earlier cycles of technological development. Gutenberg's 15th century invention of foundry-cast, movable metal type opened the way for widespread printing and publication of books. It meant that access to the storehouse of knowledge was no longer to be confined to the political, religious or economic elites, but was then open for the first time to a wider audience. Literacy levels also developed exponentially, and information-based structures such as public libraries, newspapers and schools all emerged on a more popular basis and were structured in response to the printed word. It is literacy, learning and experimentation which form the essential backdrop to participation in today's age of information. Gutenberg's innovation, marked by the printing of new editions of the Bible, was itself based on the invention of clay and wooden imprints by Chinese and Korean inventors four hundred years earlier.

It is these and other early technologies which have laid the foundations for developments in the current era. Much in the same way that a convergence of computer systems, digital technology and satellites have already begun a revolutionary transformation of industry, trade and productivity, so too did the harnessing of the steam engine, iron and steel smelting, electricity and telegraphy transform global economic development and communication in the 18th and 19th centuries. The technological antecedent of 20th century optical fibre, microwave and satellite technologies included the innovations of Morse code and the telegraphic signal from both wireline and wireless communication. Many of these early technological convergencies facilitated and were a part of the Industrial Revolution in the same way that the new communication technologies are integral to the Information Revolution of the late 20th century. The rapid developments in information processing and dissemination could not have occurred without the underpinnings of the preceding industrial and communications innovations.

Today, almost five and a half centuries after Gutenberg and a century and a half since Morse and Marconi, we see a further and even more revolutionary wave in the development of communication and information technologies and their related systems of classification, storage and retrieval of information. These technologies are creating dramatic changes in the techno-economic paradigm, fundamentally affecting the ways businesses and institutions operate and the manner in which people across the globe relate to each other. The innovations emerging from research and development (R&D) centres, located mainly in the global north, are creating unprecedented transformations in the significance of distance, time, space and scale as barriers to human progress. The immediacy with which distant parts of the world can be linked electronically represents only one dimension of the change. Simultaneous access to a global audience means marketing and production on a scale hitherto unknown. Production becomes less dependent on location of raw materials, while marketing can be tailored to the specific requirements of identifiable segments of the global population.

THE KEY TECHNOLOGIES

This revolution in the processing and transmission of information is founded on the development and increasing convergence of various streams of innovation. Four of these technologies have provided the main sources for the transformations in the present era. These are *Satellite Technology*, particularly in the form of communication satellites; *Computing Technology* using integrated circuits mounted on tiny semi-conductor boards or microchips; *Optics and Laser Technologies* used particularly in optical fibre and Compact Disc/CD-ROM applications; and *Digitalization* — using zeros and ones as universal digits for the efficient storage and transmission of high volumes of information. In the section following, we discuss these core technologies in both their historical emergence and their modern communications applications.

Satellite Technology

Satellites have been in use in communication since July, 1962 when the Telstar communications module was launched by the National Aeronautics and Space Administration (NASA) in the United States. Telstar relayed the first international television pictures from the United States to Britain and France thereby establishing the inaugural linkage between satellite technology and the mass medium of television. The venture was funded by the American Telephone and Telegraph Company (AT&T), indicating an early liaison between broadcasting and telecommunications interests, via satellite. These diverse interests in the United States were brought together even more closely with the passage of the Communications Satellite Act of late 1962. Using this legislation, the Kennedy administration established a single company, Communications Satellite Corporation (COMSAT), to deal with integrated US policy planning and implementation for international satellite communication.

COMSAT later evolved into an intergovernmental satellite consortium, now widely known as INTELSAT (the International Telecommunications Satellite Organization). This global agency, alongside the operators of the Soviet SPUTNIK space programme, has dominated the use of this technology since the 1960s. The INTELSAT Consortium operates over 15 satellites linking with some 200 large earth stations and 300 special aerials located in about 120 countries worldwide.

In addition to INTELSAT, a number of nationally- or regionally-owned domestic satellite systems are also currently in use both in the industrialized countries and in the primary producing nations. In the U.S., domestic satellite systems have been produced by General Electric (GE), Radio Corporation of America (RCA), General Telephone and Electronics (GTE), Western Union and Hughes Communications Corporation. Among satellite operators in the South are Mexico which has launched its second generation of Morellos satellites, Indonesia which has played a pioneering role with its Palapa satellites and some Arab states which operate the ARABSAT system. Some of these systems operate in a collaborative relationship with INTELSAT while others represent competing interests. They all seek to provide global or regional services in broadcasting, data transmission, weather forecasting among other uses.

In 1965, INTELSAT launched its Early Bird module, inaugurating a new and specialized type of communication satellite which has had a profound impact on global broadcasting and data communication. Early Bird was the first of the geo-stationary satellites, operating in synchronous orbit around the earth. From a position of 37,000 kilometres or 22,300 miles above the equator, these intensively wired modules travel at a orbital speed similar to the speed at which the earth rotates on its axis. And like two buses travelling side by side at the same speed, the effect is as if both the earth and the orbiting satellite are standing still. This enables electronic signals to be bounced directly between them, one off of the other to establish direct two way communication. This type of satellite enables the provision of direct broadcasting by satellite (DBS) and the related satellite services for immediate access to data as well as television and radio channels.

Caribbean broadcasting systems have traditionally operated receive-only antennae for obtaining the international (down-link) transmissions. They have relied on the established international telecommunications carrier, Cable and Wireless or its subsidiaries, for the provision of the up-link leg of the satellite transmission process. However, since 1994, two Caribbean agencies, the Caribbean News Agency (CANA) and the Caribbean Broadcasting Union

(CBU) have been operating their own uplink transponders to originate radio and television programmes and data transmissions via the global INTELSAT systems. Although the uplink facilities are initially located only in Barbados, this indigenous service has already made a difference to the speed and cost of Caribbean news and public affairs programme distribution regionally, through the UNESCO-sponsored CARIBVISION programme exchange scheme and the more commercially operated CANA news feed.

Although United States television programming still dominates, these satellite-based regional initiatives point the way in terms of beneficial regional use of the emerging technologies. Given the high volume and technical quality of competing flows of United States programming into the region, the challenge of this era is to increase the volume and quality of the counterflow emanating from our own culturally rich and artistically innovative region, from Caribbean people throughout the world and from other countries of the global south. Efforts in the mid-1980s to secure support and funding for the launch of a Caribbean regional satellite system (CARISAT) and an African system (AFROSAT) have been aborted for lack of resources [See Demac 1987:81]. In addition, substantial spare capacity on Mexico's Morellos satellite system has also limited the number of potential investors in a Caribbean satellite system. However, this idea is likely to re-surface as the region moves into the twenty first century. To be feasible, such a system may need to demonstrate that satellite is a more cost effective system of information distribution than terrestrial fibre optic systems. It will also need to link-up with similar efforts in the Central American and Andean regions as part of a wider and more integrated regional approach.

Computing and Electronics

A second foundation technology for global innovations in information processing and communications is computing technology. The predecessor of modern computer networks was the punch card tabulating machines used by International Business Machines (IBM) as early as the 1890s. These early systems were developed initially to service large clients and assignments such as the processing of data from the US government's Census Bureau, with which IBM had a contract. By 1945 a small American company Mauchly and Eckert progressed beyond basic tabulation to produce the UNIVAC 1, regarded as the first modern generation of computing equipment. The greater scope and capacity for cross tabulation offered by the UNIVAC series enabled M&E to win the UN Census Bureau contract from IBM. However, in 1950 M&E soon merged with the typewriting firm Remington Rand, which was itself interested in more effective competition with IBM. Perceiving a threat from UNIVAC/RAND, IBM began to make significant investment in Research and Development towards an electronic computer of its own. In 1953, its first computer emerged — the 701 — which was followed by a simplified 650 version for less technical customers.

These prototypes, each of which occupied entire rooms and required constant staffing and servicing, used the earlier inventions of the transistor and the vacuum tube as important elements of their electronics. Their size and limitations provide sharp contrasts with the increasing miniaturization and expanding computational features of today's personal computer. The keys to the dramatic transition are the technologies of the integrated circuit and microprocessor. Precoded data are entered on a minute piece of semi-conductive material to create the microchip. An integrated circuit accepts these coded instructions for execution. This combination, together with other associated electronics, can create minor or vast computational, storage or integrative capacities capable of use in a diverse range of applications. These include uses in complex spacecraft and satellite programming, in regular personal computers, calculators, communications systems and other consumer applications.

Optics and Laser

A third plank of the innovations affecting how we communicate are the technologies of optics and laser. This involves encoding electronic signals within tiny beams of light, which are transmitted along hair-thin cylindrical filaments of pure glass. The use of light as a medium has been under study for over a century. Message transmission by laser techniques has been in an experimental stage since 1870, when the Englishman John Tyndall attempted to use water as a means of transmitting messages with light. His efforts foundered on the tendency of the light beams to reflect, refract and stray when it encounters impurities, bubbles or other flaws. Alexander Graham Bell, the American researcher credited with development of the modern telephone, also attempted to build on the work of Tyndall to create a photophone. However he was unsuccessful in his bid to transmit images and sound by way of light beams down a tube. Experimentation has continued since then, but it was not until 1967 that the technology of using light-driven digital bit streams down thin fibres of covered glass emerged as a major prospect for message transmission.

Today's modern optical fibres consist of a thin glass core of light emitting diodes (LEDs) overlaid by several claddings of plastic and other casings to prevent loss of intensity. A single-mode, hair-thin strand can carry vast quantities of encoded data, images and voice messages substantially in excess of existing copper cables. This innovation represents a major breakthrough for telecommunications carriers, who can transmit millions of land-based telephone calls more efficiently and cheaply down a small bundle of optical fibres. With appropriate additional cladding and optical repeaters, these fibres are also now a major transoceanic message carrier capable of transmitting hundreds of global video channels in different directions simultaneously. Other consumer applications of optics and laser technology include the compact disc (CD) and CD-ROM (Read Only Memory) systems.

The technical quality, great bandwidth capacity and relative economy of fibre optics have made it an important competing medium with satellite systems for the transmission of telephone, cable television and data services internationally. It is already providing the backbone of the so-called digital information superhighway in the United States. In the Caribbean, the greater part of the telephone switching and distribution networks have been converted from copper cables and analog techniques to fibre optic cables and digital methods. And a Digital Eastern Caribbean Fibre System is already replacing the microwave system linking the territories in that part of the region.

Digitalization Technology

Digitalization technology offers another important application for the use of light in information generation, storage and reproduction. The digital system provides an alternative to the analogue mode of transmission in that it uses rapid on/off pulses of light, rather than a continuous electrical wave for processing signals. The older, analogue waveform method which was in extensive use, is now being superseded by this digital system. We see a graphic representation of this system almost every day in the rapidly changing digits on the clock or modern metre. Looking closely, we will notice that the movement through 1 to 9 are all variations on the digits 0 and 1. The pulses reflected in changes of the digits are BITS of information in binary codes. The term BITS is simply a contraction of the longer term BInary digiTS, which form basic units of data communication. Digitalization of music transmission, for example is the process by which every detail of the sound is rapidly pre-sampled by beams of light, and numbers assigned to every element corresponding to different notes. Replay can be precise and of high quality because it reflects a reproduction of the exact numbers stored in the form of binary codes.

MULTIMEDIA CONVERGENCE AND MINIATURIZATION

In their industrial and communications applications, these four technologies have been converging both to reinforce the efficiency of each other and to create new interactive and multi-media systems which can revolutionize both the home and workplace. Satellite, computing, optics and digitalization are only a selection of the more fundamental, core technologies. Many more innovations are both in use and in development, but most of them incorporate substantial aspects of the technologies discussed here. The additional communications and information technologies include High Definition Television (HDTV), the magnetic video-tape, video discs and other products of consumer electronics.

The combination of several of these technologies into multimedia systems represent the latest phase in the application of the technologies to daily life in some countries. Simultaneously with this merging of the technologies is the processes of making more compact the various application and units being produced. It is a process of both convergence and miniaturization. Greater volumes of storage space and processing capacity can he located in much smaller and more sophisticated equipment which carry out multi-media functions at a faster and more interactive pace. The combined application of the technologies in a mix of voice, data, text and image has been referred to as *Integrated Services Digital Network* (ISDN). The existence of true ISDN is questioned by some observers while several manufacturers claim to have already incorporated it into their marketing strategies.

While in the 1970 and 80s, the innovations took the form of development mainly of hardware, the emerging pattern is one which now recognises the critical role of software development and manufacturing. Substantial research and development efforts are being directed at customised software applications and increasingly sophisticated designs for specialized markets.

TECHNOLOGY ASSESSMENT

While selective application of the technologies can bring immense benefits to under-developed societies, uncritical use can lead to a worsening of economic and social disparity and capital outflow. In the reality of many countries of the global South, choice of technological innovations are dictated less by internally-generated policy guidelines and more by financial lines of credit and the marketing strategies of manufacturers. Since the imported technologies themselves are not neutral and the process of choosing among them not entirely free, underdeveloped countries are forced to pay a significant social cost in addition to the immediate financial costs reflected in the usage arrangements.

Both the political and technocratic leadership in these societies are only now beginning to gear themselves to deal with the requirements of bargaining and critical assessment of available technologies. Nevertheless, in many countries the public and private sector leadership still lack the economic power, expertise or political will to apply independent critical judgements to products and processes in the new global marketplace. They are finding that the systems and technologies are being intensively marketed as essential tools by the manufacturers with the backing of the governments in the industrialized countries from which both the product and the loan capital often come. Policy-makers in the Caribbean and elsewhere, therefore face the daunting challenge of achieving that elusive balance between the political and economic advantages to be gained from the use of the technologies and, on the other hand, the longer term socio-cultural price to be paid for an uncritical approach to technological innovations.

VIRTUAL REALITY VS REALITY

In an edition of Business Week focusing on the wonders of multi-media technologies in the industrialized North, a scenario of family life in a tele-environment of 'virtual reality' was painted. [September 7, 1992]. Walls decorated with digital art on changing flat panel displays, electronic diaries linked to remote computer units, and on-line digital newspapers complete with sound were among the hi-tech applications envisaged or already in use. It was a story of a dramatic social re-ordering involving the combined use of the computer, consumer electronics, and the output of the entertainment and information industries. It is a measure of the global reach of communications technologies that a parallel, realistic scenario can easily be painted of life among the affluent, technophile minority in the tropics.

Consider this equivalent Caribbean scenario:

> Michael and Shakira Anderson are home for the night to their plush suburban neighbourhood of Graham Heights in residential St Andrew, Jamaica. Mike's mobile sales occupation requires that he wears an active electronic badge which tells his employer's computer network, located in Kingston where to reach him at any time in the flexible workday. As he settles in at home, he can unpin the badge, thereby putting himself out of active computer deployment and into the standby mode. Although on standby, Michael's miniature cellular telephone is automatically switched to the ON position. The video-phone linking him to his workplace is also on standby with terminals both at head-office as well as in his living room.

> On that same video-phone terminal, Mike and his family can call-up any of the 50 video channels which are being brought into his home via cable. He chooses to watch *Cool Runnings 2*, with life-size images projected on a large wall-mounted screen in his digital den. Michael is receiving the images in the traditional NTSC (US) TV standard, but expects to replace this technology with the new High Definition Television (HDTV) format shortly. His modern compu-tv carries an option for transporting the viewers into the make-believe world called 'virtual reality'. At the flick of a button, Michael and his family can take a nostalgic dive with the Jamaican bobsleigh team from the ice rinks of Calgary, complete with ear-phones, motion seats and special glasses.

But Mr Anderson's teenage daughter, Maya, does not wish to take the 'virtual trip' because of an assignment in her distance education course. She had just picked up her assignment details on the electronic mailbox wired into her home via fibre-optic cables. She will be researching biology tonight. Using her personal password she can gain access to learning resources from overseas data-bases, including the INTERNET. She chooses to use the CD-ROM version of the Encyclopedia Britannica, by which she can study realistic video clips of the inner workings of the human heart, displayed in motion, in cross section and in living colour.

Mike's wife, who is an architect, doesn't go out to work. Instead, Shakira operates by day the same domestic network which is used at night for homework and entertainment. The central unit, known as the family's INFOTAINMENT network, can be accessed as her computer work-station for an in-house office in the foothills of the Blue Mountains. Designs, cost analyses, graphics and other engineering data produced by her home-based company can be downloaded to clients across the country as well as to overseas clients, using the computer network. It is linked, electronically, to a newly acquired interactive switching device known as the Asynchronous Transfer Mode, or ATM for short.

At weekends, tele-shopping for anything can be done from the terminals at home, with the supplies delivered by a fleet of drivers linked by cellular telephones. The wedding of a close friend is coming up in a week and so clothes for the occasion have to be ordered. Details of the clothing requirements of the Anderson family are transmitted on-line to the design network of Material Things Limited in Kingston or its equivalent in Miami. The clothing company then beams back realistic images of the array of suits and outfits to be chosen for the event. Selection and payment are done electronically and the clothes are delivered by couriers within 24 hours without the family leaving home.

INTERFACING WITH REALITY

Soon enough, however, the Andersons will have to fall off the edge of this functional but de-humanizing world. Alas, their hair will have to be cut or styled for the wedding, a task which, despite robotics, the computer has not yet figured out a way to do. Mike, Shakira and Maya will have to leave the confines of virtual reality if they want to have physical contact with the real world. Just occasionally, they may also wish to shake hands and say good morning, not to their computers, but to the very real human neighbours next door and to relate to the all too human household helper, Advira, whom they still need for assistance with some daily human chores.

Still, that starry-eyed trip typifies the electronic environment in which one part of the human society already exists, and in which many more will reside before the year 2000. All the technological innovations described here already exist and are in use in various section of the region. New prototypes or updated programmes are in circulation or in advanced stages of development.

But in considering the scenario, an important underlying question is what are the social and psychological consequences of existing in this synthetic environment. And what of those not able to buy their way into this world of virtual reality.

Let us take the second scenario of Advira Beckford, the Anderson's household helper.

> Advira comes from the rural parish of Westmoreland where according to the latest (1991) Jamaica census, approximately 70% of her female parishioners are 'economically inactive'. Like a large number of other rural dwellers, she has migrated to Kingston in search of work. In her parish of birth, Advira would share one telephone for every 100 other residents, reflecting the rural downside of a still low national average of 5 lines per 100 of population. Ownership of television sets in her community would be at a level lower than the national average of one set to every 170 potential viewers in 1993. It is unlikely that households in Advira's poor, rural neighbourhood would have individual access to a satellite receiver. Their main electronic medium would be radio, for which the national average is one set per household.
>
> In joining the futuristic urban household of the Andersons, Advira left behind a social situation which has not changed significantly over the last two decades: Of the private households in Westmoreland, 6% are without toilet facilities and 79% of households use a pit latrine in 1991. Over 7% get their water supplies untreated from springs, rivers or public tanks. Water is piped into only 13% of the private dwellings, and close to 30% of households still rely on public standpipes. More than half of the households (53%) use wood or charcoal for cooking and 46% use kerosene lamps for lighting at night.

Many of the household gadgets and communication equipment in the Anderson household would be unfamiliar to Advira because she is economically, socially and geographically from 'a different world'. For her, the information technologies has not brought her closer to the elites who own these products. Rather, it has contributed to an increase in the social, economic and personal distance between her dispossessed rural parishioners and the more fortunate minority, who are able to enjoy the high tech, cosmopolitan lifestyle of the Andersons. One hundred years after its invention, the plain old telephone is still a new technology for Advira and her folk in rural Jamaica, and despite the technological advances, the radio remains the main medium for her community. Their immediate struggle is for clean water, sanitary domestic conditions and decent roads, public transport and jobs. However, like other neighbourhoods in rural Jamaica, Advira's district will soon be receiving offers for cable television, and those residents with TV already receive imported television programmes from the domestic station in Kingston. The main immediate benefit for her family from the new technological innovations takes the form of entertainment: a bonding with American soap opera personalities and exposure to global advertising.

Except for variations in degree, the situation in Westmoreland, Jamaica, reflects rural conditions elsewhere in the Caribbean and in the so-called third world: acute social deprivation, sharply contrasting living conditions between rural and urban areas and between the information rich and the information poor. This is reflected in a vast disparity in knowledge and use of the information and communications technologies. However, the gap narrows in the levels of exposure to media content, particularly television, which originates mainly from overseas and which is transmitted with the use of the emerging technologies. The situation has not changed in favour of local programme content in over a decade since Brown's 1987 study indicated an 87% imported content in television output in the Caribbean region. Instead, the increased output of such programming which has arisen from the spread of United States-supplied cable television programming in the region, spells a further emphasis on the entertainment end-product of technology adoption for the majority of people like Advira and members of her community.

OPTIONS IN THE USE OF THE TECHNOLOGIES

In looking from the south at the corporate strategies and technologies, it is clear that the issue of financing the selective introduction of the innovations is a critical hurdle, which if overcome could make a major difference in the quality of life of people from all social strata. Efficiency in the delivery of public services, in professional practice and in private and public sector administration could also be enhanced. Non-governmental organizations (NGOs) have been able to gain access to some of the technologies by beginning at the so-called low end, but with important spinoff benefits for communities and small businesses. Desktop publishing, facsimile transmission and video-tape systems, for example, have been used to establish effective global networks for community development, sharing and international collaboration. Such basic-level approaches seek to deploy the new tools to meet the needs of the sector and to its resource endowments. They represent important methods for entry level use and wide diffusion of the technologies. Such a strategy can more easily be built upon for later access (where this does not already exist) to more advanced facilities such as electronic mail, global data bases and direct satellite up-linking and reception. The benefits of these more advanced services are already available, even if on a limited scale, to the region from the Caribbean News Agency (CANA) and the Caribbean Broadcasting Union (CBU), among others.

In rural communities, farmers who often operate in remote locations require the extension of the basic telephone network to obviate the need for long and time-consuming physical travel by road to get veterinary and other agricultural extension advice or market information. Equally, fishermen operating large or small vessels should be able to benefit from cheaper and more efficient ship-to-shore communication, enabling them to market their catch even before returning to shore. Remote sensing devices and small radar systems which allow easy identification of geographical locations should help to reduce the number of small craft lost at sea.

The capacity for information storage, rapid transmission, interaction and visual presentation make the multi-media possibilities of the present era particularly attractive for use in education at all levels of society. As a strategic approach, computer literacy should be taught at the primary school level, and reinforced with training in communications techniques as a requirement in secondary education. In societies where access to secondary and tertiary education is severely limited, the benefits and prospects for distance learning, pioneered in the Caribbean region by the UWI's UWIDITE system, are being more widely recognised. Access to such global data bases as offered by the INTERNET provide an important resource base for both teaching and learning. The build-up of our own national, regional and south-south data bases and exchanges would constitute an equally important qualitative advance in the use of the technologies.

However, attempts to gain access to the new systems of data storage and retrieval are frequently confronted by adherence to the traditional methods of record-keeping and bibliographical services. The physical stocks and operating systems on offer in many of our libraries still reflect almost exclusively the product of Gutenberg's technology, namely books. At the human level as well, it has been noted that many practitioners do tend to approach the new technologies with the psychological and sensory responses of the old. In a way it makes good sense to be cautious and not to hastily abandon long established systems in response to technologies which are expensive and largely commercially driven. But where clear opportunities for renewal present themselves, they should be explored. Instead, as Rosario de Horowitz of the International Federation of Library Associations has noted at the international level, there is a tendency for many librarians to remain, in her words 'prisoners of the psychological, emotional and intellectual conditioning of the world of print'.

She found that not enough librarians were prepared to re-evaluate their role in terms of the perspectives of alternative systems of information storage and distribution. Confronted with the inevitability of change many practitioners have opted to regard the sound and visual media as 'a subordinate order to be contained rather than a new order to be adjusted to.' (de Horowitz

1993:173-174). It becomes particularly important not simply to adjust to the technologies, but to seek ways of adjusting the technologies themselves to our needs. This is especially vital in regions like the Caribbean and Africa, where a strong tradition of oral communication could be augmented by the use of modern electronic systems. Academics, planners and professional practitioners will also need to adjust their working practises and our attitudes to accommodate methods which can offer enhanced services to students, customers and other users of the learning and information facilities.

MASS MEDIA AND TECHNOLOGY

Of course, journalism and the mass media are areas which have historically been subject to changes and the emergence of new branches. The messages now diversely communicated by the media were, up to fifty years ago, confined to the print outlets. The branches we now call the electronic media of radio and television are relatively recent additions. It is true to say however, that the changes we have witnessed over the last decade are unprecedented in their radical impact on the scope and diversity of the profession and on the way in which practitioners carry out their tasks. Entire departments of the printed media have been retooled and re-staffed with the consequent loss in old jobs. New departments requiring different skills have been introduced and the methods of editing and reporting in both the printed and the audio visual media are becoming indistinguishable. In addition, the electronic media has been merging with telecommunications to create such new channels as cable television and other services.

As these changes take place, the protocols and ethical issues surrounding the new technologies become increasingly important. The matter of privacy of the individual versus the right of the public to information is among the aspects generating significant debate. How far can the media, for example, use the technology of miniature cameras or microphones to probe into the private lives of citizens and even public figures. In the United States, fierce battles have raged over privacy rules in relation to intelligent telephone networks. Intelligent services, such as automatic call return, selective call rejection, anonymous call rejection, selective call forwarding have given rise to concerns about the identity of both senders and receivers of telephone messages. In our professional environment, this issue would arise, for example, in a situation where a highly confidential source calls a newsroom to provide a tip or a fax message. Part of the issue is whether the sender's telephone number automatically appears on the tiny screen of certain modern phones and faxes. Since many such sets are equipped with an automatic call back button, it means that a third party could simply press re-dial and establish the identity of the informant.

Another privacy issue emerging from the data storage capacity of the technologies is citizen access to data about them stored in information systems. The nature of use to which such data-bases can be put, and the accuracy of the stored information are issues of concern. In the UK, a Freedom of Information Act prescribes the rules of access to such information and data bases. In the US, the Right to Financial Privacy Act requires a government investigative department to inform an individual before it can look at his or her financial records. And in Washington, Bill Clinton, during his bid for the US presidency, proposed the insertion of a right to privacy clause into the Consumer Bill of Rights.

In the case of the Caribbean, the most urgent legislation should apply to the right of the public to information held by either government or private corporations, the release of which is in the public interest. In that way, while protecting against unwarranted intrusion, the press and the public could demand more information on such issues as the terms of government contracts, privatization arrangements and access to early drafts of legislation.

Other thorny issues relate to whose space satellite information is coming down into and what controls, if any can be exercised to limit, mitigate or utilize the incoming information. And if that last option is taken, then there is the issue of who owns the data, the information or the entertainment packages being transmitted. The passage of new Copyright legislation in Jamaica and elsewhere is an attempt to acknowledge that all users and countries have the responsibility to respect the authorship of materials received and in turn to expect an equivalent measure of respect and recognition for their works of art, literature or technical innovation.

CONCLUSION

With the emergence of information as a key profit-generating resource, the service-providing firm has been acquiring increasing importance in the 1990s in the same way that the extractive and manufacturing TNCs dominated the global economy in the previous era. In the global competition for 'market share', where size and global reach are important factors, the tendency has been towards dominance by a few very large transnational operators and for take-overs, mergers and joint corporate ventures. The bigger and more interlocked these companies become, the more difficult it is for governments and the local private sector in resource-strapped countries to monitor or regulate them. The challenge is to design policies and regulatory arrangements which are flexible enough to accommodate changes, but which aim to secure significant benefits for the wider society and the economically disadvantaged. The transnationals in communication and information need or markets and access to our geographical locations. They are in competition with each other, a fact which offers client countries the opportunity to select and bargain for access to appropriate technologies.

Strategies for selecting and modifying the incoming technologies and their software content appear to be more feasible than attempting to restrict the inflow and limit access to the global products. Underdeveloped countries have to value, preserve and develop their own methods and resources, even while they incorporate and adjust to the incoming content and technologies. The experiences of later industrializing economies such as Japan, the Republic of Korea and other south east Asian countries suggest that the design of a clear industrial policy which emphasises the build-up of a resource bank of trained specialists capable of assessing and adapting the technologies to local needs, provide a feasible basis for reaping some of the benefits of the innovations.

Such frequently reviewed industrial policies which target technology and its application to all sectors of the economy will constitute a critical strategic advance, linking into similar global processes. These policies should explicitly place at their centre, the improvement of the living standards of PEOPLE, and establish benchmarks by which they can be evaluated on these terms. Related to this is the need, at the level of human resource development, to create a national culture which is secure and comfortable with its own self-worth and heritage and which is therefore open to critically relate to new methods of addressing old problems. It is argued here that such a long term process begins with primary and secondary level training in new applications of science and technology and in techniques of marketing and human communication, even as we strengthen early education in the history, arts and culture of the peoples of our regions.

SELECT BIBLIOGRAPHY

Bittner, John R. — Broadcasting and Telecommunications — Prentice Hall, New Jersey, 1985.

Business Week — Your Digital Future — September 7, 1992 pp 56-64

Commonwealth Secretariat — 'Technological Change: Enhancing the Benefits': Report by a Commonwealth Working Group, Commonwealth Secretariat, London, 1985.

de Horowitz, Rosario — Technology and Librarianship — IFLA Journal 1993 pp 173-174.

Demac, D and Brown A. — '10 Future Regional Satellite Systems: The Case of the Caribbean' in Satellite International, New York, 1987.

Dror, Y — 'Muddling Through: Science or Inertia?' — Public Administration Review No 24, 1964 pp 153-157.

Dunn, Hopeton S. — Upgrading Our Libraries — Caribbean Affairs Vol 7 No 2, May/June 1994 pp 3-6.

Economist — Making Way for Multi-media — October 16, 1993

Enderwick, Peter — Multinational Service Firms — Routledge, New York, 1989.

Etzioni, A — Mixed Scanning: A Third Approach to Decision-making -Public Administration Review No 27, 1967 pp 285-392.

Ferguson, Marjorie (Ed) — New Communication Technologies and the Public Interest: Comparative Perspectives on Policy and Research — Sage, London, 1986.

Girvan, Norman — A Strategic Approach to Technology — in Lewis, Patsy — Jamaica Preparing for the 21st Century, Ian Randle Publishers, Kingston 1994 pp 194-203.

Girvan, Norman — Technology Policies for Small Developing Economies: A study of the Caribbean — ISER, UWI Kingston, 1983.

International Telecommunications Union (ITU) — Telecommunications: Visions of the Future — Geneva, 1993.

Kubr, Milan — 'How to Select and Use Consultants: A Clients Guide' International Labour Office, Geneva, 1993.

Lasswell, Harold — The Policy Orientation — in Lerner D. and Lasswell H. — The Policy Sciences, Stanford University Press, 1951 pp 131-155.

Lindblom, C.E. — 'Still Muddling — Not Yet Through' — public administration Review No 39, 1979 pp 517-526.

Newsweek — Your Electronic Future — June 6, 1994 pp 16-31.

Newsweek — Eyes on the Future — May 31, 1993

Rist Ray C. (Ed) — Policy Studies Review Annual — Transaction Books, Vol 7, New Brunswick, USA, 1985.

Simon, Herbert A — Administrative Behaviour — Free Press, Glencoe, Illinois, 1945.

Statistical Institute of Jamaica — Population Census 1991 — Vol 1 Part 10 Parish of Westmoreland, Kingston 1994.

Winsbury, Rex — 'Privacy, Media and Telecom: An Essay' — Intermedia, August/September 1993, Vol 21 No 4-5.

3

CARIBBEAN CULTURES AND MASS COMMUNICATION TECHNOLOGY:
RE-EXAMINING THE CULTURAL DEPENDENCY THESIS

Aggrey Brown

INTRODUCTION

A variety of interpretations can be brought to bear on the concepts of culture and technology. It is therefore appropriate before proceeding, to define how both concepts are being used and to show their relationship to each other.

   Defined holistically, culture constitutes the symbolic, instrumental and social responses of collectivities of people to their environment. Technology refers to the physical and intellectual tools that extend our capacity to relate to our environment as they simultaneously mediate our relationship with our environment. Environment then, is a common factor to both culture and technology. And in this context, 'environment' comprises more than physical external space. It is descriptive of all that is outside of the ego self and is therefore dynamic: impacting on individuals as they in turn impact on it.

   Culture and technology then, are analytically distinct but dialectically related phenomena. Technology helps to shape and produce culture as culture creates and employs technology. Thus, societies in their myriad manifestations are products of a complex dialectic: the interplay between cultural expression — itself a dialectic — and technological application. However, there is another narrower sense in which the concept of culture is generally understood, and that is as emanation of the creative imagination. Art, dance, drama, music, etc. are forms of such creative expression.

However, whether or not we are concerned with culture in its holistic or narrower sense does not change the basic dialectical relationship between culture and technology. Close analysis of all forms of creative expression will always reveal this irreducible relationship between culture and technology. So for instance, 'pan' music would not be possible without the steel drum, the technology through which it is expressed.

The unique vision or perception of each individual artist is always subject to the tools at his disposal for realising his imaginings. In this sense, the 'primitive' artist is only 'primitive' because of the limits imposed on his expression by the tools available to him. Contemporarily, the genre 'primitive' has taken on new meaning reflecting more a style of creative expression than the use of archaic tools to realise products of imagination.

Although some traditional skills and techniques for realising creative imagination may be lost to us contemporarily, available tools permit us to mediate our relationship with our environment in ways unheard of in the past. Some of these technologies, as we shall see, have also altered our temporal and spatial relationship to and with our environment, giving rise to forms of cultural expression that are more globally embracing than local and/or parochial.

More specifically, contemporary information/communication (infocom) technologies have ushered in an era in which humanity's environment has become global, giving rise to forms of cultural expression which, transcending both time and place, are themselves global. However, access to, and the development and control of these media(ting) technologies by a few, limits the participation of the majority in creating this nascent global culture both in its physical-technological as well as in its expressive forms. As long as this remains the case, the potential richness of global creative expression cannot be realised.

The pertinent questions to be addressed in assessing Caribbean cultures and mass communication in the 21st century therefore, are both structural and instrumental. What are the extant and foreseeable mass communication technologies? What form or forms do ownership and control of these technologies take? What instrumental value do they have for those who have access to them? Finally, what are the infocom options for those who do not have access to them?

While these questions are applicable to all the mass media, the focus here will be on the electronic media because they are internationally ubiquitous; they do not rely on literacy for their impact; and they are mesmerising. Particular attention will be paid to the visual media.

MASS MEDIA TECHNOLOGIES:
FROM EVOLUTION TO REVOLUTION

Among other things, the invention of the printing press led to the development of newspapers — the first form of mass media — from as early as the first decades of the 19th century. This was a virtual revolution since no longer would the written word be limited to the few, but information in the medium would be available to the many. This was followed almost a century later by radio broadcasting, and less than a few decades beyond that by television broadcasting.

In their earliest manifestations, the broadcast media had relatively limited reach. The technologies were cumbersome and expensive and in application required skills that were only readily available to a few. Furthermore, because of the fact that the Earth's electromagnetic spectrum constitutes an environmentally scarce resource, from the very beginning broadcasting, which utilises the spectrum, has been subject to official national and international regulation. The international regulatory agency, the International Tele-communications Union (ITU), was established from as early as 1865. Most importantly, the broadcast media were, and remain essentially potent point-to-multipoint information transmitting technologies. They allow a single message source to reach multiple receivers simultaneously but not vice versa. And precisely because they are non-interactive, strictly speaking, they are not communication technologies. The most significant, durable and far-reaching socioeconomic consequence of this observation is that the mass media as technologies, separate potential producers of cultural product from the consumers of cultural product and consequently, influence how both producers and consumers relate to the technologies.

In Europe, the regulations governing the use of the electromagnetic spectrum, that is, the context within which broadcasting developed, was paternalistic. For the most part, European governments adopted a proprietary approach to the application of these technologies in the service of the 'public good'. The broadcast media in the US, on the other hand, were from the very beginning cast in a competitive environment in which government merely regulated, by licensing private citizens, the uses to which these media could be put. The 'public good' was market-determined and not what government prescribed as being desirable. Therefore two entirely different broadcasting practices emerged in Europe and North America. In the former, radio and television broadcasting were government-supported and controlled activities whereas in the latter, the free enterprise ethic led to the emergence of commercial broadcasting.

Additionally, in television broadcasting three different and incompatible technical standards for propagating signals emerged in Europe and North America (PAL, SECAM and NTSC). Programmed material originating in one system cannot be broadcast in the others without first being converted technically.

These historically different approaches to broadcast media ownership and control as well as to technical standards on both sides of the Atlantic continue to affect the evolution of broadcasting internationally in spite of the presence of the ITU. In fact the politics of the ITU is defined by the need to ameliorate differences between international actors of differing capacities.

For well known colonial historical reasons, we in the Anglophone Caribbean inherited the British regulatory approach to the broadcast media. Economic as well as geopolitical imperatives however, gave rise to a hybrid form which combined government media ownership with commercial broadcasting — a nuanced departure from the strictly tax-supported BBC model. However, the potency of the broadcast media for influencing mass opinion and shaping popular values, was recognised by the colonial government from the inception of broadcasting in the region in the late 1930s and early 40s. Governments or government surrogates would become the arbiters and purveyors of culture (in its narrow sense) and the masses of Caribbean people consumers of cultural product. Consequently, throughout the region, private ownership of radio broadcasting facilities was limited to the British-based Rediffusion broadcasting group.

That is, in the colonial dispensation, broadcast media ownership and control meant either government ownership and control or British private ownership and control albeit in the case of the former with a liberal, paternalistic slant.

Forms of ownership and control in radio broadcasting evolved to include private ownership and control in the post-independence era. However, the tradition of government ownership and control was maintained even after independence with the introduction of the new technology of television broadcasting in the decade of the 60s. Implicitly, governments felt that the potential of the 'new' medium for influencing opinion and 'culture' in its narrow sense, was too great to cede to popular control.

Governmental authority notwithstanding, technological considerations also imposed limits to popular access to and use of broadcast technologies. Widespread consumption of the cultural products of radio and television was influenced by infrastructural supports such as limited distribution and availability of electricity; availability of the relevant repair and maintenance skills as well as by the bulk, size and cost of radio and television receivers and their consequent lack of mobility. In their infancy, the specialised skills required for producing programmes for the broadcast media, in particular television, also contributed to if not ensured the transmission of elitist values through these media.

However, by the 1970s, with the introduction of revolutionary new technical components and common use of transistors (particularly in radio receivers), mass consumption of electronic media had become a reality not only in the Caribbean region but also globally. Simultaneously, the means of propagating and transmitting broadcast signals were being revolutionised with the digitising and compression of electronic signals. Improvements in Frequency Modulation (FM) transmission as opposed to Amplitude Modulation (AM) made for clearer, cleaner, crisper sound broadcasting as well as greater accessibility to broadcasting technologies by potential new owners and managers.

By the end of the decade, the reach of broadcast signals also became global with the widespread use of satellite transmitting technologies. Audio and video cassette recording devices such as compact and laser discs would also become popular mass consumption technologies allowing consumers time-shifting capabilities hitherto limited to all but a few. In essence, a new revolution, similar to that which was unleashed by the newspaper as a mass medium, was being consummated in the last decades of the 20th century.

The dramatic and rapid developments in electronics that characterise the infocom industry today, led one analyst from as early as 1980 to observe that

> the latest developments in telecommunications make it possible for all the internal mail of major companies, all of the content of radio and television stations, all the material which passes into newspapers, all of the monetary transactions between large organisations and within them, all of the new sensing devices which analyse weather, harvests, troop movements and mineral deposits, to be conducted electronically rather than by normal physical means. (Smith, 1980).

In short, contemporary media technologies have expanded enormously human consciousness of the environment. They have transformed the local and parochial into the global and universal. As the drama continues to unfold it is futile to predict the ultimate impact of these technologies on mankind. However, in terms of the structure of the entertainment sector of the global infocom industry, certain trends have already begun to emerge which indicate the role and scope of the sector in human affairs.

THE GLOBAL ENTERTAINMENT INDUSTRY: THE PRODUCERS

There are two intrinsic limiting aspects of infocom technologies that define the parameters of their use. First, as already observed, they are not communication technologies. Rather, they are potent information transmitting technologies. Secondly, and as a consequence, they separate the producers of cultural product from the consumers of cultural product. Moreover, they are simultaneously physical as well as intellectual tools. That is, they have both a 'hardware' and a 'software' dimension. To illustrate: the consumer of a television receiver (the hardware), also consumes television programmes (the software). The consumer of a Compact Disc player (the hardware), also consumes the compact disc (the software). The consumer of a VCR (the hardware), also consumes video tapes with programmed material (the software). The consumer of a satellite dish receiver (the hardware) also consumes video information (the software), and so on.

The production of both hardware and software for global consumption therefore constitutes gigantic business which, particularly in the case of the former requires enormous financial outlays in research and development as well as investments in highly technical electronic engineering skills. Needless to say, the returns on hardware research and development are extremely rewarding.

It is estimated that by the end of the first decade of the 21st century, the entertainment hardware market alone will be worth US$3 trillion, that is, three million, million US dollars. (The Economist, Dec. 23, 1989). After aerospace, the entertainment industry is the USA's second largest source of foreign earnings generating $5.5 Billion or 5.5 thousand million dollars in 1988.

The incipient hardware-software nexus that arose out of the development of television technology in mid-century, and which initially saw the emergence of a division of labour between hardware manufacturers and software producers, has today resulted in the convergence of the two. This is a direct consequence of the development of inexpensive global information transmitting capabilities which have generated an almost insatiable demand for software. The deputy president of the Sony Corporation of Japan, one of the world's largest and best known industry participants, is on record observing that the 'hardware and software parts of the entertainment industry can no longer be talked about separately'. (The Economist, Dec. 23, 1989).

It is therefore not surprising that the intrinsic economic logic of hardware/software technological convergence has resulted in the emergence of an oligopolistic structure of the global infocom industry, in which it is estimated that by the turn of the 21st century there will be no more than approximately three vertically and horizontally integrated players. (Chesterman and Lipmann, 1988). By itself this would be cause for concern. That the technologies involved are consciousness-altering technologies makes this development doubly so.

Contemporarily, among the megaconglomerates vying for a permanent niche in the global industry are:

1. Time-Warner (a $13 billion merger in 1989), Thorn EMI, Gulf and Western and MCA which subsume such well known names as Home Box Office (HBO), Cinemax, Paramount and Universal Studios, Time Magazine, Sports Illustrated, Simon and Schuster, as well as lesser known entities involved in defence

systems, electronic security systems, computers, semi-conductors and telecommunications.

2. RCA, General Electric, Coca Cola-Citicorp subsuming NBC television, Random House and lesser entities involved in cable television, electronic hardware, defence and security systems, home appliances and consumer electronics.

3. Sony Corporation, Columbia (Sony) Pictures, CBS (Sony) Records (the world's largest record manufacturer), Loews and the News Corporation (Rupert Murdoch) including Twentieth Century Fox, Fox TV network, Sky Channel (which carried for the first time from the Caribbean live global satellite transmission of the 1990 Test series between England and the West Indies), and lesser entities involved in telecommunications, consumer electronics, including the Walkman, the Watchman, digital audio tape (DAT), CD players, Betamax VCRs and newspaper publishing.

4. Fujisankei Communications which includes television and radio stations, newspapers, records (including Virgin Records which acquired Island Records which had previously acquired the rights to the Bob Marley legacy) and video and film production.

5. Matsushita with its popular Panasonic range of technologies including audio and video electronics, photocopying machines, among others.

There are as well a handful of large, independent transnational entities that participate in the global industry in either the hardware or software dimensions, and whose size allows them to compete effectively for the time being. These include The Japan Victor Company (JVC) whose Video Home Service (VHS) video recording and playback system became an industry standard in the 70s and the well-known — though comparatively speaking, small — Turner Broadcasting system, a subsidiary of which is the world's first global and best known television news service, Cable News Network, (CNN).

A noticeable feature of all these players in the global infocom industry is their multinational character comprising Western European, North American and Japanese participants. Transnational, vertical and horizontal integration of the conglomerates give them strategic access to the world's major media markets. And, brooking no opposition, their dominance allows them to determine when and what technologies — both hardware and software — are introduced to the global marketplace.

By way of example, when in 1988, the Sony Corporation planned to introduce digital audio tape (DAT) on the world market, its initiative was resisted by CBS records, at the time the world's largest record manufacture. CBS perceived in the move by Sony a threat to the record industry since DATs would allow technically perfect multiple tape recordings of audio material. It proceeded to lobby the United States Department of Commerce to ban the sale of DAT equipment in the US. Undaunted and unwilling to have its strategic designs subverted, the Sony

Corporation acquired CBS records and proceeded to put DATs on the global market. DAT has not yet become a popular consumer item globally but the Sony Corporation's influence in the hardware and software sectors guarantees that it will at least find a niche in due course. The Corporation will not only be able to produce DAT recorders and tapes, but also will be able to guarantee, through CBS (Sony) Records, programmed material to be played on the hardware. (Quite incidentally, Mr. Michael Jackson is a contractee of CBS records).

The limited high-stakes competition within the global media marketplace also propels technological innovation. So the JVC company, Sony's homegrown archrival, has recognised that 'Digital sound is the wave of the future ...' (Chesterman and Lipmann, 1988), and has introduced its own version of digital sound on its internationally dominant VHS video recording system. In order to ensure that the new technology takes to the market, JVC makes its blank video tapes (the software) compatible with older hardware models and has invested over $100 million in a Hollywood joint venture to develop appropriate programme software.

At the macro level therefore, the global infocom sector is not only structurally vertically, horizontally integrated and dominated by a handful of mega-conglomerates, but also it is divided into discrete but interrelated subsectors comprising information, entertainment, news; hardware and software manufacturing, research and development, and distribution and marketing. Competition within the sector in the global market place continues to spawn even newer hardware and software technologies which, in turn result in expansion of product consumption internationally. Planned obsolescence, a tested technique of transnational hardware marketing, helps to delay the onset of entropy within the sector as a whole. Paradoxically as well, the consciousness raising capacity of the industry has helped to expand temporally and spatially the human environment even as the electronic gimmicks, gadgets and gizmos result in passive participation in an emerging global culture by the majority of the world's people. It is to the consumers of these technologies that we now turn our attention.

THE GLOBAL ENTERTAINMENT INDUSTRY: THE CONSUMERS

With but a few exceptions, every man, woman and child of planet Earth is a potential consumer of the products of the global infocom sector. Video and audio signals can be transmitted to and received from any place on the Earth's surface where the sun shines, thanks to the wonders of solar power. Satellite information transmitting technologies will have entered their fourth generation by the turn of the 21st century by which time as well, the globe would have been encircled by an interconnected network of the cheaper and even more reliable distribution technology of optical fibres.

Events occurring in any part of the world can be witnessed vicariously in real time (as opposed to delayed broadcast) by anyone with access to receiving equipment. The release of Nelson Mandela in South Africa in February 1990, was witnessed in such a manner by approximately a quarter of the human race. So too were the events in Tiananmen Square in Peking and the destruction of the wall separating East from West Berlin in the latter part of 1989.

Of course it is only a very small fraction of all globally transmitted material that is as momentous as the foregoing. By far, the vast majority of electronically transmitted material is made up of entertainment — the vehicle for advertising messages — with the bulk of it originating in the USA.

From as early as 1974, the authors of a comparative study on international television programming trends concluded that most television programmes in international distribution are produced to satisfy audience tastes in the United States, Canada, Australia, Japan and Western Europe . . .

> (T)here are two indisputable trends to be discovered in international flow:
>
> 1) a one way traffic from the big exporting countries to the rest of the world; and
>
> 2) dominance of entertainment material in flow.
>
> These aspects together represent what might be called a tendency towards concentration. (Nordenstreng and Varis, 1974).

Other studies conducted in the mid 80s, drew similar conclusions although one researcher found that globally, approximately one third of television programmes were imported.

Two studies conducted in the Caribbean by Hosein and Brown respectively in the mid 70s and mid 80s revealed that an average of over 70% of television programmes transmitted in the region originated from outside the region. The Brown study of the late 80s found an increase in the percentage of foreign content in regional television over that found by Hosein in the mid 70s.(Caribbean Quarterly, 1976). Comparison with international data led Brown to conclude that the Anglophone Caribbean, with an average of over 80% imported content, was the most penetrated region of the world by foreign television content.(Brown, 1987).

As of the beginning of the decade of the 90s, together Latin America and the Caribbean accounted for approximately 10% of the world's television audience having approximately 35 million television receivers. The extended region formally accounts as well for 5% of the world's television programme purchases. (Telecommunications Update No 19). However, when private satellite reception and video tape recordings are added, the figure more than doubles.

The vast majority of formal programme purchases are of course, from the USA, not only because it is the world's largest supplier of software, but also because of geographic proximity and familiarity. The fact too that the population of South America comprises a larger market than North America, is not lost on the scions of the infocom industry. A report on the 1989 convention of the US National Association of Television Programme Executives (NATPE) — a major annual trade meeting — concludes that

> Latin Americans generally have been more in tune with [the] commercial orientation of the US market than Europe. Latin broadcasters tend to show a disdain for Europe's long tradition of government-dictated content restrictions. The Latin love affair with action-adventure programming seems impossible to satiate, and police dramas or detective series are often at the top of the broadcasters' shopping lists. Latin viewers are accustomed to the US style of pacing, as reflected in their keen interest in US movies and miniseries. However, few situation comedies or reality-based shows seem able to bridge the culture gap. (Telecommunications Update, No 17)

What is clear from this is that access to video technologies affords the consumer some degree of choice regarding what he will or will not watch and when. However, the viewer's choice is predetermined by those responsible for selecting and transmitting programmes. Often, the latter's choice is determined by commercial advertising expedience and not by what is necessarily culturally relevant to a particular audience segment.

In the CARICOM region, a number of corollary factors determine consumer choice. The first of these is geography. Unlike the rest of the hemisphere, the region's proximity to North America permits easy access to signal spill-over from North American domestic satellite transmissions. In the Northern Caribbean which is closest to the US mainland, a dish antenna as small as six feet in diameter is capable of accessing such materials. And the owner of such an antenna has access to over 432 channels. Ku band direct broadcast satellites (DBSs), planned for launch by mid-decade, will permit access to signals by dishes no larger than 18 inches diameter. Video compression techniques will allow these satellites to double the number of channels already being transmitted. What is more, 'it is an axiom of satellite broadcasting that as the dish size shrinks, the market grows'. (Telecommunications Update, No 20). The reason for this, esthetics aside, is that the economic cost of dishes correlate positively with size.

In the Southern Caribbean, access to Ku band signals will be possible with dishes varying in size from 4 to 6 feet in diameter. Since the channel capacity of satellite dishes more than quadruples the capacity of coaxial cable which is used extensively in the Southern Caribbean, we can anticipate widespread consumption of DBS technology within a few years throughout the region with highest concentration in the Northern Caribbean.

A second corollary factor determining growth in consumption of video technologies in CARICOM in the near future is that of shared language and by extension culture, in its narrow sense. With the exception of shortwave radio broadcasting, English is the language of international broadcasting, particularly for television. While it may therefore take longer to 'bridge the culture gap' as in the case of Latin America, that is not the case in the CARICOM region where the 'Cosby Show' is almost as popularly received as 'Oliver at Large'.

A third corollary factor is the continued monopoly of television broadcasting by governments in the region. It is a little perceived paradox that government monopoly of the television medium since its introduction in the 60s, contributed significantly to the high consumption of video technologies subsequently throughout the region. Certainly in the instances of Trinidad and Tobago, Jamaica and Barbados, government monopoly limited consumer choice at the very moment that the global entertainment industry was taking off, that is, when dishes and VCRs were being introduced as consumer technologies.

While cost and other factors, including domestic politics, contributed to the maintenance of government monopoly of the medium, consumer awareness of alternatives led them to exercise their options. That in the case of Belize, St. Lucia and Guyana, extra-regulatory initiatives were taken by private entrepreneurs to introduce cable services, merely substantiates the point. The mesmerising effects of the medium are particularly demonstrated in the case of Guyana whose government from the late 1960s had consciously adopted a 'no television' policy.

Finally, the ease of travel between CARICOM and North America has also had an impact on the consumption of media technologies in the region. Relatives, friends, returning residents and guests have all been sources of supply of media consumer electronics hardware and software throughout the region. The burgeoning of video cassette rental shops throughout CARICOM in the mid to late 1970s, with most of the tapes recorded directly from North American transmissions, including commercials and station identifications, testifies to the impact that these supply sources have had in the regional media marketplace. The ready availability of Orbit and other publications of satellite television programme attractions throughout the region, including daily listings in some newspapers, also testifies to the permanence and high consumption of visual media technologies in the environment.

REGIONAL IMPACT AND RESPONSES:
CONSUMERS AND OFFICIALDOM

The notion of 'cultural imperialism' gained prominence throughout the region beginning in the late 1970s and continuing up to the present especially in official, academic and professional circles. While the two studies mentioned earlier by Hosein and Brown generated some useful empirical data on the amount of foreign content on regional television, there has been virtually no research done to measure the impact of the visual media on regional cultural expression. There is nevertheless, some documented and undocumented empirical evidence that supports the assumption that the visual media in particular, have had some impact on regional culture.

Popular responses to such local television productions as 'Gayelle' and 'No Boundaries' (Trinidad), and 'Oliver at Large' (Jamaica), would indicate a yearning on the part of regional television viewers for more regional programming. The explosion of music videos of local soca and reggae hits, reflects as well external influences and the popularity of the genre within the region.

Efforts by the Caribbean Broadcasting Union (CBU) to produce regional news exchange programmes and documentaries, albeit with external financial and technical assistance, and the popular acceptance by regional audiences of these efforts, also indicate the importance that regional viewers attach to such fare.

On the other hand, the importance that a growing number of local community self-help groups throughout the region attach to alternative media and to alternative uses of mainstream mass media, would indicate that there is some disagreement concerning the instrumental significance and cultural relevance of the mass media to citizens. As consumers, these citizens do not attach as much importance to the entertainment value of the mass media as many other citizens do. Rather, they wish to see the media used to enhance real communication possibilities in the service of development as well as individual and collective self-actualisation. (Brown and Sanatan, 1987).

At the political level, some regional leaders have, during the decade of the 80s, voiced appropriate platitudes about the role of the media in national and regional development but, for the most part, were found wanting in terms of meaningful policy formulation and decisive action.

Governments of the more developed Caribbean countries continue to monopolise television even as they reluctantly expand the scope of radio broadcasting by licensing new entrants to the field as is the case in Barbados, Jamaica and Trinidad and Tobago. For the most part they however remain oblivious of the fact that contemporary media technologies and delivery systems, have all but nullified the official cultural gate-keeping role and the paternalism of a past era. Citizens in the less developed parts of the region have long since coopted the visual media to their commercial and entertainment purposes.

RETHINKING THE CONCEPT OF 'CULTURAL IMPERIALISM'

Earlier on, some of the salient characteristics of contemporary mass media technologies were cited and it was suggested that, among other things they are not communication technologies but potent information transmitting technologies. Too, that they have the capacity to expand consciousness of the human environment spatially and temporally. By affecting human consciousness, they are also, as technologies, products of culture and products through which culture is expressed. However, their most potent feature is that, as technologies, they separate the producers of cultural expression in its narrow sense, from the consumers of cultural expression as product.

The formative phase of a global oligopoly of megaconglomerates that control both the hardware and software aspects, especially of the visual media, will be consolidated by the close of the decade. Given present trends, this competitive oligopoly, through research and development, will continue to produce and market globally new hardware — the core of the infocom industry — for which software will be required and not all of which they will be able to produce. In other words, the demand for video programming exists on a global scale. By the turn of the 21st century, the infocom industry as a whole will be the world's largest industry and its entertainment subsector, the most financially lucrative.

In light of all of the foregoing, present conceptions of cultural imperialism and the limited, tangible response to it in the region, are misconceived. This is inevitably so, since the very concept of cultural imperialism constitutes a misdiagnosis of the situation.

As is true of all the mass media, but particularly so of the visual media, Caribbean citizens have been willing consumers of both hardware and software. We have not been coerced into consumption. That the images reflected on the region's television screens are not often enough likenesses of ourselves, cannot be denied. However, cultural ennui is the price we pay for passive consumption.

Furthermore, the majority of our countries are members of the ITU, which formulates the regulations governing the use of the Earth's electromagnetic spectrum. While we do face some disadvantages — primarily lack of cutting-edge technical information and political/economic clout — vis-a-vis the industrial countries, we do participate in the decision-making process.

The obvious ascendancy of capitalism in the world at the close of the 20th century and the imminent dominance of the infocom sector in the world economy, are auguries of what can be called the globalization of culture (in the narrow sense). The geography and history of the Caribbean can be used to its strategic advantage to participate fully in the evolution of world culture.

More specifically, while the enormous sums required for research, development, production and distribution of infocom hardware will be beyond our collective capacity perhaps permanently, CARICOM does possess the technical skills and creative imagination to participate decisively in the development, production and distribution of visual media software.

The region's international successes in music in particular (reggae, soca, calypso), as well as in dance and drama, demonstrate the obvious, namely, that no nationality has a monopoly on creative imagination. This is what our poets, novelists, playwrights and other artists have demonstrated for over half a century. The Walcott Nobel prize for literature in 1992 testifies to that!

Meaningful participation in the evolution of global culture through the visual media however, will require the formulation and implementation of regional and national infocom policies that will nurture the requisite skills and mobilise the needed resources for doing so. That Caricom governments would have endorsed such a regional Infocom Policy by the mid 90s holds out some hope that Anglophone Caribbean citizens will not be excluded from such meaningful participation.

In light of CARICOM's political economy; the emergence of Japan as a global power; the evolving European union, as well as the North American Free Trade Area (NAFTA), it is incomprehensible that the region has so far all but neglected the infocom sector of the global economy which, by the first decade of the 21st century, will be worth over three thousand billion dollars and which is already having profound impact on human consciousness and global culture. The region possesses the potential to participate in the sector by producing software, if not hardware, that could earn significant revenues while simultaneously contributing to the evolution of global culture.

In this regard the Miami-based, Jamaican-owned and West Indian run Caribbean Satellite Network (CSN) specialising in Caribbean and Third World cultural expression, was a positive augury although regrettably it has since ceased to function. The planned acquisition of a satellite transponder to be shared by members of the CBU also signals the seriousness of purpose of the region's television practitioners to participate in the evolution of global culture through the medium.

The Steel Pan, reputedly the only original musical instrument (hardware) to have been developed in the 20th century, emerged out of the cultural dialectic of Trinidad at the start of the century and Reggae (software) out of a Jamaican dialectic near the end of the century. Facing the technologically mediated global environment of the 21st century, Caribbean people need only be reminded of and inspired by these two singular human achievements in order to make equally significant contributions to global culture via the electronic media.

BIBLIOGRAPHY

Brown, Aggrey and Sanatan, Roderick, *Talking With Whom: A Report on the State of the Media in the Caribbean,* Kingston, Carimac, 1987.

Caribbean Quarterly, Vol.27 #s 2 and 3, 'Mass Media in the Caribbean II', June-September, 1981.

Caribbean Quarterly, Vol.22 # 4, 'Mass Media in the Caribbean', December 1976.

Chesterman, John and Lipmann, Andy, T*he Electronic Pirates*, Lon. Comedia, 1988.

The Economist, 'Survey: The Entertainment Industry', December 23, 1989.

Nordenstreng, Kaarle and Varis, Tapio, *Television Traffic - A One-way Flow?*,UNESCO, 1970.

Smith, Anthony, *The Geopolitics of Information*, NY: OUP, 1980.

Telecommunications Update, Vol.V Nos. 17, 19 and 20.

PART TWO

Imported Media Content and Cultural Identity
Case Studies from the Caribbean and Canada

4

AMERICAN MEDIA IMPACT ON JAMAICAN YOUTH:
THE CULTURAL DEPENDENCY THESIS

Hilary Brown

INTRODUCTION

Are Jamaican youth the subject of a massive cultural assault from the unending flow of American television, magazines, books, films and music that bombard them daily?

This is the central question of this study which explores whether prolonged exposure to exogenous media products, results in dependency relationships which establish a set of foreign norms and values, and cultivate unsustainable levels of consumerism in recipient countries. The study seeks to determine whether differences in levels of cultural appreciation among Jamaican youth are related to higher or lower levels of foreign media consumption.

This area of international communication research, widely known as *media imperialism*, has been the subject of polemical debates in international fora, in academia and among media professionals over the last two to three decades, but has suffered from inadequate systematic research to enhance or refute the claims being made. This study was undertaken to help fill the void, particularly with regard to the media imperialism debate in the Caribbean.

Caribbean researchers, scholars and media professionals, as well as specialist interests from outside the region, have long been expressing concern over the potential threat to indigenous Caribbean culture by the unprecedented global penetration of new-age media technologies (Brown & Sanatan, 1987; Browne, 1987; Hoyte, 1986; Knaack, 1987; Lent, 1979; Lent, 1987). These have been unleashed by the enormous capacities for information access, storage, transmission and retrieval of satellite, fibre-optic, microwave, micro-electronic, digital, and micro-chip technology.

The hegemonic activities of North American media have been characterized in strong terms by Nettleford (1993:129), the foremost and most prolific scholar of Caribbean culture as 'the hijacking of the region's media, the invasion of the Caribbean people's intellectual space and the cultural bombardment of the entire region by every means possible from North America....'.

The English speaking Caribbean is particularly susceptible, as it shares a common language with the United States (US) and the United Kingdom (UK), the world's two largest producers of media content; its geographical proximity to the US facilitates programme importation, exchanges and training of personnel. Tourism as a major regional industry facilitates further interaction with Americans; and because many West Indians reside in the US, linkages are even more personalized.

HISTORICAL AND THEORETICAL CONTEXT

The concept of media imperialism rose to prominence in the late 1970's, within the context of the call for a New World Information and Communication Order by the developing world. The notion was fueled by the failure of the 1960's approaches to modernization and development through the rapid adoption of Western media technologies by developing nations, and by the all-pervasiveness of primarily American media in the marketplace.

Tapio Varis (1984) documented the global flow of television programmes which showed that Latin America and the Caribbean and parts of Africa and Asia, had the highest levels of imported content. The lowest importer was the United States (2%); Western Europe imported approximately 30% and Canada 38%. In the Caribbean, the level of importation ranged from a 'low' of 76% in Jamaica to a high of 95% in Montserrat in the mid 1980's (Brown, 1987).

In addition to television, the term 'media imperialism' has been invoked with reference to the operations in the developing world of transnational news agencies, transnational advertising companies, conglomerates in print, and in the recording industry. Media imperialism is also said to be reflected in the foreign ownership of media in the developing countries and in the transfer of media conventions in print and electronic journalism.

The majority of the early research in this area was macrosocial investigations of the concept, which had a primarily historical, critical and qualitative approach to the problem, focusing on the operations of transnational media, multinational corporations and on the impact of other social and economic factors such as tourism and trade (Schiller, 1969; Smith, 1980; Tunstall, 1977; Hamelink, 1983).

These investigations usually pointed to technological media dependency (for programmes, spare parts, technical expertise, and software), little local programming and high importation of foreign programmes and other media products. The demand for Western consumer products and the resulting high importation of consumer goods was another consequence of the dependency relationship frequently cited (Katz & Wedell, 1977; Wells, 1972; Tunstall, 1977; Lee, 1979; Hamelink,1983).

It has also been asserted that the traditional Western values in journalism and production are perpetuated by media managers in the developing world (Golding, 1977). Consequently, in spite of the fact that Latin American tele-novelas have successfully reduced dependence on US imported programmes, the main producers — Mexico's *Televisa* and Brazil's *TV Globo* — are said to represent the same commercial television values as US network TV.

A number of studies have found some erosion of traditional values and aspirations in favour of those emphasized on American TV, including studies of the cultural impact of American media on the values of Filipino high school students (Tan, Tan & Tan, 1987), Korean college students (Kang & Morgan, 1988), Algonkian Indians (Granzberg, 1982), and the Inuit people (Coldevin, 1979).

A number of other studies in Taiwan and Mexico (Tan, Li & Simpson, 1986; Tsai, 1970), Thailand (Tan & Suarchavarat, 1988) and Israel (Weimann, 1984), found that the viewing of American television affected views held about Americans.

However, the majority of the studies have been criticized as placing too much emphasis on television and news (Hamelink, 1983; Tunstall, 1977), and Fejes (1981) suggested the need for greater attention in research to the historical dimension, to culture and to forms of communication other than mass media.

CHALLENGES TO THE MEDIA IMPERIALISM CONCEPT

Early challenges to the media imperialism concept were asserted by Read (1976) who argued that dependency through media imports was a myth. He contended that the impetus was economic expediency and that the profits, though significant were not phenomenal. He also argued that it was primarily the élite in the developing world that had access to foreign media and that they constitute an insignificant minority.

However, as Brown (1990) contends, it is the region's élite who are the policy-makers and decision-makers and as a result of their ready access to foreign media, they are at greatest risk, as Nettleford (1993) argues, of cultural conditioning away from a national or regional 'sensibility.'

However, in keeping with Read's position, one West Indian scholar argued that 'a generation of West Indians have grown up on the tradition of Hollywood westerns, but West Indians remain West Indians and not duplicates of John Wayne. The impact of foreign programming is thus exaggerated' (Hosein, 1976: 11).

Tracey (1985) challenges the idea that the media 'are agents of domination. He suggests that the cultural domination theory is too simplistic and lacks evidence. He argues that national audiences prefer their own, that they discriminate rather than 'slavishly' pursue imported programmes, and as such home produced programming can and does exceed the popularity of imported programmes. Further, that it is 'the real genius of American popular culture, to bind together, better than anything else, common humanity', by what it 'taps' rather than what it 'imposes' (Tracey, 1991: 304).

The paradigm shift in communication theory and research in the 1980s from a conception of audiences as passive consumers to active consumers of media products as posited in reader reception or reader response theory has sought to challenge the media imperialism theory, thus heightening the debate.

Katz and Liebes (1984 &1987), conducted cross cultural research on the decoding of *Dallas* among audiences of different ethnic origins in Israel (Israeli Arabs, new immigrants from Russia, first and second generation immigrants from Morocco, and kibbutz members), suggesting that foreign audiences may construct different 'readings' and rely on a different frame of reference to decode a cultural artifact than Americans in Los Angeles. US viewers appeared to 'read' less into a programme which they knew from experience did not represent the average American household.

This finding however, suggests that there is the potential for even greater assimilation and cultivation among foreign audiences whose 'experience' is largely mediated. Roach (1990) further contends that the media imperialist school of thought has been faulted for what it never set out to address. She maintains that the school never intended to establish a theory of message (or media) reception. Rather, that the arguments are structural, based on the assumption that the economic structures of capitalist exploitation are complemented by communications structures and cultural industries.

It has also been argued that there is evidence in the case of the Caribbean that the imbalanced flow of cultural products from the North has been countered to some degree by the success of Caribbean music with foreign audiences (Dunn, 1993), most notably reggae and calypso (McCann, 1993; Nettleford, 1978; Nettleford 1993; White, 1993).

CARIBBEAN RESEARCH

One of the few studies conducted in the Caribbean to date, which has informed this study, was a survey of music preferences among Jamaican youth. Higher socio-economic status (SES) was accompanied with greater preferences for foreign over local music (Cuthbert, 1985).

Surlin (1990), in a cross cultural investigation of American, Canadian and Caribbean university students concluded that the 'reality' projected in US TV was far too removed from the reality of Caribbean life to have a major impact on fundamental values. Surlin (1988) reported that Caribbean students consistently projected a more 'humanistic' value profile while the American and Canadian students projected a more 'materialist' profile.

A study which was conducted in Belize, Central America, found support for the hypothesis that the amount of time an individual spends watching US TV is positively correlated with a person's attitude towards the consumption of US products and negatively associated with a person's attitude towards the consumption of Central American products (Oliveira, 1986).

An investigation of the impact of US television programme viewing on national allegiances, was conducted in Trinidad and Tobago (Skinner, 1984; Skinner & Houang, 1987), which focused on social and psychological dependency, through a survey of 400 subjects. Skinner reported that 75% of Trinidadian's viewing time was devoted to American programming, 19% to local shows and 6% to British shows. US TV viewing was positively correlated with US values, appeal, dependency and appreciation.

THE JAMAICAN CASE

In Jamaica, certain trends have been identified as evidence of cultural dependency, with little systematic investigation. Among the indicators are the desire to migrate to the US in various groups in the society, evidence of the 'brain drain' of the professional classes, the demand for consumer products that are not realisable for many in the context of a developing country and the extreme popularity of day-time soaps such as *Santa Barbara* and *Generations*.

Additionally, the tendency of those who work in the tourist areas to acquire American accents from interacting with tourists, the love of American music among upper and middle class youth and their disdain for local traditions, dances and reggae music are also frequently cited manifestations.

The sentiment that what is local is inferior is still quite prevalent and status is often conferred by the extent to which one adopts North American fashion and technology, and the frequency of travel to the US.

Home VCRs and satellite dishes have become exceedingly popular, estimated at 294,000 and 34,000 respectively (Market Research Services, 1994), further facilitating the unimpeded, unregulated flow of American entertainment into the country. In addition, cable television is increasingly available from illegal operators islandwide, a situation which is currently being addressed by the government. There is also an estimated 699,000 television sets and over 1.8 million radios in a population of just over 2.3 million in the 1991 population census.

The media in Jamaica and the rest of the Caribbean have a history of foreign ownership dating to the days of colonialism which has been documented elsewhere (Dunn, 1991; Lent 1977; Lent, 1990; Wolfe, 1991). The introduction of media to the region by external forces, resulted in the unplanned adoption of radio and TV technology which has an insatiable appetite for content and relies on commercial enterprises for operating revenue, which are relatively few in most Caribbean countries. Without the productive capacity and resources, it is almost impossible to depart from the cycle of dependency.

Although the region has a rich cultural heritage which fuels a thriving theatre industry, many factors mitigate against tapping this source. The common problems identified include the prohibitive cost of local production and the relative inexpensiveness of foreign imports; limited resources; the absence of an industry to keep producers and talent gainfully employed and the lack of government support to foster such an industry.

THEORETICAL DEFINITIONS

It is the global entrepreneurial activities of transnational media and their perceived effects that the terms *media imperialism* (Lee, 1979), *electronic colonialism* (McPhail, 1986), *cultural imperialism*, *cultural domination* (Schiller, 1976), *cultural synchronization* (Hamelink,1983), *cultural dependency* (Smith, 1980), *enculturation* and *cultural penetration* have been applied.

It has justifiably been argued that the lack of conceptual precision or consensus in terms has been a major obstacle to the development of a precise theory to inform research on media imperialism (Fejes, 1981; Lee, 1988). However, it is the concept of *cultural dependency* which provides the theoretical justification of this empirical study, as this concept best describes the nature of the *impact* of exposure to foreign media on a given audience. Domination, imperialism, penetration and synchronization all connote the activity of the exporters of media products which result in cultural dependency.

For the purposes of this study, cultural dependency is a process in which an exogenous system of meaning and symbols (culture) is learned by another society, and their indigenous culture simultaneously subordinated and demeaned. The definition incorporates the essential notion of cultural dependency as a process, and defines culture as a learned system of meaning and symboling which defines the unique identity of a people (Kottack, 1986; Benedict, 1945; Steward, 1950; Hockett, 1950). That that culture is learned and symbol-based rather than genetic makes it possible for cultural traditions to extend beyond national boundaries, through diffusion and borrowing (Kottack, 1986). The definition also captures the essential element of subordination of the indigenous culture subject to media imperialism.

STATEMENT OF HYPOTHESES

Prolonged exposure to foreign media is presumed to result in negative attitudes towards the local culture, and positive attitudes towards the foreign culture depicted, giving rise to the following hypotheses tested in the study:

Hypothesis 1

The more time spent with foreign media the less is one's orientation towards Jamaican culture and the greater one's orientation towards American culture.

Hypothesis 2

The higher the level of foreign media use the higher the level of personal consumerism.

It should be noted that notwithstanding the focus of the study on media impact, resulting in the stated hypotheses, there was recognition of the fact that the media are merely part — albeit an influential part — of a complex environment of socio-psychological influences.

Other variables besides media exposure which were believed to significantly affect cultural dependency, were rural versus urban residency, and non-media contact with Americans through tourism and travel.

The rural areas do not have as much access to American consumer goods or American media as urban areas, and higher socioeconomic groups have greater access to foreign media. The tourist areas allow high non-media contact between Americans and Jamaicans, and travel allows first-hand experience with American culture.

These variables in addition to media exposure were therefore investigated and controlled in the study and treated as an interrelated model of cultural dependency. That is to say that the effect or *contribution* of media exposure to evidence of cultural dependency if any, was evaluated within the context of other intervening and contributing variables.

This approach seeks to depart from the previous narrow, direct causal effects or 'hypodermic needle' type conceptualizations of media impact in the effects research tradition, enhanced by utilizing more sophisticated methods of statistical analysis which allow for model testing and which account for the interdependence of social scientific variables.

METHOD

Subjects

A survey of 1734 Jamaican adolescents, ages 10-19, was conducted in 31 secondary educational institutions, in eight geographical areas in the island, between October 1992 and January 1993. However, for the purposes of this chapter, preliminary analyses of a subsample of 952 subjects from 17 schools in three areas were conducted.

Sampling procedure

The three areas selected represent the following combinations of independent variables under study:

1. **Kingston**: urban, non-tourist, high media concentration
2. **Montego Bay**: urban, tourist, high media concentration
3. **Seaforth, Hector's River, Golden Grove and Trinityville**[1]: rural, non-tourist, low media concentration

The sample was drawn from eight schools in the capital city, Kingston; five schools in the island's second city and main tourist area, Montego Bay; and four schools in four rural, non-tourist areas in the parishes of St. Thomas and Portland, namely Seaforth, Golden Grove, Trinityville and Hector's River.[2]

The schools were selected randomly from a stratified list of schools by school type, in each area. The different secondary school types represented in the subsample were: *high, secondary, technical and comprehensive. All age* schools were represented in the wider study but did not fall within the reduced sample. All secondary school types were included in the wider study as they represented differences in curriculum as well as differences in social class in the composition of the students.[3]

A systematic random design yielded the sample of students, using the aggregation of class registers as the sampling frame. All the year groups in the schools were represented in the sample.

Questionnaire Administration

As literacy levels varied by SES, rural/urban residency and school type, two methods of administration were used. The questionnaires were *self administered* in the high schools and some secondary schools in the sample where the subjects were literate. In the remaining schools, *group administration* was conducted, where the questions were read aloud by the researcher and time allowed for the subjects to respond.

The respondents required between 30–45 minutes to self administer the questionnaire and the group interview took 1.5 – 2 hours to conduct.

Reliability Assessment

The reliability of the instrument was established with the test-retest method of assessment on a sample of 30 students from the target population at Ardenne High School in Kingston. The test yielded an $r = .9385$.

Instrument Construction

The questionnaire was designed with the following types of questions: media-use and music preference measures, knowledge items, attitude items, a consumerism index, questions on travel experiences and aspirations, educational goals and demographic items.

Statistical Procedures

The main statistical procedures used in the study were Analysis of Variance (ANOVA) and Multivariate Analysis of Variance (MANOVA). These procedures test the significance of the differences in the means which may occur between groups, on specified dependent variables. In these analyses, the differences between the different areas, school types, high, medium and low SES groupings and high, medium and low media users, among others were tested.

The Cultural Dependency Model

The conceptual model of cultural dependency tested in the study was that depicted in Figure 1. The theory informing the model is that the underlying, unobserved concept of cultural dependency has multiple observed causes, namely travel experiences, SES, tourist/ non-tourist, rural/urban residency and foreign media exposure; and multiple observed indicators, namely a manifested cultural orientation away from Jamaica and the Caribbean, high levels of consumerism, a preference for foreign music, and high knowledge levels of the US, compared with local and regional knowledge.

That is to say that we do not directly observe cultural dependency but rather observe some important though not exhaustive manifestations of the concept. The effect of the predictor variables are therefore simultaneously evaluated within the presence of the effects of all the other independent variables for significance, through the MANOVA *F test*.

The Independent Variables

A brief description of the composite measures of all the variables used in the analyses would be instructive.

The (foreign) *media exposure* variable (MUSE) is a composite measure of media ownership, access, and time spent with the media. Respondents were asked about the different media they had at home, namely TV, radio, records and tapes, VCRs, computers, telephones, newspapers, magazines, comics, books, and satellite dishes. The respondents indicated how much time they spent with each medium on weekdays and weekends, making selections from six or seven categories in two-hour increments.

Given the dearth of local television programming, comic books, movies, and fictional books for the specified age group, and the significant foreign music programming on local radio stations with the exception of *Irie FM*,[4] the use of media in general was operationalized as being synonymous with the use of foreign media in this study. However, the time spent with local newspapers, local magazines and *Irie FM* was omitted from the measure of foreign media exposure. The range of possible scores on this composite variable was 0-77.

Each subject was assigned a number between one and four to distinguish between *school types* (SCHTYP) in the sample. However, for the purposes of the analyses, the technical and comprehensive schools (types three and four) were treated as one group.[5]

The SES variable was composed of four measures, namely, parents occupation rated on a 6 point scale; an 18 item home appliance list (for example, air conditioner, dishwasher, iron, oven, washing machine); an 8 item media appliance list; and 8 leisure activities (for example going to plays or to the zoo, weekends at resorts, extracurricular activities). High, middle and low SES were determined by using the median and upper and lower quartiles of the distribution of the new composite variable as classification margins. The variable range was 0-91.

To facilitate analyses by the independent variable *area*, each subject in the survey was assigned the appropriate code for his or her geographical area which defined it as tourist or non-tourist, rural or urban, and high or low in media concentration.

The *travel* variable is a summed index of responses to five questions on individual travel experiences, which were whether the respondent has visited the US, if so the approximate number of times; whether the respondent has travelled to any other country in or outside the Caribbean; and a general question on whether travel is a part of their family's leisure activities. Points were awarded for affirmative responses, resulting in a range of possible scores of 0-32.

The Dependent Variables

The points assigned for correct responses to 11 true-false questions tapping aspects of Jamaican and Caribbean geography, politics and culture were summed to constitute the local/regional knowledge variable (KNOW1). Points were also assigned for the correct explanation of two West Indian proverbs.[6] The resulting variable range was 0-15.

A similar assessment of general knowledge of the US (KNOW2) was based on the responses to 8 true-false questions and one item of American slang. The range was 0-10.

Figure 1. The Dependent Variables

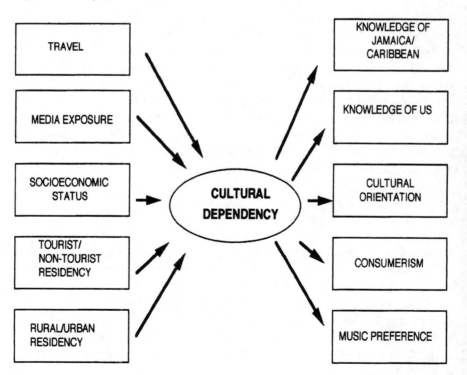

The cultural orientation variable (CULTURO) was composed of the summation of a 21 item, five-point agree-disagree Likert scale developed by the researcher. It consisted of items such as 'I would prefer to live in the United States,' and 'I am proud of my cultural background.' The scale yielded a *Cronbach alpha* reliability coefficient of .64. High scores on CULTURO signified a pro-Jamaican orientation. The index range was 21-105.

Points were assigned on a 20-item consumer index (CONSUME), also developed by the researcher, to constitute the consumerism variable, which had a range of 0-27. Respondents indicated whether they owned or had access to items such as make-up, jewellery, designer clothing and brand name sneakers at home. Separate lists were constructed for males and females although there was some overlap between the lists.

Three variables pertaining to musical preference were developed by measuring the degree of liking for calypso and soca (MUSIC1), reggae and dancehall[7] (MUSIC 2) and the foreign forms disco, soul (rhythm and blues), and rap (MUSIC3), on a five-point scale (don't know, not at all, a little, quite a lot, very much). The MUSIC1 and MUSIC2 variable ranges were both 0-8 and the MUSIC3 range was 0-12.

RESULTS

Sample Profile

The sample was comprised of a relatively equal male-female ratio (49% and 51% respectively) and age group ratios, where 54% of the sample fell in the 10-14 age group and 46% in the 15-19 age range.

Differential weighting in sampling based on school population, was applied to the three geographical areas under study, which resulted in 47% of the sample being drawn from Kingston; 27% from Montego Bay; and 26% from the combined areas of Golden Grove, Hector's river, Trinityville and Seaforth.

With respect to school type, some 58% of the sample was high school students, 25% secondary school students, 11% was from technical schools and 6% from comprehensive schools.

Media Profile

As shown in Table 1, it was not surprising that 99% of the respondents reported having at least one radio at home, in view of the well documented evidence of radio as the most widespread medium in Jamaica and the Caribbean (Brown & Sanatan, 1987; Market Research Services, 1994; Nettleford, 1993).

Table 1. Media Profile by Area (in percentages)

Media	Total	Kgn	MoBay	St. Thom/Port*
Radio	99	98	100	99
Newspapers	96	95	95	98
Television	93	95	96	85
Magazines	88	89	85	88
Comics	82	83	82	78
Tape Recorders	76	79	83	63
Books	74	74	78	70
Record Players	65	72	64	55
Video (VCRs)	63	72	63	48
Cinema	45	58	42	24
Telephones	45	62	42	18
CD Players	23	29	23	13
Satellite Dishes	15	28	7	1
Computers	12	21	5	2

*Note: The areas have been abbreviated as follows: Kingston (Kgn); Montego Bay (MoBay); St. Thomas/Portland (St. Thom/Port).
Each area column is not a break-down of the total column. All entries in the table are computed out of 100%

Having access to newspapers was next in popularity (96%), where the *Star* was the most read publication in the age group (87%), followed by the *Gleaner* (89%), then *Children's Own* (64%), all of which are published by the Gleaner Company Limited, the oldest and most established media house in the country.

Television was also widespread in the group under study, where 93% of the sample reported having a television at home. The four least popular appliances at home were telephones (45%), compact disc players (23%), satellite dishes (15%) and computers (12%).

Comparisons between areas revealed the greatest concentration of satellite dishes in Kingston, where 28% of the Kingston respondents had a 'dish' at home compared with 7% of the Montego Bay respondents and 1% in St. Thomas/ Portland. The subjects in the latter area (98%) surpassed both the Kingston (95%) and the Montego Bay (95%) respondents in reported newspaper use and were on par with Montego Bay and Kingston with regard to the prevalence of radio and magazine use. St. Thomas and Portland as expected, lagged behind the other two areas with respect to the least popular media previously mentioned — computers, CD players, satellite dishes, and telephones. This group also reported significantly less movie-going activity, where 58% of the Kingston respondents, 42% of those in Montego Bay and only 24% of the St. Thomas and Portland respondents reported this type of activity.

These results confirmed the expected patterns with regard to media concentration in the areas chosen for the study. A comparison of mean media use between the three areas resulted in the highest average in Kingston, followed by Montego Bay, then St. Thomas/ Portland.

MANOVA Tests for Significance

All the independent variables attained significance on each of the MANOVA tests of overall significance — *Wilk's Lambda, Pillai's Trace, Hotelling-Lawley's Trace, and Roy's Greatest Characteristic Root*. The levels of significance were p.0005 for the media use, school type and SES variables, p.001 for area and p.01 for travel.[8]

Hypothesis 1

The more time spent with foreign media, the less is one's orientation towards Jamaican culture and the greater one's orientation towards American culture.

Support was found for this hypothesis as evidenced in the level of significance of the media use predictor variable on the cultural orientation variable (F=8.72, p.<0005). That is to say that the differences between the means on the cultural orientation scale of the high, medium and low media users were sufficiently significant to suggest a relationship between attitudes and media use. The high media users expressed more pro-foreign sentiment than those in the middle strata and averaged orientation scores which were close to the low media users (see Table 2).

Other significant variables on the cultural orientation scale were school type (F=3.93, p.<05) and socio-economic status (F=4.45, p.<05). Of the three school types in the analysis, the technical/ comprehensive grouping expressed the strongest pro-Jamaican/ West Indian sentiment, followed by the high then the secondary school respondents.

With respect to SES, the high SES subjects averaged the lowest scores on the cultural orientation scale and the middle class group the highest scores.

Hypothesis 2

The higher the level of media use, the higher the level of personal consumerism.

Support was found for this hypothesis as media use was also a significant determinant of differences in levels of consumerism as measured by the consumer index (F=33, p.<0005). High media users averaged the highest scores on the consumer index, followed by the medium users then the low media users. In addition to significance on the cultural orientation and consumerism variables,

Table 2. Mean Scores on the Dependent Variables by Media Use, School Type and Socioeconomic Status

	Know1	Know2	Culturo	Consume	Music1	Music2	Music3
MUSE							
HIGH	7.849	6.116	76.258	19.124	4.600	6.702	8.933
MID	7.954	4.521	77.624	14.445	4.277	5.857	8.595
LOW	7.187	3.240	75.321	10.850	4.085	5.561	7.915
SCHTYP							
HIGH	8.297	5.290	76.732	16.145	4.295	5.918	8.505
SEC	6.546	3.496	75.731	12.357	4.357	6.160	8.538
TECH/COMP	7.526	3.641	78.071	12.686	4.256	5.929	8.417
SES							
HIGH	8.039	6.721	75.000	19.699	4.336	6.358	8.598
MID	7.792	4.281	77.605	14.121	4.290	5.969	8.682
LOW	7.351	3.183	76.615	11.061	4.302	5.672	8.092

foreign media use was also related to all the other dependent variables with the exception of KNOW1, where the three groups averaged almost equal scores.

It was therefore a significant determinant of group differences in knowledge of the US (F=5.32, p.<01), where the high media users had the highest scores, followed by the medium then the low users. With respect to the music variables, the high media users expressed greater degrees of liking for all three categories of music — calypso and soca (F=7.71, p.<001), reggae and dancehall (F=12.65, p.<0005), and rap, disco and soul (F=9.62, p.<0005) than the medium and low users.

School Type

In addition to being a significant predictor of differences on the cultural orientation scale, school type was significantly related to group differences in knowledge of Jamaica and the Caribbean (F=24.66, p.<0005), and knowledge of the US (F=14.41, p.<0005), where high school subjects averaged the highest scores on both measures, followed by the technical/ comprehensive group then the secondary school group.

On the music variables, the secondary, followed by the technical/comprehensive group expressed greater degrees of liking for reggae and dancehall than the high school students. However there were no significant differences on the calypso/soca or foreign music forms investigated.

Area

Area was significant on the knowledge of the US, the consumerism and all the music variables, with all p values less than .05 and .01 in some instances. The Kingston respondents were most knowledgeable of the US, and the St. Thomas/Portland group the least knowledgeable. A similar pattern obtained on the consumer index variable (see Table 3).

The St. Thomas/Portland group expressed the greatest degree of liking for soca and calypso and for the foreign forms, followed by the Kingston then the Montego Bay respondents, with a reversal of this pattern with respect to reggae, where the Kingston respondents averaged the highest scores, followed by the St. Thomas/Portland group, then the Montego Bay respondents. Area did not attain significance on the cultural orientation scale.

Table 3. Mean Scores on the Dependent Variables by Area and Travel

	KNOW I	KNOW2	CULTURO	CONSUME	MUSIC1	MUSIC2	MUSIC3
AREA							
KGN	7.570	5.546	76.152	16.398	4.309	6.382	8.464
MOBAY	8.008	4.352	76.707	13.961	4.055	5.594	8.418
ST.T/PORT	7.725	3.072	77.657	12.187	4.550	5.673	8.641
TRAVEL							
HIGH	7.957	6.914	75.216	20.185	4.451	6.556	8.833
LOW	7.683	4.083	77.008	13.475	4.274	5.862	8.429

Socio-economic Status

Socio-economic status was not a significant determinant of differences in knowledge of Jamaica and the Caribbean and was surprisingly not significant on any of the music variables. It was significant on the US knowledge variable ($F=6.83$, $p.<005$), where higher socioeconomic status was associated with higher knowledge levels; on the cultural orientation scale ($F=4.45$, $p.<05$), with the middle class group averaging the highest scores on the scale, as previously discussed; and on the consumer index ($F=13.78$, $p.<0005$), where higher SES was associated with higher levels on the index of consumerism.

Travel

The dependent variables which were significantly affected by the amount of travel overseas, were US knowledge ($F=11.74$, $p.<001$), and the consumerism variable ($F=16.61$, $p.<0005$) where the more frequent travellers averaged higher scores in both instances than the low travel group.

DISCUSSION

The support which was found for the first hypothesis with regard to foreign media and cultural orientation, was in keeping with the prior expectation that socio-economic status and foreign media use would be the primary determinants of attitudes to Jamaica and attitudes to the United States.

The pattern of cultural dependency towards the US was expected to be highest in the urban tourist area (Montego Bay) and among the upper middle and upper class youth who have the greatest access to foreign media, if the media are indeed primary in the cultivation of these attitudes.

However, in view of the severity and harshness of the current economic environment, it was also possible that to the extent that the more depressed classes saw the US as a form of escape from local poverty, then the converse would have obtained, with lower SES being associated with more expressions of pro-foreign sentiment.

However it was the high SES grouping which expressed the highest levels of these attitudes, and the middle class group which expressed the highest levels of pro-Jamaican sentiment, followed by the low SES group.

Further, with regard to media use, the high media users (which consisted primarily of high and upper middle SES respondents) again failed to exhibit the highest pro-Jamaican scores on the cultural orientation scale, falling second to the medium media users. The students in the technical and comprehensive schools averaged the highest scores in cultural orientation (indicating more pro-Jamaican sentiment), followed by the high school subjects, then the secondary school respondents.

These patterns suggest the tendency for greater expressions of loyalty, confidence and commitment to country and region from the upper end of the low socio-economic group and from the middle class. However, this is not inconsistent with historical patterns in the development of Jamaica, as traditionally, the Jamaican middle class has exhibited significant levels of nationalism and regionalism. These forces, spearheaded by the middle class, accounted in large measure for the independence movement of the early 1960s, and the prior West Indies Federation in 1958.

Some 42% of the sample reported having relatives in Canada with whom they were in contact, 75% had relatives in the United States, 51% in Europe, primarily the United Kingdom and 13% in other Caribbean countries. When asked where they would ultimately like to live and work, 63% indicated a preference for Jamaica and 32% expressed a desire to live overseas. Of the 32% which expressed the latter preference, the most frequently given reason for choosing an overseas option was to earn higher salaries and capitalize on the exchange rate advantage (12%), followed by the perception that a foreign option offered a better standard of living and more opportunities (10%). Some 4% indicated a desire to join relatives overseas or to pursue further studies; 3% expressed a desire for a change of environment, to experience other cultures, or to learn a new language; and 1% expressed the wish to gain experiences and skills that would enable them to return to Jamaica and make a contribution to the development process.

The majority (17%) selected the US as the preferred destination for relocation; 3% Canada; 3% Western Europe and 1% selected a Caribbean country, Cayman being a popular choice. It should be noted that a significant proportion of 9% did not name a country and as such were classified as missing data. However, the term 'foreign' is almost synonymous with the United States in the context of rural Jamaica and among the lower SES groupings, and as such many may not have seen the necessity to specify their foreign selection beyond a 'tick' next to that option.

That the area variable was not significant with regards to cultural orientation suggests that the effect of tourism and the rural versus urban factors do not supersede, but rather interact with the more marked effects of SES, school type and media use. The apparent absence of within-group homogeneity by area resulted in the lack of significant difference in attitudes to Jamaica, local culture and cultural heritage between subjects resident in a tourist mecca like Montego Bay, and the rural areas like those selected in St. Thomas and Portland.

With respect to the second hypothesis, there were no unusual or unexpected patterns as regards media use and levels of consumerism. High media users, Kingston respondents, high socioeconomic group subjects and the more frequent travellers overseas all scored significantly higher on the consumer index than the middle or low group in each case.

These patterns are not surprising as there is a close relationship between media use, socioeconomic status and consumerism. Many media items such as satellite dishes, magazines and CD players are also relatively exclusive consumer goods which are more affordable to the élite social groups.

One might then engage in a circular argument to debate whether high media use *causes* consumerism or whether high media use is merely a manifestation of a consumeristic lifestyle afforded by affluence. Whatever the outcome, there is a positive linear relationship between media use, consumerism, and externally driven cultural orientation, as operationalized in this study.

Whereas school type was the only significantly related variable to knowledge of Jamaica and the Caribbean, all the independent variables — media use, school type, area, SES and travel — were significant on the knowledge of the US variable.

The expectation with regard to the knowledge variables was that the higher SES and higher media users would average lower scores on the KNOW1 measure, higher scores on the KNOW2 measure and vice versa for lower groupings. However, the high school students followed by the technical and comprehensive students were more knowledgeable in both instances.

This is undoubtedly a reflection of the fact that high school students and higher SES subjects have better educational opportunities and more access to resource persons and materials. Coupled with the fact that the Jamaica/Caribbean knowledge scale combined true-false general knowledge (and hence more academic) items such as 'Belize, Guyana and St. Kitts are members of CARICOM' with more grass roots cultural phenomena such as explaining the meaning of a West Indian proverb, it is perhaps not surprising that the lower SES groupings did not perform as well as expected on this measure. A separation of these two types of questions in two different scales may have yielded results along the expected lines, as the lower SES gave the highest percentages of correct answers to the following items: 'The Maroons were runaway slaves,' 'Pocomania is an African-based religion,' 'Every hoe 'ave 'im 'tick a bush,' 'Patois is the language of the slaves passed on through time,' and 'Blue drawers is something you wear.'[9]

Music

Music was viewed as a profound cultural icon in the study as music and indeed dance, are essential everyday cultural practice in Africa and the African Diaspora. Nettleford (1993:86) takes this even further, with his view of music and dance as the two most effective weapons available to Caribbean people in their battle for inward and outward space. He contends that these 'elemental creative acts' help to define Caribbean identity and contribute to cultural survival:

> To function in the modern world, Caribbean citizens, despite the presence of expressive Creole tongues, may indeed have to write and speak in the masters language (French, English, Spanish or Dutch); yet they can survive, dancing their own movements and singing their own music. Because of such modes of existence this civilization may be unique (p.98).

Differences were observed in levels of appreciation for reggae along school type lines. The secondary school subjects were the greatest lovers of reggae, followed by the technical and comprehensive, then the high school subjects. When asked to name their five favourite artistes, a greater percentage of high school students named at least one foreign artiste (58%) compared with the secondary (37%) and the technical/ comprehensive (43%) students.

In the overall sample, 53% named four or five local artistes compared with 11% naming the same numbers of foreign artistes, and 89% named at least one local artiste compared with 50% naming at least one foreign artiste also. Whereas 98% of the sample did not name any proponents of the calypso or soca genre, this finding is not in keeping with the 30% who expressed a strong liking for soca and the 27% who were similarly appreciative of calypso. This suggests either a lack of familiarity with the names of these artistes and merely an appreciation of the art form, or that these artistes were not short listed in the top five choices.

Reggae was the most popular form with the sample, where (76%) expressed a strong liking for reggae in the top two categories on a five-point scale (don't know, not at all, a little, quite a lot, or very much), followed by soul or rhythm and blues (69%), gospel (61%), rap (59%), dancehall (58%), soca (30%) and calypso (27%).

These results suggest that although there is the tendency for a greater degree of preference for foreign music and foreign artistes among the high SES, high school and high media users compared with the other class groupings, there is nonetheless a very significant appreciation for Jamaican music among the high SES subjects, and indeed across the entire sample.

Cultural Orientation

A closer evaluation of the individual items constituting the cultural orientation scale reveals some interesting patterns of attitudes.

The earlier reported finding that 32% of the sample would prefer to live overseas received relative confirmation in the responses to two items in the Cultural Orientation Index, where 34% disagreed with the statement 'I would only like to live in Jamaica,' and 29% agreed with 'I would prefer to live in the United States.'

However, the sample nonetheless demonstrated strong loyalties to the country and their heritage on some of the other items. Some 94% agreed that 'It is important to know your history and your culture;' 90% expressed agreement with 'I am proud to be Jamaican,' 87% were in agreement with 'I feel good about my cultural background,' and 73% agreed with 'I enjoy Jamaica's folklore, ring games and proverbs.'

The items which pertained to the economic conditions of the country ellicited less agreement and more uncertainty. The statement 'The Jamaican economy will never get better,' elicited a 23% agreement, 50% disagreement, and 25% undecided. In response to 'My generation will find the solution to Jamaica's problems,' there was 43% agreement, 21% disagreement, with 34% undecided. When asked whether they felt that 'Jamaica should seriously consider becoming one of the states of the US, 36% agreed, 52% disagreed, and 13% were undecided. Some 36% agreed with 'Most Jamaican-made products are not as good as imported ones,' 50% disagreed, and 13% were undecided.

With respect to the rest of the region, 61% agreed that 'Jamaica is similar to the rest of the Caribbean,' a surprising 76% expressed agreement with 'I think of myself as West Indian as well as Jamaican,' and 88% were favourably disposed towards 'I would like to learn more about the rest of the Caribbean.'

On the matter of psycho-cultural links with Africa, there was an expected lack of consensus. Some 35% agreed with the statement 'I have difficulty identifying with the culture of African people,'[10] with 32% in disagreement and 31% undecided. However, 54% disagreed with 'There is no such thing as African influence in Jamaican culture,' 22% agreed, and 23% were undecided.

These results suggest that although there is the tendency for the high SES and high media users to be most pro-foreign on the cultural orientation scale, there is nonetheless an encouraging level of appreciation of cultural identity — pride in what sets them apart as being Jamaican, assuming that the questions did not elicit 'knee-jerk' or socially appropriate responses. That is to say that it is now politically correct, widely acceptable and essentially the norm, to speak in terms of self reliance and black pride — a legacy of the black power and self reliance movements of the 1960s and 1970s in Jamaica, the Caribbean and black America. These philosophies have been in circulation since and before those periods in the region's history.

When coupled with the levels of appreciation expressed for the local reggae, we perhaps find evidence of strains of resistance to the cultural bombardment from outside (returning to an earlier citation) made possible by the new age media of global communication which Jamaican youth notwithstanding, seek out and enjoy.

It may be that the Jamaican youth of the present have developed cultural and psychological strategies to reconcile myriad simultaneous images and influences with their 'Jamaicanness' in order to survive culturally in an increasingly smaller world.

The people of the region however have always shown a remarkable capability for cultural survival historically, particularly in the face of European domination and repression during the creolization process under slavery and colonial rule, when Africans, Indians and later Asians and Middle Easterners were in the main coerced into re-establishing their domicile in the West Indies.

CONCLUSION

The *preliminary* results which have been the subject of this discourse should be regarded as only a part of a wider conceptualization of a study of Jamaican youth which is based on twice the present sample size, and a sample drawn from eight locales rather than three. The study's final conclusions are therefore reserved until the completion of the wider project analysis, which is forthcoming.

However, the trends based on the sample presented, suggest that the youth of the 1980s and 1990s have far more diverse interests and levels of appreciation for myriad phenomena, afforded by the greatly increased scope of access to foreign cultures and cultural artifacts through a multidimensional media environment whose technologies are increasingly cheaper, accessible and personalized.

The development challenge for those nations for which this objective remains an elusive goal, is to create an economic, psycho-social and cultural environment which will inspire its citizens, particularly its youth, to believe in and realize the self-actualization they seek.

It is apparent that the youth investigated in this study are seeking a better quality of life, and the alarming ratio of one in three youth perceives the United States or some other foreign option as the means to that end. The youth who expressed the least pro-Jamaican sentiment as hypothesized, were those who classified as high SES, with the middle class group demonstrating the greatest desire to persevere in spite of the odds.

The preliminary findings of the study lend support to the often articulated urgent need for more culturally relevant media products for consumption by the region's people and in particular the region's youth. The current images are still irrelevant to Caribbean reality and the region's media are not fulfilling the storytelling function which will contribute in the words of Nettleford (1993), to cultural certitude, continuity and survival in language, religion, kinship patterns, ethnicity and artistic manifestations.

It is clear that the foreign images are here to stay, and further, that Jamaican and indeed Caribbean people choose to attend to these images. As such the real challenge as expressed by Nettleford (1993:ix) is to develop 'a unique and distinctive sensibility, capable of coping with *difference* without resort to intolerance or deterioration into psychic despair. This is likely to be a major challenge for a planet that is growing smaller in the face of instant communication.' That is, to develop critical skills for decoding and deconstructing the media in the region's people.

This study demonstrates the advantages of a more comprehensive measure of media use beyond television viewing, in arriving at better approximations of reality. The statistical procedures also depart from those which treat social scientific effects in isolation in an attempt to arrive at better assessments of reality.

The broad scope of this study was intended to provide baseline data for future studies which on a smaller scale can better assess psychological attitudes and conditioning, viewing patterns and interpretations as regards the highly complex cultural phenomena under study. The broad scope of this study did not afford the exploration of deep seated cultural questions like whether kinship and community oriented values were being eroded as a result of the external domination of local media. What has been argued, investigated and supported is evidence of a complex structure of influences of which the media are but one component part.

Although the study does not directly assess the adult population of Jamaica, the adolescents nonetheless give a good indication of the nature of influence of older siblings, parents, teachers and other opinion leaders. Adolescent's media access is afforded by parents and guardians, their levels of consumerism are determined by those on whom they depend, and their attitudes are conditioned in the home, the school, the church, by the media and their peers. We therefore gain some insights into processes at work within the wider society through the youth under study.

While more research is urgently needed, of even greater urgency is the need for action in the development of national information policies to guide and nurture the development of vibrant cultural industries and culturally appropriate media, the demand for which is evident in the popularity of regional television productions such as the Jamaican *Oliver at Large*, and the Trinidadian *No Boundaries* and *Gayelle* (Brown, 1990).

As Nettleford (1993:167) contends, the network of national television and radio stations throughout Africa, the Caribbean and the Americas need to propagate material created by African people about African people, 'so that the people of Africa and the Diaspora can interpret themselves faithfully to themselves and to the rest of the world.......'. He further points out that even the United States, despite its initial dependence on 'Mother Europe,' has understood the urgency of creating and projecting its own expressive cultural forms.

The region's cultural milestones include the development of the only 20th century musical instrument — the steel pan — in the early 1940s in Trinidad and Tobago and the previously mentioned international success of the region's music, which in the case of reggae has resulted in the inclusion of a reggae category in the prestigious American Grammy Awards.

The region's annual cultural exposés such as Trinidad and Tobago's annual carnival and Jamaica's *Reggae Sunsplash* continue to attract phenomenal levels of visitor arrivals from around the globe, and the region's artists, novelists and poets continue to receive international recognition for excellence in their respective fields, most notably the recent Nobel Laureate for Literature, 1993, St. Lucian Derek Walcott (Dunn, 1993, Brown, 1990).

If Caribbean culture is indeed demonstrating some resilience in the face of adversity, as this study's preliminary trends suggest, and which tireless investigation can only help to elucidate, then such resilience demands the reinforcement of the modern world's most effective centre for creative cultural expression — the media.

NOTES

1 Four areas were combined to constitute this rural category in order to generate sufficient schools for comparison with Kingston, Montego Bay and other areas in the wider study. The four areas are all in eastern Jamaica and share similar social, economic and demographic characteristics.

2 The schools in the sub-sample were as follows: Campion College, Jamaica College, St. Andrew High, Hillel Academy, The Priory School, Vauxhall Secondary, Donald Quarrie Secondary, Charlie Smith Comprehensive (**Kingston**); Montego Bay High, Cornwall College, Montego Bay Secondary, Herbert Morrison Technical, Harrison Memorial High (**Montego Bay**); Seaforth High (**Seaforth**); St. Thomas Technical (**Golden Grove**); Happy Grove High (**Hector's River**); Trinityville Secondary (**Trinityville**).

3 The high schools are the most prestigious secondary educational institutions in the country which emphasize a traditional academic curriculum. Success at the national Common Entrance Examination which is sat at the age of 11, is a prerequisite for entry to high school. All the other school types do not have this requirement. They also emphasize mixed curricula, incorporating a wider variety of vocational, commercial, technical and agricultural subjects than the high school. Upper and middle class students are almost exclusively found in the high schools.

4 Irie FM, launched in August 1990, is the island's only radio station with an all-reggae programming format.

5 In order to better facilitate comparative statistical analyses, the technical comprehensive school types which share similar characteristics, were combined as each of these school types was not represented in all three areas.

6 West Indian proverbs or sayings are part of the oral cultural heritage of the region, passed down through the ages from the days of slavery. They are maxims which seek to describe and to prescribe human behaviour.

7 The contemporary sound in reggae which involves the fast and lyrical 'toasting' of a deejay over a back track (a form on which American rap drew heavily as an influence) is loosely referred to as dancehall music and was understood as such among the population under study. However, it should be noted that all forms of Jamaican reggae grew out of the dancehalls (an open-air space in a yard or street where the sound systems and patrons gather) and as such a more appropriate name for the current trend in reggae is *ragga*.

8 Interaction effects between pairs of the independent variables in the study were tested, resulting in a significant school type-area interaction on the knowledge of the US ($F=13.16$, $p.0005$), the consumerism ($F=2.76$, $p.05$), and foreign music variable ($F=2.87$, $p.05$), and a significant area-travel interaction on the foreign music variable ($F=4.22$, $p.05$).
Two independent variables are said to interact if the difference between treatment means for two levels of one variable (A) is not the same for all levels of the other variable (B) as they relate to a third (dependent) variable (C). That is, variable A does not have the same effect at all levels of variable B, with the converse also being true (Byrkit, 1987).

9 The Maroons were runaway slaves who fled the cruelty of plantation life, hid in the hills and established new settlements. Pocomania is an indigenous religious syncretism of Christian teachings and African spiritualism and revivalism. 'Ev'ry hoe 'ave 'im 'tick a bush,' a West Indian proverb which literally translates to 'Every hoe has its stick somewhere in the bushes,' means that every person has a suitable match somewhere for marriage or partnership. Patois or Jamaican Creole, which is spoken today by the majority of the Jamaican people, is a mixture of English, Spanish and various African languages, which developed during slavery to facilitate communication among the many cultures banded together on the plantations. 'Blue drawers' is a corn or cornmeal pudding which is wrapped in banana leaves, tied with a piece of the bark of the banana tree and boiled. It is popular in rural Jamaica.

10 Whereas the researcher recognizes that Africa does not present one uniform culture, these differences are not widely appreciated in Jamaica and as such were not tapped in this statement.

REFERENCES

Benedict, R. (1945). *Race,science and politics*. (rev. ed.).New York: The Viking Press.

Brown, A. (1990). Effects of the New World Information Order on Caribbean Media. In S. Surlin & W. Soderlund (Eds.), *Mass Media and the Caribbean* (pp. 251-271). New York: Gordon and Breach.

Brown, A. (1990). *Caribbean Cultures and Mass Communication Technology in the 21st Century*. Round Table Discussion paper, Caribbean Studies Assn., Trinidad, 1990.

Brown, A. (1987). *TV Programming Trends in the Anglophone Caribbean: The 1980s* (Report No. 367348.6). Kingston, Jamaica: UNESCO.

Brown, A., & Sanatan, R. (1987). *Talking With Whom: A Report on the State of the Media in the Caribbean*. Kingston, Jamaica: CARIMAC, UWI.

Brown, H. (1993, October). *Dancehall Soca: Fusion in Caribbean Popular Music*. Paper presented at the annual conference of the Canadian Association of Latin American and Caribbean Studies (CALACS) Ottawa, Canada.

Browne, E. (1987). *Caribbean Voices - Caribbean Images*. Ottawa: Peak.

Byrkit, D. R. (1987). *Statistics Today: A Comprehensive Introduction*. Menlo Park, CA: Benjamin/Cummings.

Coldevin, G. O. (1979). Satellite Television and Cultural Replacement Among Eskimos. *Communication Research*, 6, 115-134.

Cuthbert, M. (1985). Cultural Autonomy and Popular Music: A Survey of Jamaican Youth. *Communication Research*, 12, 381-393.

Dunn, H. (1993, October). *A Tradition of Resistance and Survival in Caribbean Culture: Re-examining the Cultural Dependency Thesis*. Paper presented at the annual conference of the Canadian Association of Latin American and Caribbean Studies (CALACS) Ottawa, Canada.

Dunn, H. (1991). Monopoly or Competition in Communications: The Case of the British Caribbean. *Intermedia, 19* (1), 29-32.

Fejes, F. (1981). Media Imperialism: An Assessment. *Media, Culture and Society, 3,* 281-289. Reprinted (1982), in *Mass Communication Review Yearbook, 3*, 345-353.

Golding, P. (1977). Media Professionalism in the Third World: The Transfer of an Ideology. In J. Curran, M. Gurevitch, & J. Woollacott (Eds.). *Mass Communication and Society* (pp. 291-308). London: Arnold.

Granzberg, G. (1982). Television as a Storyteller: The Algonkian Indians of Central Canada. *Journal of Communication,* 32, 43-52.

Hamelink, C. J. (1983). *Cultural Autonomy in Global Communications: Planning National Information Policy*. London: Longman.

Hockett, C. (1950). Language and Culture: A Protest. *American Anthropologist, 52,*113.

Hosein, E. N. (1986). The Problem of Imported Television Content in the Commonwealth Caribbean. *Caribbean Quarterly, 22* (4),7-25.

Hoyte, H. (1986, June). *The Influence of Foreign Television on Caribbean People*. Paper prepared on behalf of the Caribbean Publishing and Broadcasting Association. Bridgetown, Barbados.

Market Research Services (1994). *Jamaica Media Survey*. Kingston, Jamaica: Market Research Services.

Kang, J. G., & Morgan, M. (1988). Culture Clash: Impact of U.S. Television in Korea. *Journalism Quarterly, 65,* 431-438.

Katz, E. & Liebes, T. (1984). Once Upon a Time in Dallas. *Intermedia, 12* (3), 28-32.

Katz, E., & Wedell, G. (1977). *Broadcasting in the Third World: Promise and Performance*. Cambridge, MA: Harvard University Press.

Knaack, K. (1987, October). *Foreign Media versus Caribbean Culture*. Paper presented to the meeting of the Caribbean Broadcasting Union, Plymouth, Montserrat.

Kottack, C. P. (1986). *Cultural Anthropology*. (4th ed.). Random House.

Lee, C. (1979). *Media Imperialism Reconsidered: The Homogenising of Television Culture*. Beverly Hills, CA: Sage.

Lee, P. S. (1988). Communication Imperialism and Dependency: A Conceptual Clarification. *Gazette, 41*, 69-83.

Liebes, T. & Katz E. (1987). Patterns of Involvement in Television Fiction: A Comparative Analysis. In M. Gurevitch & M.R. Levy (Eds.), *Mass Communication Review Yearbook 6*. Beverly Hills, CA: Sage.

Lent, J. (1977). *Third World Mass Media and Their Search for Modernity: The Case of the Commonwealth Caribbean 1717-1976*. Lewisberg (Pa) & London: Bucknell University Press & Associated University Presses.

Lent, J. A. (1979). *Topics in Third World Mass Communications: Rural Developmental Journalism, Cultural Imperialism, Research Education*. Hong Kong: Asian Research Service.

Lent, J. (1987). Mass Media in the Leeward Islands: Press Freedom, Media Imperialism and Popular Culture. *Studies in Latin American Popular Culture, 6*, 245-258.

Lent, J. (1990). *Mass Communications in the Caribbean*. Ames, IA: Iowa State University Press.

McCann I. (1993, July 10). Planet Skank: The International Face of Reggae. *Billboard*, July 10, 1993, pp. R-2 - 3.

McPhail, T. L. (1987). *Electronic Colonialism: The Future of International Broadcasting and Communication*. Newbury Park, CA: Sage.

Nettleford, R. (1978). *Caribbean Cultural Identity: The Case of Jamaica: An essay in Cultural Dynamics*. Kingston, Jamaica: Institute of Jamaica.

Nettleford, R. (1993). *Inward Stretch Outward Reach: A Voice from the Caribbean*. London: MacMillan.

Oliveira, O. S. (1986). Satellite TV and Dependency: An Empirical Approach. *Gazette, 38*, 127-145.

Read, W. H. (1976). *America's Mass Media Merchants*. Baltimore: Johns Hopkins University Press.

Roach, C. (1990). The Movement for a New World Information and Communication Order: A second wave? *Media, Culture and Society, 12*, 283-307.

Schiller, H. I. (1969). *Mass Communications and American Empire*. New York: Kelley.

Schiller, H. I. (1976). *Communication and Cultural Domination*. New York: International Arts and Sciences Press.

Skinner, E. C. (1984). *Foreign TV Programme Viewing and Dependency:A Case Study of US Television Viewing in Trinidad and Tobago*. Unpublished dissertation, Michigan State.

Skinner, E., & Houang, R. (1987). Use of United States Produced Media in Caribbean Society: Exposure and Impact. *Studies in Latin American Popular Culture, 6*, 183-195.

Smith, A. (1980). *The Geopolitics of Information: How Western Culture Rules the World*. New York: Oxford University Press.

Steward, J. (1950). Area Research: Theory and Practice. *Social Science Research Council, Bulletin 63*.

Surlin, S. H. (1988, July). *North American and Caribbean Perceptions of Values Projected in Television Content*. Paper presented at the annual conference of the International Association for Mass Communication Research (IAMCR), Barcelona, Spain.

Surlin, S. H. (1990). Caribbean Cultural Identification, Cultural Consciousness and Mass Media Imperialism. In S. Surlin & W. Soderlund (Eds.), *Mass Media and the Caribbean* (pp. 299-317). New York: Gordon and Breach.

Tan, A. S., Li, S., & Simpson, C. (1986). American TV and Social Stereotypes of Americans in Taiwan and Mexico. *Journalism Quarterly, 63*, 809-814.

Tan, A. S., & Suarchavarat, K. (1988). American TV and Social Stereotypes of Americans in Thailand. *Journalism Quarterly, 65*, 648-654.

Tan, A. S., Tan, G. K., & Tan, A. S. (1987). American TV in the Philippines: A Test of Cultural Impact. *Journalism Quarterly, 64*, 65-72.

Tracey, M. (1985). Popular Culture and the Economics of Global Television. *Intermedia, 16* (2), 9-25.

Tracey, M. (1991). The Poisoned Chalice: International Television and The Idea of Dominance. In A. A. Berger (Ed.), *Media USA: Process and Effect* (pp. 297-306). (2nd edition). New York: Longman.

Tsai, M. K. (1970). Some Effects of American Television Programmess on Children in Formosa. *Journal of Broadcasting, XIV,* 229-238.

Tunstall, J. (1977). *The Media are American: Anglo-American Media in the World.* New York: Columbia University Press.

Varis, T. (1984). The International Flow of Television Programmes. *Journal of Communication, 34,* 143-152.

Wells, A. (1972). *Picture-tube Imperialism? The Impact of US Television on Latin America.* Maryknoll, New York: Orbis Books.

White, T. (1993, July 10). Real Situation: Introducing the Billboard Reggae Charts, *Billboard*, p. R-2.

Wolfe, S. (1991). *Colour and Class Representations in Jamaican Television Commercials: A Content Analysis 1970-1989.* Unpublished master's thesis. University of Windsor, Canada.

5

TELEVISION AND THE AMERICANIZATION OF THE TRINBAGONIAN YOUTH:
A STUDY OF SIX SECONDARY SCHOOLS

Lynette M. Lashley

INTRODUCTION

The flow of information from both print and broadcast media, emanating from the United States and other industrialized western countries has always been of concern to many countries, particularly those of the third world. The emergence of new technology in some third world countries, mainly in the form of satellite television, has led many national leaders to express concerns about national identity, and cultural sensitivity. This is because a voluminous amount of mostly American and western programming enters these countries. Within UNESCO and in other fora, third world governments have been engaged in deliberations on the qualitative and quantitative flow of mass media programming from the developed countries to the developing nations.

Many third world countries have seen American and western programming as threatening to drag emergent countries back into a dependent status (Sterling and Head, 1987). More importantly, others have complained that United States cultural and political influence globally gained strength from the dominance of American programmes in their countries (Sterling and Head). In light of this, an issue that needs to be addressed is the effect of American programming on third world countries, since the United States is the world's greatest supplier of programming to the rest of the world.

It has been pointed out that citizens of the less developed countries must depend on foreigners, particularly the United States, to a significant degree, for their print materials, television programming, and films. Tunstall (1977) has shown that the United States is by far the most dominant communication power in the world. Emery and Smythe (1986), state that the United States and the west, by virtue of being dominant in world communications, are likely to spread their standards and style universally. Against this background, many third world leaders and citizens are concerned about their countries becoming a part of the American media village. This has been expressed repeatedly within the vulnerable Caribbean area.

Trinidad and Tobago was the first country in the English-speaking Caribbean to have introduced television technology. It did so at the same time that it gained independence from Britain in 1962, under the government of the People's National Movement (PNM). The country now has three television stations, state-owned Trinidad and Tobago Television (TTT) is the oldest, having been in existence since 1962. The other two stations, CCN TV6 (CCN) and AVM TV4 (AVM), are both privately owned, and have been in operation since 1991, just under three decades after the start-up of TTT.

The *raison d'être* for TTT was to provide public service information, education, and entertainment. However, there was never any regulation of the amount of locally-originated or foreign-originated programming to be aired. Opting for cheaper overseas canned products, TTT's programming, since its inception, has been dominated by American fare. However, there has been some local information, education, and entertainment.

It should be pointed out that since TTT came into existence in 1962, no other licences had been granted for the operation of television or radio in Trinidad and Tobago until 1991 under the National Alliance for Reconstruction (NAR) government. Since their inauguration CCN and AVM both provide a substantial amount of American fare in their programming. AVM airs programmes from the ABC network, and CCN from the CBS network. The programme schedule in Table 1 illustrates the offerings of the three stations on a given broadcast day.

Trinidad and Tobago has even distribution of television sets throughout the country. Unlike many other third world countries where the concentration of ownership of television sets is in the urban areas, Trinidad's 273,000 television households are distributed evenly throughout the country. Approximately 820,000 adults (over 15 years of age) out of a population of 1.1 million are served (Hoyos, 1992).

From this information, one can easily glean that television viewing is widespread and that the overwhelming majority of programmes on all the channels is American. The situation has been exacerbated because of the competition among the three television stations. Each is vying for audiences, which translate into advertising dollars, and therefore, Trinidadians are being bombarded with more American fare than ever before. This situation in Trinidad and Tobago is disquieting, since it is the author's perception that the level of exposure to US output is bound to have an effect on the psyche of the average Trinbagonian, particularly the youth. This is what motivated the study.

RELATED LITERATURE

In a study done by the Caribbean Institute of Mass Communication and UNESCO, it was reported that between 1976 and 1986, the amount of imported fare in Trinidad and Tobago television increased from 71 per cent to 89 per cent. Among the Caribbean countries surveyed, Trinidad and Tobago showed the highest increase of 17 per cent, in the importation of foreign content (Brown, 1988). At the time only TTT was in operation. The situation today has worsened, since on all three stations, American fare constitutes more than 90 per cent of the programming. There is an increase in the absolute volume as well as in the ratio of foreign to local input.

According to another study, United States television viewing in Trinidad and Tobago is positively related to United States values, appeal, dependency, and appreciation (Skinner, 1984). Similarly, a study of viewers in the Corozal district of Belize showed that those who had a choice of satellite relayed television from the United States, and watched United States programmes, tended to prefer United States imported goods. Those who had direct reception of Mexican television across the border, and who watched more Mexican programmes, did not have the same bias against local goods (Laird, 1987).

Commenting on the preponderance of American fare on the Trinidadian airwaves, William Demas has observed that the Caribbean has a rich treasure of not only cultural heritage, but also cultural achievement. He noted, however, that more and more of the region's cultural identity was being undermined by foreign programmes, many of which were of an extraordinarily poor quality, with a negative impact on the societies (Demas, 1986). Though not in reference to the Caribbean specifically, but to other developing countries, others share Demas' sentiments (Granzberg, 1982; Kang & Morgan, 1988; Tan, Tan & Tan, 1987). Television is a cultural industry. A cultural product has symbolic content, and has or creates meaning for its audience (Astroff, 1982).

> In terms of psychological influence, television might have little or no impact if only a few people pay relatively little attention to it. But the opposite is the case: just about

everybody watches some television, it has almost universal appeal. ...The first basic principle of influence has to do with exposure. Although the relationship is not perfectly linear, in general the more exposure the more influence. Certainly the more exposure the more potential for influence... (Condry, 1989, p.4).

Nordenstreng and Varis (1974) assert that American-produced television programmes were dominating a great part of the world. According to Schiller (1991), global television still plays a part in cultural domination in the 1990s because of the new delivery systems — communication satellites and cable networks. With the consistent bombardment of such foreign fare on a country such as Trinidad and Tobago, the more the people are exposed to it, the more will be the potential for influence.

The influence of US television entertainment programming on the youth of Trinidad and Tobago has sometimes been disastrous. An 11 year old boy hanged himself trying to emulate a stunt he saw in the movie 'Han 'Em High' on television. Another child died when she tried to imitate the hanging which the television character MacGyver performed (Treavajo, 1992).

In an article by Yearwood and Richards (1989), both authors contend that the potential of the mass media as a powerful force in social communication is evident.

It is the ideological dimension of mass media which comes through its programming, its themes and points of view that can have potent long term influences on society. The media are capable of legitimizing ideas, personalities and a way of life as social norm... (Yearwood and Richards, 1989:1-2).

The mass media are also endowed with the agenda-setting function.

...they establish the agenda of items about which we talk..., they select and present particular topics, themes, social concerns, and persons as objects of social discussion. Because the mass media have the potential to command national attention, those persons, issues and points of view selected as media content, either in the news or through media entertainment, are conferred with a special social status (Yearwood and Richards, 1989:2).

Because of the potential socio-psychological impact of foreign programming on third world countries in particular, there continues to be concern about the consequences. This study explores the following research questions:

1. How deep an influence is American television entertainment programming on the youth of Trinidad and Tobago ('Trinbago')? and

2. Is there a preference for American television entertainment programming over Trinidadian programming?

METHOD

In order to answer these questions, survey research was employed for the study. A list of all the secondary schools in Trinidad and Tobago was obtained from the Ministry of Education. A representative sample of six schools was selected. This was done in order to ensure an adequate representation from the North, Central, East, and South Trinidad, and from Tobago. These represented the major geographical and populated areas. The sample also took into consideration, the various ethnic and socio-economic groupings of the country. The schools in the sample also represent the various secondary school systems in the country. The Belmont Junior Secondary is co-educational and generally caters to the lowest achieving students. Sixty-three students from this institution participated in the study. Couva Secondary and Northeastern College are also co-educational, and cater to those of middle to low achievement. The subjects for this aspect of the study totalled 146 and 174 respectively. Presentation College, an all boys' institution, Naparima Girls' High School, and co-educational Bishop's High School are three schools which have the elite or highest achieving students. For the first, there were 190, the second 175, and the third 166 subjects. It should be pointed out that the sample also took account of the fact that the East Indian population in Trinidad and Tobago is about 50 per cent of the total. As such, Naparima, Presentation, Couva, and Northeastern were selected as schools with good representations of East Indian students. One class from each year, was sampled from each school. The ages of the students ranged from 11 to 18. The sample yielded a total of 914 respondents. Questionnaires containing 25 close-ended questions were distributed to the students. They were self-administered in the classrooms, under the supervision of teachers.

RESULTS

There is little doubt that American television entertainment programming has a significant effect on the Trinbagonian youth. Table I shows the results of the aggregate responses of the six schools.

Viewing Patterns

An average of sixty-seven per cent of the students viewed television every day, and 16 per cent, a few times a week. Twenty-six per cent viewed over five hours a day, and 32 per cent viewed three to four hours daily. Thirty-one per cent viewed one to two hours daily. These results indicate that television viewing is fairly high among the students.

Table 1. Responses by Schools

ITEM	N = 166 Bishop's %	N = 190 Presentation %	N = 175 Naparima %	N = 174 Northeastern %	N = 146 Couva %	N = 63 Belmont %	N = 914 Aggregate %
Frequency of TV viewing							
Everyday							
Over 5 hrs.	39	14	17	27	17	41	26
3-4 hours	31	36	28	36	33	25	32
1-2 hours	21	37	39	26	39	23	31
Less than 1 hr.	6	11	13	8	6	6	8
Station mostly viewed							
TTT	40	6	7	11	5	14	14
AVM 4	14	68	56	18	61	36	42
CCN 6	43	21	31	68	29	47	40
Rating of programmes on TTT							
Excellent	3	1	3	6	6	7	4
Good	37	33	37	33	42	33	36
Fair	42	50	43	41	30	38	41
Poor	14	15	14	16	17	15	15
Rating of programmes on AVM 4							
Excellent	27	45	45	29	52	57	43
Good	54	43	46	47	41	31	44
Fair	9	9	4	18	2	4	8
Poor	1	0	2	2	0	1	1
Ratings of programmes on CCN 6							
Excellent	42	15	30	61	35	46	38
Good	43	64	58	32	52	46	49
Fair	8	16	7	4	9	4	8
Poor	3	2	2	0	0	0	1

Of the three television stations, AVM turned out to be the one most heavily viewed by the respondents — 42 per cent of them indicated this. CCN was next with 40 per cent, followed by TTT with a low of 14 per cent; 4 per cent did not respond. It should be pointed out that in reacting to criticism over the years, TTT has made an effort to feature more locally originated programming, and this might probably be the cause of their low viewership by the youth.

When it came to the rating of the programmes on the three stations (Table 2), CCN and AVM emerge at the top; 38 per cent of the students rated CCN's programming as excellent and another 49 per cent of the subjects rated them as good, while 43 per cent of the students rated AVM's programming, as excellent, and another 44 per cent rated them as good. In comparison, only 4 per cent of the respondents rated TTT's programming as excellent and 36 per cent indicated that it was good. It is noteworthy to see that 15 per cent of the subjects rated TTT's programming as poor and 41 per cent rated them as fair. For CCN only 1 per cent found the programming poor and 8 per cent found it fair, while 1 per cent found AVM's output poor, and 8 per cent found it fair. The message is clear here, and can be supported by Appendix 2. The more American the fare, the more it is preferred by the youth.

Forty per cent were either very satisfied, or satisfied with the absence of local programmes on television. Only 5 per cent had no real feelings about it. When asked if the Trinbagonian youth did not care for local programming, 22 per cent of the respondents strongly agreed, and another 28 per cent agreed. Only 7 per cent strongly disagreed and 17 per cent disagreed. About 21 per cent remained undecided. Furthermore, 27 per cent strongly agreed that the Trinbagonian youth desired American programming to continue without local fare, and 26 per cent agreed. Six per cent however strongly disagreed, 21 per cent disagreed, and 17 per cent were undecided. These responses seem to indicate some uncertainty in some respondents, despite the overwhelming preference for the programming on CCN and AVM.

The responses to the quality of the American programmes as opposed to those locally produced showed that 47 per cent strongly agreed that the American programmes were better than the local ones aesthetically, and 33 per cent agreed that they were. Eighty per cent either strongly agreed or agreed that the US programmes are more attractive in presentation. Only 2 per cent strongly disagreed, and 4 per cent disagreed.

As far as programme content is concerned, 29 per cent of the students strongly agreed that American programmes were better in content than the local ones, and 32 per cent agreed with this. Five per cent strongly disagreed, and 9 per cent disagreed. The great majority of youth — 61 per cent approved in varying degrees of the US programmes.

Table 2. Student Responses Local vs Foreign Programmes

ITEM	N = 166 Bishop's %	N = 190 Presentation %	N = 175 Naparima %	N = 174 Northeastern %	N = 146 Couva %	N = 63 Belmont %	N = 914 Aggregate %
Satisfaction with absence of local progammes							
Very satisfied	16	25	32	24	28	11	23
Satisfied	14	20	14	13	10	28	17
Somewhat satis.	15	12	15	9	15	9	13
No real feelings	21	30	21	25	24	22	24
Very dissatisfied	8	1	4	6	2	9	5
Dissatisfied	12	4	6	10	7	7	8
Somewhat Dissat	12	6	5	9	8	4	7
T & T Youth doesn't care for local programmes							
Strongly agree	16	25	27	23	30	12	22
Agree	24	34	33	31	20	23	28
Undecided	25	24	17	20	20	20	21
Disagree	22	14	14	17	15	20	17
Strongly disagree	9	0	5	5	8	15	7
Youth's desire for American programmes to continue without local							
Strongly agree	24	31	31	28	33	15	27
Agree	25	30	34	17	23	25	26
Undecided	16	17	12	22	15	19	17
Disagree	28	14	16	24	19	22	21
Strongly disagree	7	5	5	7	5	6	6
American programmes better than local aesthetically							
Strongly agree	50	41	57	56	52	25	47
Agree	32	44	29	25	34	34	33
Undecided	9	7	7	7	7	20	10
Disagree	4	4	4	6	2	6	4
Strongly disagree	2	1	1	1	0	7	2
American programmes better than local in content							
Strongly agree	34	29	37	37	28	11	29
Agree	29	33	33	32	32	31	32
Undecided	20	17	12	13	19	22	17
Disagree	6	11	7	8	10	12	9
Strongly disagree	4	2	5	5	3	12	5

OPINIONS ON THE INFLUENCE OF AMERICAN TELEVISION

Sixteen per cent of the students strongly agreed that American programming influenced the way the youth speaks, while 31 per cent agreed. Ten per cent strongly disagreed and 26 per cent disagreed.

Eighty-two per cent strongly agreed or agreed that American programming influenced the way the youth dresses. Two per cent strongly disagreed, while 6 per cent disagreed.

Do American programmes influence the youth's preference for American culture over his or her own? In answering this question, 20 per cent strongly agreed, and 32 per cent agreed. Six per cent strongly disagreed, and 20 per cent disagreed, with 19 per cent remaining undecided.

Twenty-seven per cent of the respondents strongly agreed that American programmes influence the youth's longing to live the life seen on television, and 47 per cent agreed with this. Two per cent strongly disagreed, and 9 per cent disagreed, leaving 13 per cent undecided.

Do American programmes influence negative behaviour in some of the Trinbagonian youth, for example, drug use, violence, sexual promiscuity? Twenty-one per cent strongly agreed, and 38 per cent cent agreed. Seven per cent however strongly disagreed, while 15 per cent disagreed and 14 per cent were undecided. A significant 36 per cent of the youth do not identify social deviance with US programme contact although nearly 60 per cent agreed that it was an important factor. There is at present in Trinidad and Tobago, an upsurge of indiscipline in the schools. All of the teachers whom I interviewed for the study have attributed this type of behaviour to the American television shows. A few of them mentioned to me that many of the students were suffering from a 'Bart Simpson' syndrome.

As can be seen from the responses, the majority of the students in the study tended to concur with the teachers to a reasonable extent, that American programming somewhat influenced negative behaviour in some of the youth.

Programme Appeal

Three American and three local programmes with possible youth appeal were listed on the questionnaire, and the students were asked to select which one was their favourite. All three American programmes had higher preferences than the local ones; 85 per cent listed 'The Fresh Prince of Bel Air' as their favourite, while 3 per cent of the students liked 'Wheel of Fortune' and 5 per cent favoured 'Wonder Years'. Less than 1 per cent of the students chose the local 'Indian Variety'. Students from Couva Secondary, one of the schools with a sizeable East Indian population accounted for this. Only 3 per cent chose 'Teen Talent', and

Table 3. Influence of US Programmes on Youth

ITEM	N = 166 Bishop's %	N = 190 Presentation %	N = 175 Naparima %	N = 174 Northeastern %	N = 146 Couva %	N = 63 Belmont %	N = 914 Aggregate %
American programmes influence youth's speaking							
Strongly agree	31	14	16	19	17	12	18
Agree	30	28	38	35	23	31	31
Undecided	8	17	10	7	18	7	11
Disagree	18	28	25	21	30	34	26
Strongly disagree	10	10	7	15	8	9	10
American programmes influence youth's dress							
Strongly agree	59	39	40	46	35	31	42
Agree	30	48	45	39	39	39	40
Undecided	2	9	5	5	9	11	7
Disagree	6	2	5	4	7	14	6
Strongly disagree	1	0	2	4	6	1	2
American programmes influence youth's preference for that culture							
Strongly agree	28	16	20	22	15	19	20
Agree	30	34	35	31	35	28	32
Undecided	25	20	14	12	20	20	19
Disagree	12	20	23	23	19	23	20
Strongly disagree	2	8	4	10	8	4	6
American programmes influence youth's longing to live the life seen on TV							
Strongly agree	38	21	21	29	26	28	27
Agree	39	45	51	44	42	41	47
Undecided	10	16	12	12	13	15	13
Disagree	8	10	10	10	14	9	10
Strongly disagree	1	5	3	3	4	1	3
American programmes influence negative behaviour in some of the youth							
Strongly agree	19	15	22	24	21	23	21
Agree	40	38	42	40	34	36	38
Undecided	14	16	10	9	21	11	14
Disagree	12	20	14	12	8	22	15
Strongly disagree	10	8	8	10	0	3	7

Table 4. Programme Appeal and Youth Preferences

ITEM	N = 166 Bishop's %	N = 190 Presentation %	N = 175 Naparima %	N = 174 Northeastern %	N = 146 Couva %	N = 63 Belmont %	N = 914 Aggregate %
Favourite programmes							
Indian variety	0	0	0	0	3	0	-1
Wheel of Fortune	3	3	3	2	1	6	3
Teen Talent	3	0	1	2	0	1	1
Fresh Prince	89	90	82	84	80	87	85
12 and under	0	0	0	0	0	1	-1
Wonder Years	1	3	8	7	8	1	5
Programmes with most appeal to youth							
Indian Variety	0	0	2	2	5	0	2
Wheel of Fortune	0	2	0	4	1	12	3
Teen Talent	17	2	10	4	13	30	13
Fresh Prince	68	91	76	81	65	42	71
12 and under	8	0	2	3	6	9	5
Wonder Years	3	2	5	4	6	3	4
TV Programming in Trinidad							
Remain same	8	8	22	9	14	9	12
50% local/50% foreign	30	20	13	39	21	36	27
90%local/10% foreign	0	0	1	0	0	3	-1
75% local/25% foreign	4	1	4	2	2	11	4
50% local/50% American	13	9	8	9	11	12	10
90% local/10% American	0	0	0	0	0	1	-1
75% local/25% American	1	0	0	1	2	1	-1
90% American/10% local	42	59	47	36	45	23	42

less than 1 per cent chose 'Twelve and Under' both local youth shows. Belmont Junior Secondary represented 1 per cent of the students who favoured the latter programme.

When asked to choose which one of these programmes had the most appeal to the youth, 'Fresh Prince of Bel Air' also emerged at the top with 7 per cent. 'Teen

Talent' ranked second with a distant 13 per cent. It is noteworthy to mention that 'Indian Variety' as a programme with appeal to the youth, had an aggregate of 2 per cent, and as seen in Appendix I, this has been attributed to Presentation College, Couva Secondary, and Northeastern College. These three schools have sizeable East Indian student populations. The results clearly show that the youth will choose an American programme over a local one.

The final item on the questionnaire was how the students would like to see entertainment programming presented on Trinidad and Tobago television stations. Surprisingly, 12 per cent wanted it to remain the same. More specifically, 42 per cent wanted 90 per cent American and 10 per cent local programmes. The results do show a majority preferable for a predominance of American programming. The 42 per cent that indicated 90 per cent American programming, and the 10 per cent that wanted 50 per cent American programming were significant enough to predict a majority leaning towards American programming. On the other hand, when one looks at those who support 90 per cent local programming and 10 per cent American programming, there was less than 1 per cent. The same was true for those who affirmed 75 per cent local and 25 per cent American programming. Only 10 per cent agreed to 50 per cent local and 50 per cent American programming. One is able to discern a disinclination towards local programming.

DISCUSSION

From what has been seen in the findings, in response to the first question 'How deep an influence is American entertainment programming on the Trinidadian youth?', it can safely be concluded that there is a fairly deep influence. Forty-nine per cent of the respondents agreed that American programmes influenced the Trinbagonian youth's style of speaking. Another 82 per cent agreed that the programmes influenced the way the youth dresses, and 52 per cent agreed that these programmes influenced the youth's preference for American culture. These programmes influenced the youth's longing to live the life he or she sees on television, and this was affirmed by 74 per cent of the subjects. American programmes do have an influence on the negative behaviour of some of the Trinbagonian youth, and 59 per cent of the students agreed with this. These responses clearly show that the youth do agree that the American entertainment programmes have significant influence on them.

The second question: 'Is there a preference for American programming over Trinidadian programming?' was affirmed to a reasonable extent. Fifty per cent of the respondents agreed that the Trinbagonian youth did not care for local programmes, and 24 per cent disagreed. Again 53 per cent of the students agreed that the youth preferred American programming to continue without local programming, and 27 per cent disagreed interestingly enough, even though 40 per cent of the subjects indicated satisfaction with the absence of local programming, and 13 per cent was somewhat satisfied; only 20 per cent were dissatisfied, 24 per cent had no real feelings.

The respondents overwhelmingly endorsed 'The Fresh Prince of Bel Air' as their favourite programme over the three local ones, with 85 per cent of them indicating this. This programme was also perceived to be the one that appealed most to the Trinbagonian youth, 71 per cent of the students agreed with this. While this specific result could be expected, given the nature of that black American comedy, the evidence as a whole from the study, does show that the Trinbagonian youth has a greater preference for American programming over the local.

From the results of this study, American television programming does have an impact on the Trinbagonian youth. The fault lies in the programming policy of the television stations. The most common argument put forward to support the continued importation of television programmes in Trinidad and Tobago is that it will not make economic sense to produce local programmes. This view was supported when the author interviewed two of the three programming directors. They all indicated that economics was the reason for the deluge of American programming on Trinidad and Tobago's airwaves. One of the interviewees however, hastened to add that if quotas were legislated for locally-originated programming, then the stations would have to comply, and find the money to make the programmes.

One irony of the situation in Trinidad and Tobago, is that although US programmes dominate the country's television fare, it should be guardedly construed that the local audiences have a preference for US entertainment over those produced locally. A case in point is the soap opera 'No Boundaries' produced by TTT. That is one of the highest rating programmes on the airwaves of Trinidad and Tobago, in the face of competition with US programming. The author believes that once a country has the ability to produce its own television fare, that these indigenous programmes will prove more popular than imports. Unfortunately however, many countries are not able to produce enough of their own entertainment to fill all their programming needs. Were this possible, the youth of Trinidad and Tobago may not have been as partial to American programming.

Table 5. TV Programme Schedules - Trinidad & Tobago -January 1993

AVM

5.59 a.m.	Sign on	3.30 p.m.	Mr. Dress Up (R)
6.00 a.m.	F.I.T.	4.00 p.m.	Fred Penner's Place
6.30 a.m.	ABC World News Now	4.30 p.m.	G.I. Joe
7.00 a.m.	ABC World News This Morning	5.00 p.m.	Police Academy
8.00 a.m.	Good Morning America	5.30 p.m.	Words, Books and Letters
10.00 a.m.	Neighbours	6.00 p.m.	Invention
10.45 a.m.	General Hospital	6.30 p.m.	Jeopardy
11.30 a.m.	ABC News Nightline (R)	7.00 p.m.	The AVM Evening News
12.00	The AVM Midday Show	7.30 p.m.	ABC World News Tonight
1.00 p.m.	The MacNeil Lehrer News hour	8.00 p.m.	Tarzan
2.00 p.m.	ABC Primetime Live (R)	8.30 p.m.	The Oprah Winfrey Show
3.00 p.m.	Ebony Jet Showcase	9.30 p.m.	Movie: Blind Vision

TTT

6.00 a.m.	CNN	4.30 p.m.	Style with Elsa Klensch
9.00 a.m.	Sesame Street	5.00 p.m.	Dateline
10.00 a.m.	Ministry of Education	6.00 p.m.	Santa Barbara
10.30 a.m.	CNN	7.00 p.m.	Panorama
12.00 p.m.	The Young and the Restless	8.00 p.m.	Murder She Wrote
1.00 p.m.	Generations	9.00 p.m.	Secrets
1.30 p.m.	Showbiz Today	10.00 p.m.	Supertime
2.00 p.m.	Crossfire	11.00 p.m.	Cricket Highlights
2.30 p.m.	Documentary	11.30 p.m.	Panorama (late night edition)
3.00 p.m.	CNN		Sign Off
3.30 p.m.	Sesame Street		

CCN

5.00 a.m.	Up to the Minute	6.00 p.m.	Wheel of Fortune
6.30 a.m.	TV6 News (R)	6.30 p.m.	TV6 News
7.00 a.m.	CBS Morning News	7.15 p.m.	Caribbean Evening
8.00 a.m.	CBS This Morning	8.00 p.m.	Tour of Duty
10.00 a.m.	Channel America	9.00 p.m.	Infovision Feature
4.06 p.m.	Sign on/Prayer	9.30 p.m.	The Bold and the Beautiful
4.10 p.m.	700 Club	10.00 p.m.	CBS Evening News
4.40 p.m.	Another Life	10.25 p.m.	European Football
5.05 p.m.	The Price is Right	11.20 p.m.	Channel America

REFERENCES

Astroff, R. (1987) Communication and Contemporary Colonialism: Broadcast Television in Puerto Rico. In H.E. Hinds, Jr. and C.M. Tatum (eds.), *Studies in Latin American Popular Culture,* Vol. 6 (pp 11-26). University of Arizona Press, Tucson.

Brown, A. (1988) *TV Programming Trends in the Anglophone Caribbean: The 1980s.* University School of Printing, Mona, Jamaica.

Condry, J. (1989) *The Psychology of Television.* Lawrence Eribaum Associates, Inc., Hillsdale, New Jersey.

Emery, M. and Smythe, T.C. (1986) *Readings in Mass Communication.* 6th ed. Wm. C. Brown Publishers, Dubuque.

Granzberg, G. (1982) 'Television as Storyteller: The Algonkian Indians of Central Canada', *Journal of Communication.* 32 (1), 43-52.

Hoyos, P. (1992) 'T and T's Broadcast Wars'. *Horizons,* Vol. 1, No. 1, pp. 15-17.

Kang, J.G., and Morgan, M. (1988) 'Culture Clash: Impact of US Television in Korea'. *Journalism Quarterly,* 65, 431-438.

Laird, C. (1987) *Inside the People TV: Television for National Development.* Banyan, Port of Spain.

Read, W.H. (1976) America's Mass Media Merchants. Johns Hopkins University Press, Baltimore.

Schiller, H. (1991) 'Not Yet the Post-Imperialist Era'. *Critical Studies in Mass Communication.* 8, 13-28.

Skinner, E. (1984) 'Foreign Television Viewing and Dependency: A Case Study of US Television in Trinidad and Tobago'. Unpublished dissertation, Michigan State University.

Sterling, C., and Head, S.W. (1987) *Broadcasting in America.* 5th ed. Houghton Mifflin Co., Boston.

Tan, A.S., Tan, G.K., and Tan, A.S. (1987) 'American TV in the Philippines: A Test of Cultural Impact'. *Journalism Quarterly,* 64, 65-72, 144.

Treavajo, T. (1992, August 7) 'Careful With TV Shows, says Grieving Granny'. Trinidad Guardian, p. 1.

Tunstall, J. (1977) *The Media are American.* Columbia University Press, New York.

Yearwood G. and Richards, M. (1989) *Broadcasting in Barbados: The Cultural Impact of the Caribbean Broadcasting Corporation.* Lighthouse Communications, Bridgetown.

6

LOITERING ON COLONIAL PREMISES AFTER CLOSING TIME:
AN ANALYSIS OF TELEVISION PROGRAMMING POLICY IN BARBADOS

Cheryl Renee Gooch

INTRODUCTION

A country with nearly thirty years of independence, Barbados faces numerous development tasks, including the formidable challenge of fostering cultural identity. On the eve of independence in 1966, the late Prime Minister Errol Barrow proclaimed that his country would 'not be found loitering on colonial premises after closing time',[1] envisaging that Barbados would emerge as a culturally and politically autonomous nation. Following independence, some of the early expectations of Barbadian television were that it would help Barbadians to rediscover themselves and establish their national culture. Yet today, the country's television schedule displays a dominance (nearly 92 per cent) of US programming;[2] virtually unregulated, that is perceived to emphasize foreign lifestyles to the detriment of indigenous customs and values.

   Although field research for this article was conducted in Barbados in 1992, the data, analysis and conclusions remain valid. It examines the confluence of factors and circumstances that influence the nature and direction of television programming policy in Barbados. Subjects for this study included key actors from media, cultural and educational, economic, government and political sectors involved in the development and implementation of television programming policy. They included ministers responsible for broadcasting, statutory board chairmen and members, advertising executives, media managers and practitioners, educators and community activists.

The findings indicate that television programming decisions are informed more by popularity cost factors, and partisan political influences stemming from the structure of the Caribbean Broadcasting Corporation (CBC) than by development and programming objectives. Fragmentation at institutional and decision making levels in the communications sector has weakened endogenous capacity to address pertinent programming policy issues, and external influences often are reflected in television programming and policy decisions.

While potential leaders in Barbados have acknowledged the vital role of television in nation-building, there is a dearth of coherent communications policies designed to help preserve national cultural identities through the development of programming with local dimensions. The inappropriateness of policy governing Barbados television stems, in part, from a vagueness about the function of the national television system, and the relationship between national development goals and the programming objectives of television.

GOVERNMENT OWNED AND OPERATED TELEVISION SYSTEM

The Caribbean Broadcasting Corporation Act which established the CBC became effective November 11, 1963. According to Part II Section (3) of the CBC Act, the CBC's function is to provide 'broadcasting services of high quality both as to the transmission and as to the matter transmitted'. Beyond parliamentary debates on the Act, there was limited original public discussion and explication of the goals and objectives of the Corporation. For instance, the purpose CBC would serve is not mentioned in the government development plan for the period during which the CBC was established.

De facto, however, there seem to be two general perspectives about the early expectations of Barbadian television. One view is that television was seen as a mechanism that would help Barbadians forge a national culture, a crucial achievement denied them by the former colonial 'taskmasters'. Another, more critical view, holds that Barbadian television, like services introduced into other Caribbean territories in the 1960s and 1970s, was brought in as an 'independence trapping'. Observes one Barbadian communicator: 'When Jamaica got independence, we got television. So everybody, once they could afford it, got a television station' (J. Wiltshire-Forde, personal interview April

23, 1992). Some scholars further argue that these television systems generally were introduced more in response to local elite demands than as a result of deliberate, informed decision making, and that the concepts which help to define communication in the region are largely received, unanalysed and unappropriated (Cuthbert and Hoover, 1990; Cuthbert and Emke, 1988; Brown, 1987).

In Barbados, the first official responsible for the CBC was the Minister of Education. The placement of CBC under the Ministry of Education suggested that a strong public service thrust was intended for the station. Yet over the years, successive governments have placed the CBC under different ministries including Tourism, Culture and Information, and even directly under the Office of the Prime Minister.

Down through the years, administrations have addressed how information generated by governmental ministries, departments and agencies should be transmitted, and the role public information should play in the development of the country. Although the CBC is a statutory corporation with some implied autonomy, it is regarded by government as a part of the communication services of the government which include Government Information Services (GIS). Therefore, the objectives of the government with respect to its communications services encompass the CBC television. Within that context, for example, the 1988-93 government development plan stresses the strong public service role of communications services, and reaffirms the educational function the radio and television services of the CBC are expected to assume. The radio and television services of the CBC, the plan states, are to be maintained '... as public organs for the transmission of information, education, culture and ideas of citizens, in much the same way as public educational institutions are publicly maintained for similar purposes ...' (p. 110). The strategy advanced by the government to attain the latter objective is to retain the present policy of not privatising these services.[3]

Sixteen key administrators responsible for broadcasting between 1973-1992, including Cabinet ministers, GIS staff, Broadcasting Authority (BA) and CBC chairmen and board members of both the Authority and the Corporation were asked to express their views, and justifications for those views, about the function and objectives of the national television system. In a small developing country where the government is seen as 'the guardian of law and order ... protector of the underprivileged ... the regulator of public and private activity, and as the planner for the development ...' (Government of Barbados Development Plan 1988-1993, p. 109), the most prevalent view expressed among these informants is that the development role, especially that of nation building, can only be achieved if television remains in the hands of the government.[4] While many did not deviate much from the abstract 'to inform, educate, and entertain' definition of television, some did buttress the argument by stating that the public broadcasting system is intended to help prevent the social and economic disenfranchisement of the majority of Barbadians.

The function of the government owned media system, of which television is a part, is vaguely stated, but strongly suggests an intended developmental role for the system. However, the lateness of attempts to further explicate that developmental objective, appears to have precipitated a process whereby programming decisions are informed more by considerations originating from outside of the public policy domain. Before examining those considerations, attempts to formally establish the relationship between national development goals and television programming objectives of the CBC are analysed for their policy implications.

THE RELATIONSHIP BETWEEN NATIONAL DEVELOPMENT GOALS AND TELEVISION PROGRAMMING OBJECTIVES

Apart from the CBC Broadcasting Acts and the Corporation's licence, up until 1986 there were no formal written policies pertaining to television programming to which the management and staff regularly adhered. In 1986, some twenty-two years after the establishment of the CBC, policy documents pertaining to news and programming were developed and later, partially implemented. The two documents, the 'News Broadcasting Policy' (effective 1986) and the 'Programming Policy' (effective 1987), were developed by the board of management in conjunction with the staff. Partly intended to help curtail political interference in programming decisions, and to provide a general statement of mission for the CBC, these documents, for the first time in CBC's history, formally related national development goals to television programming objectives. It should be noted that these programming policies were developed and implemented during the tenure of a Minister of Information, board chairman and political administration who no longer occupy those posts. Also, there is evidence that succeeding boards do not embrace all of the policy suggestions set forth in these documents.

In accordance with the CBC Act, the stated overall objective of CBC's programming 'is to provide the finest programmes of information, education, culture and entertainment' (CBC Programming Policy, 1987, p. 3), and as a public institution, CBC's role is to create 'a national awareness' (p. 1). The strategy proposed for achieving this goal is the increased production of local materials.

The proposed programming policy provides for the consideration of audience interest and need, availability of material, intrinsic worth of content, standard of production and social relevance. Some highlights of the policy are proposals to ensure that:

1. programming caters to the entire community;

2. feedback opportunities are made available to the public;

3. interaction between the CBC and other educational and cultural organisations take place to provide for the further development of programmes reflecting local and regional content;

4. programming reflects acceptable morals and standards of taste of the local community;

5. no one particular group monopolised local programming; *and*

6. equitable opportunities to participate in programming are allowed.

In keeping with these policy suggestions, the CBC implemented the 'Open-line' programme in 1991. Developed by the public relations office and marketing manager, 'Open-line' was designed to help viewers and listeners better understand the CBC policy and programming. The public relations officer would respond to selected letters (inquiries ranging from types of programming to technical failures), and during each programme, encouraged viewers to continue to submit inquiries, criticisms and suggestions to the CBC. 'Open-line' which appeared to have been designed to address issues of public concern about programming and policy was discontinued with the resignation of both members of staff.

The policy document refers to the Broadcast Rules section (9b), clause (25) of the CBC's licence which states that the licencee must ensure

> ... that a reasonable portion of broadcast material is local or Caribbean in content and character, and that such material includes programmes featuring prose, poetry, drama, music and other arts of the region. (CBC Programming Policy, 1987, p. 12).

In keeping with that rule, the policy stipulates that the CBC maintain a 40 per cent local programming ratio for television.

Acknowledging circumstances likely to impede the attainment of the 40 per cent local television programming goal, the document addresses the most ideal circumstances under which this achievement would occur. It states:

> This percentage is not fixed and will vary from time to time as the board deems fit. The television percentage should increase with the acquisition of new equipment, improved studio facilities and resource personnel. Local programming must increase in a quantitative, as well a qualitative nature. The end result must appeal to the audience, and be able to compete favourably with foreign productions. (CBC Programming Policy, 1987, p. 12).

In suggesting a goal of 60-40 per cent (foreign-local) content for television, the document reaffirms that 'the policy of the Corporation is not to eliminate foreign programmes but to reduce the dependence on these programmes,' (1987, p. 12).

The policy recognises the importance of cultivating cooperative, working relationships with educational, cultural, health, religious and other institutions which share similar or related development goals in the interest of developing programming materials for broadcast. Yet, there is documented criticism of the lack of coordination among government agencies concerned with information, communication, and culture issues. For example, members of the Cinematic Censorship Board (Censorship Board) which is responsible for screening movies shown at theatres and which aims to help preserve the moral fabric of Barbados, are often critical of the programmes shown on the CBC. According to one board member, films barred from cinemas are often shown on the CBC television. The informant also stated that the Censorship Board has no input into policies regarding what is shown on CBC TV, and has been trying to get an input for some time. The director of the National Cultural Foundation (NCF) also has been critical of the dominance of foreign entertainment programmes on the CBC, and has called for better cooperation between the agencies to enhance local production efforts more reflective of national and regional cultures.

In 1989 the government-appointed committee looking into the operations of the CBC also recommended better cooperation between the CBC and the NCF, and government departments like the GIS and the Audio Visual Aids division of the Ministry of Education. Both of these departments employ highly trained staff with useful programme development expertise. It has been further suggested that input from educational institutions like the local community college and the local campus of the University of the West Indies might help facilitate the production of much needed developmental programming. The committee also recommended more cooperation between the CBC and local companies like Barbados External Telecommunications (BET) and the Barbados Telephone Company (BARTEL) with telecommunications capability and expertise. Although the programming policy calls for the pooling of resources from these agencies and organisations, a manager at the CBC reported that government departments traditionally do not always offer full cooperation in such efforts, thus making the attainment of linking programming to development goals difficult.

The proposed news broadcast policy provides detailed guidelines for covering news stories and handling requests for air time, and is intended to ensure that no particular partisan group, or individuals dominates broadcast time. However, the specific policy recommendation of equal time for political parties is often ignored when the Opposition requests equal time to respond to political issues. This issue of equal time has been and continues to be a point of contention between the major political parties.

Although the two policy documents constitute the most thorough efforts to establish a stable approach to programming policy at the CBC, these documents are not regarded as official guidelines and procedures. They are suggestions; recommendations by which the CBC is not bound. Official adherence to these proposed guidelines would require a Cabinet decision resulting from an effort by the Minister responsible for the CBC. No such effort was made by the Minister under which the policy proposals were developed. Nor has any such effort been advanced by the current Minister responsible for broadcasting, the Prime Minister.

FINDINGS

In spite of the perception that excessive amounts of imported television programming contribute to the erosion of indigenous cultural character, the government of Barbados has not systematically assessed, planned and developed policies and regulations to redress the serious imbalance between national and foreign television content. Two major policy issues that emerged from the data collected relate to how television is financed, and the structural framework in which it operates. Stemming from these two broad, encompassing issues are factors which explain how the interrelated questions of programme sources and content, and structural considerations inform television programming decisions.

The most prohibitive factors to the development of local programming stem from the way in which the CBC is financed and structured. Such factors have facilitated an environment in which commercial and partisan interests many times supersede stated or inferred development programming objectives; often allowing advertising dollars and political endeavours to directly influence television programming decisions.

Policy Issue: Programme Sources and Content

Traditionally, the CBC is undercapitalised, and successive governments have been unable to finance on a wide scale the type of programming that reflects indigenous culture and lifestyles of the local community. Since the black community is generally unable to finance such programming endeavours, those who are not within this community ultimately pay for the bulk of programming aired on the CBC. The type of programming most consistently financed is popular, imported fare that generally perpetuates negative social stereotypes and exogenous orientation.

In Barbados, the emphasis on the importation of inexpensive, popular programmes with mass appeal has been touted as the most feasible way to fill television programming time. The systematic unwillingness of advertisers to support locally produced programmes over imported ones has resulted in little or no support of local programmes. In turn, the estimated high production costs of local programmes compared to the low costs of foreign programmes is used by the programmers to further justify expenditures on imported materials.

In addition to the interrelated constraints of limited funding and sponsorship, costs, and inadequate resources, certain attitudinal factors undergird these concerns. Most often, these attitudes that are observable across sectors of Barbadian society project the notion that foreign is better, or at least most popular. The view is that imported programmes with mass appeal are attractive to viewers who demand them, advertisers who support them, and programmers who import them.

Limited Subvention as a factor influencing decisions to import television programmes vs Development of Local Productions

The current position of the government of Barbados is that the public corporation model remains the best model for achieving the social development goals of television. Highly regarded examples are the British Broadcasting Corporation (BBC) and the Canadian Broadcasting Corporation (CBC-Canada).

CBC, though established upon an almost identical policy structure as the BBC and CBC-Canada, no longer receives the same kind of support. Both the British and Canadian public broadcast systems are regularly subsidised by government grants and subscription fees.

A wholly government owned corporation, CBC, according to Part III, section (II) of the CBC Act, is required to seek to secure revenues to '... become at the earliest possible date and thereafter continue ... to meet all sums properly chargeable to revenue account, including ... loans and interest thereon...' The same section also indicates that the CBC is expected to make provision 'for depreciation and for establishment and maintenance' of reserve funds. In short, the government has insisted that the CBC should pay its own way. To date, the CBC has been unable to meet this provision. Instead, in crisis situations, the CBC has had to rely on the government's assistance to meet budget requirements. In recent years, government subvention has amounted to the authorisation of a BD$14.5 million capital development loan from the Bank of Nova Scotia to pay for the renovated building complex of the station, and sporadic assistance to help cover losses incurred from operating expenses.

An alternative to government subvention existed between 1965 and 1986 when the CBC profited from annual television licence fees which provided substantial revenues. In 1985, licence fee revenue amounted to BD$627,888; the same year the CBC incurred an overall loss of BD$456,344 (Report of the CBC, 1990).

Other CBC informants indicate that the Corporation collected about BD$700,000 out of the BD$1 million which was collectable annually.

The CBC's inability to show that the revenues collected were being used to support local programme development drew complaints from subscribers. In 1986, partly for political reasons, the television licence fee was abolished, thereby substantially reducing CBC's takings. In 1988, the estimated loss of income of television licence fees to the CBC was BD$1.2 million dollars (Report of the CBC, 1990).

At the time of this study there was no direct government subsidy for local television programme development. Nor was there an identifiable business plan to further upgrade television production facilities and equipment needed to enhance local production efforts. Combined, these circumstances have served to increase the dependence on foreign materials. In turn, the reliance on the advertising sector for support has directly influenced decisions to import foreign television programmes.

Advertising factors and standards that influence decisions to import foreign television programmes

Advertisers traditionally support programmes that have been proven in terms of popularity and rating. However, informed broadcasters refute the popularity argument stating that advertising agencies often erroneously assume that locally and regionally produced programmes have no audiences. They assert that viewership surveys reveal otherwise.

Citing the popularity of the Jamaican-produced programme 'Oliver at Large' and 'the regionally distributed Caribscope', several professional communication informants suggested that there is sufficient evidence that people desire and enjoy programming with local and regional angles. These informants argue that more emphasis should be placed on enhancing such efforts; namely improving upon the quality of already existing popular programmes instead of endeavouring to rapidly increase the overall percentage of productions.

Yet in the case of 'Oliver at Large', the CBC reports having encountered problems convincing advertisers to support the programme. According to a management spokesperson, businesses disapproved of some of the images conveyed in the programme like that of a Rastafarian man, and indicated that the Jamaican dialect was too pronounced for Barbadians to understand. In spite of encountering disfavour from the business sector, 'Oliver at Large' became one of the most popular shows in Barbados. The CBC reports, however, that there was a paucity of sponsorship.

Along with cost and rating considerations, advertising executives assert that issues of standards and quality influence their clients decisions to underwrite programmes. Advertisers express a willingness to support programmes that reflect suitable production standards; standards which local productions are said to lack generally. Reasoned one marketing agency director:

> ... an advertiser looks at programming on television as a vehicle to communicate his business services. Therefore, if he can buy a canned programme from the United States which is made professionally at a high quality, and it is going to cost him $3,000.00 an hour to sponsor such material that has come to him in a can, why is he going to pay $9,000.00 or $10,000.00 for a similar type of exposure which might not be as well made just because it is local?' (M. Williams, personal interview, June 26, 1992).

Despite assertions by advertisers that they would willingly support quality local productions, informants from the communication and socio-cultural sectors, and even the advertising community, contend the reasons for the lack of support are insidious. A prevalent theme that emerged from the interview data was that the advertising sector, which is comprised mainly of white, middle class Barbadians and expatriates, is less than enthusiastic about supporting local productions of a culturally-oriented or racially conscious nature. Within the CBC, eight staff members (including five at the senior level) reiterated this thesis, stating that advertisers have commonly referred to such programmes as 'too grass roots' or 'anti-white'.

The controversy surrounding a lecture known as the 'Mutual Affair' appears to have perpetuated this perspective about the advertising community. Presented by an acclaimed Barbadian historian, the lecture series examined alleged racism at all levels in the Mutual Insurance Corporation, a Barbadian company. According to the historian, the CBC was pressured by advertisers to discontinue his lecture. He said:

> ... the white community in Barbados thought that it was raising the temperature of race relations in the country. And they instructed the board of management that unless it was removed that they would have to withdraw their financial support in the future, and of course, the lecture was cut short. (H. Beckles, personal interview, March 2, 1992).

The CBC declined to confirm that the 'Mutual Affair' lecture was discontinued due to advertiser pressures. However, both board and station informants did confirm that other lectures by the same historian have been run without advertising support.

In response, some advertisers deny deliberately withholding support for informative, black-oriented programming. However, some contend that advertisers persistently sponsor black comedies as opposed to politically and culturally enlightening programmes. One producer contends that advertisers

> .. will support a local programme if it makes a mockery of Barbadian culture .. the slapstick comedies, the exaggerated dialect.... Anything that will enlighten, especially

programmes of an educational nature that will uplift and cause Barbadians to question certain things, will never get sponsorship.' (O. Walrond, personal interview, July 1, 1992).

A Barbadian cultural anthropologist's observation seems to reify the perspective that advertisers tend to prefer supporting black comedies. He noted:

'Certainly the black programmes that have sponsors in Barbados have been primarily comedies. Nothing serious. And you have to ask yourself if it is a deliberate policy of the people who buy advertising time on CBC to keep Barbadians away from that serious type of social commentary; serious political commentary ....' (P. Simmons, personal interview, July 10, 1992).

Leading advertising executives refuted this argument stating that comedies are sponsored most often because of popularity, and not denigrating content. Yet, it often appears that black-oriented programming either of stellar or mediocre quality is not a priority for advertisers. During the period of this study, the CBC aired a programme regarded as containing political and social commentary relevant to the black experience; the acclaimed PBS series 'Eyes on the Prize' which chronicles the Civil Rights Movement in the United States. A nine-part series, 'Eyes on the Prize' was aired weekly during prime time. During that time, the programme did not contain any local advertisements. The researcher inquired across the target sector for reasons.

Once again, the question of whether certain sponsorship commitments, on a broad scale, are informed by social considerations, was asked of an advertising executive who had on a prior occasion emphatically denied such assertions. He restated that cost and issues of quality are the most pertinent considerations. However, after he was assured of anonymity, this informant confided that the social orientation of advertisers invariably factors into most sponsorship considerations. This advertising industry informant stated:

'... we can't hide the fact that many Barbadian companies are Caucasian in ownership. They are not going to be as eager to sponsor a documentary on civil rights in the United States unless they are encouraged to do so. Remember, it is showing people in a bad light.' (Personal interview with advertising informant).

If such views do factor into sponsorship decisions, they could stem from the publicly expressed concerns that certain types of programming might intensify racial tensions between whites and blacks. Indeed, during the study period, the researcher observed several editorials in the two local daily newspapers written mainly by whites addressing this concern. Perceiving that there were growing racial tensions between the majority of black populace and the white minority, they argued that black-oriented programming should be discouraged because of its potential to exacerbate such tensions.

A recognised calypsonian, journalist and culture critic refutes this concern of racial violence, insisting that it has always been exaggerated and used to justify the lack of support of programmes like 'Eyes on the Prize'. Stating that such attitudes have persisted among whites for years, he recalled how the 'Roots' series encountered disfavour from the white community which openly opposed its screening. He stated:

> 'There was a big controversy when "Roots" was going to be shown here because basically, all the white companies were saying 'if we sponsor this kind of show on television, all the black people are going to start wanting to kill the white people tomorrow'. But when it was shown, that didn't happen.' (Adonijah, personal interview, June 30, 1992).

There were other informants, including two former Ministers, four chairmen responsible for the CBC, and two board members who see the limited sponsorship problem in a less insidious light. They argued that generally the problem of limited sponsorship of programmes, including series like 'Eyes on the Prize', is more attributable to the lack of aggressive marketing on the part of the CBC. The CBC marketing division, however, confirmed that prospective advertisers were approached, but declined to underwrite the 'Eyes on the Prize' series. Also, the general manager of the CBC refuted assertions that marketing staff are not aggressive enough, restating that advertisers are traditionally nonsupportive of local programmes.

Throughout this discussion of factors which inform policy decisions pertaining to programme sources and content, evidence of some interrelated attitudes emerged. What follows is a discussion of the extent to which these attitudinal factors may undergird approaches to television policy. Informants from all target sectors were asked to respond to questions regarding the extent to which television could be used to further Barbadian social development. An analysis of these responses produced two general attitudinal themes relating to the cultural orientation of Barbadians; namely advertisers, viewers and programmers, and the perceived developmental role of television among these groups.

Attitudinal Factors that influence television programming decisions

A Barbadian historian's description of Barbadian culture as 'irretrievably Western' implies a certain ideological permanency; a certain social orientation. He argues that having developed a Euro-American perspective, Barbados has endeavoured 'to accommodate North American interest and thinking'. There is little question that Barbados' colonial past and its continued affiliation with the West has had a great impact on its economic, political and social institutions.

That Western orientation is observable not only in expressed views and behaviour of Barbadians, but may in fact, inform some of the television programming expectations of the viewing public as well as the decisions made by programmers in response to those expectations.

On occasion there seemed to be some optimism, (even among the more skeptical), that if the CBC, in spite of its many constraints could produce more locally originated programmes more reflective of Barbadian society, citizens would welcome and view those programmes. Yet certain attitudinal factors seem to obscure such enthusiasm; namely the widespread perspective that foreign is better. Even among the more directly informed programmers, the prevalent view expressed was that foreign fare, if not necessarily better, is at least more marketable. Such attitudes carry over into the decision making area. Moreover, the advertisers' insistence that the programmes they sponsor adhere to US programme standards and formats may further perpetuate this perspective. By effect, ratings surveys conducted in the United States determine what programmes are most appropriate for the viewers of Barbados.

Another CBC informant indicated that programming decisions are informed by neocolonial attitudes, and contends that a commitment to developmental programming needs to be better emphasised and pursued at CBC. Based on his continuous attempts to advance programme ideas, ideas not always supported, the informant observed:

> 'There is a lack of spoken, professed commitment to local programming ... I'm speaking of ... management at CBC. It sounds good to hear people talk about the need for local programming, but there is not that commitment, that belief in the necessity for local programming. They are not committed to the concept of television programming from out of which there is a wide content of things Barbadian. And that too goes back to the sociology of Barbados. We are a neocolonial society. We are only now beginning to break down the notion that everything cultural and everything else must be patterned after the British model. I am not convinced that some people have even started out of that notion yet.' (Personal interview with CBC informant).

A July 1991 viewership survey conducted by the CBC revealed that with the exception of the local evening news, the ten most watched television programmes are US serials. Moreover, according to that survey, Barbadians were pleased with the programmes shown, and in some cases, recommended extended broadcasting hours and more entertainment programmes. This survey did not include the Subscription Television Service (STV) which comprises totally foreign fare.

Since the inception of television, Barbadians have always viewed primarily imported programmes because that is what has been offered. While it is not bewildering that the viewing public, having become accustomed to foreign fare and standards of presentation, would expect and even prefer such materials, an equally significant concern to programmers is the extent to which the public would be responsive to locally produced materials that may not necessarily reflect these same themes and standards.

For example, some programming staff contend that if local programme alternatives are successfully developed, Barbadians, having been fed on a diet of American-made sitcoms and dramas, would not likely appreciate those efforts. The contention of more than one producer that 'a typical Barbadian trait is that Barbadians do not like things Barbadian', is a widely expressed sentiment. Hence, the perception that some programmer's efforts appear to end here, has repeatedly prompted commentators to criticise what they see as ineptness on the part of the CBC in living up to its development role.

Community commentators insist that in spite of the extenuating circumstances, both the CBC and the government need to be more vigorous in searching for alternative programmes which need not be expensive. Collectively, they insist that if the development and preservation of a national culture is desirable, then cost factors are subsidiary.

On the other hand, the CBC programmers and administrators contend that the public does not have a full appreciation for the precarious situation in which the CBC finds itself. With no clear, viable alternatives readily apparent, there appears to be a diminishing sense of enthusiasm among the CBC production and programming staff, although the management maintains its stated commitment to providing locally originated programmes reflective of Barbadian interests and issues.

Policy Issues: Structure of the CBC and Practices Emanating from the Structure

The structure of the CBC has functioned to allow successive governments to directly influence television content. The few attempts to develop and implement formal television programming policies more than twenty years after the establishment of the CBC have been overshadowed by de facto practices of partisan control and manipulation.

The structure of broadcasting has an unsettling effect on the management of the CBC and any attempts to establish definitive policies and practices. The Act does not provide any explicit guidelines as to what the boards of management are appointed to do. As governments change, so does the composition of boards. In parliamentary democracies where legislators are key policy makers, political agendas will also change. For example, while the 1986 'News Broadcasting Policy' and the 1987 'Programming Policy' were approved by the then Minister and adopted by that board, many of the recommended guidelines have not always coincided with the objectives of subsequent boards. After the death of former Prime Minister Errol Barrow in 1987, ministerial assignments changed. The board chairman and most of the board members also changed. Because board members do not always serve their full three year terms as provided by the Act, even less consistency is achieved, resulting in what one veteran broadcaster called a 'hodge podge' approach to communication planning and policy at the CBC.

The board, which is comprised of a chairman, deputy chairman, and nine other members including the permanent secretary to the Prime Minister, is widely perceived as an extension of political control, regardless of whatever political party is in office. Often, board chairmen and members are referred to as 'yard fowls' because their appointments result more from their political allegiance and affiliation than their broadcasting knowledge or managerial skills. Although political allegiance is not a formal criterion for appointment to the board, appointments based on allegiance are the rule rather than the exception. When asked about the validity of the allegations of political patronage on the board, all of the ministers, permanent secretaries and chairmen interviewed, acknowledged the regularity of the practice. Says one former chairman: 'There are always people on the board who are positively friendly to the party in office'.

Even without being instructed, some board members have assumed the posture of protecting the party's interests. In other cases, says a former chairman, board members have been lobbied into particular positions even before they met. The presence of the permanent secretary on the board is also regarded as yet another extension of governmental influence. In the present scenario, the permanent secretary reports directly to the Prime Minister. In defence of this practice, an informant who served eight years combined as Minister (responsible for broadcasting) and board chairman said 'the government should have a direct voice on the board'. However, a former CBC chairman refutes this practice, contending that the presence of the permanent secretary on the board as well as ministerial influence do not allow the board to think independently and to manage the CBC as it is charged to do.

Ministerial Influence on Programming Decisions

Partisan government influence in the CBC programming decisions has also been characterised by ministerial involvement. The interviews yielded a wealth of verifiable anecdotal evidence of attempts by various government and political officials to either influence or manipulate the content of news programming.

A widely documented example of an administration's attempt to influence the content of news is the June 1973 'Positive Side of News' edict issued by the then Minister of Tourism. At that time, the CBC, formerly under the Minister of

Education, was placed under the supervision of the Minister of Tourism, suggesting that government radio and television, like GIS, were regarded as public relations mechanisms.

The edict from the Minister to report only the positive side of the news was issued during a CBC general staff meeting. Recalls one staff member: 'The positive side of news meant that we should only spotlight the government ministers and anything the government was doing. Anything critical was considered the negative side of news'.

Evidently the Barbadian government is still sensitive about the news media reporting of crimes: coverage, the government contends, hurts tourism. During the period of this study, the researcher observed public statements by government officials criticising the media for emphasising the escalating incidence of crime on the island. This escalation in crime also drew the attention of the governments of the United States and Great Britain, both of which issued precautionary travel advisories for Barbados in 1992.

Some CBC news staff (both current and former) report having been contacted directly by government officials about altering the content and order of news stories. One former staff member recalled that such contact was often made around election time, usually by members of the incumbent party trying to manipulate the content or presentation of the news. The informant stated:

> ... you would get a telephone call from the chairman of the board and sometimes the Minister responsible for Information himself trying to influence ... a particular slot or news item. If the news did not reflect positively on the government, then you might get a sort of suggestion that maybe it should be played down, meaning of course dropped lower in the order of the news, or not carried at all.' (Personal interview with former CBC staff member).

Another staffer, who for nine years worked in news under different administrators, reported instances where directives were issued about what should or should not be covered, particularly controversial issues. In one case, this reporter said she received a call from the Minister who ordered her to run a story to offset a controversial story that reflected negatively on another co-Minister.

The STV system, in many ways, epitomises how ministerial liberty and inadequate feasibility planning have directly influenced programming. Conceived in 1983, STV was not actually implemented until 1987 under a different political administration. Intended to help the CBC to become more profitable and to underwrite local programming, instead, the system has beset the CBC.

From the beginning, the establishment of STV faced a series of delays because of technical problems. Some of these technical problems were attributed to inadequate feasibility planning under the previous administration. For example, an unusual feature of the system is that the programming is transmitted over UHF, not cable. The CBC is still experiencing transmission problems due to this set up and it is projected that the STV system will eventually have to be converted to cable.

After the government changed, the new Minister attempted to achieve some consistency in planning by retaining a few of the former board members who were familiar with the STV system. However, even with this effort, the intended continuity was difficult because of the absence of a written business plan. Stated the chairman of the board that inherited the STV project, '... we could not find, either in the board minutes, or in any other document, the rationale for why that system was chosen. Because of a number of interlocking decisions that were already in process, we had to go along with that decision'. (M. Walrond, personal interview, April 17, 1992). Since then, the board composition has repeatedly changed. The government sponsored committee that reviewed the operations of the CBC concluded that no comprehensive business plan for STV was developed.[5]

Direct Board Involvement in Programming Decisions

Beyond its inferred goal of setting general standards for programming, the board's efforts to influence some specific programming decisions have been regarded as politically motivated. This perspective has been spurred in recent years by the resignations of CBC staff, and the denial of programme proposals submitted by outside, independent sources.

Throughout the history of the CBC, there have been documented cases of partisan influence in programming decisions via the board of management. One of the most widely known forms of direct programming control in Barbados is banning. Some of the most renowned bannings have occurred in radio where certain calypsos, namely those critical of administrations in power, have been declined for airing. In the area of television, successive governments have pursued some policy of banning or censorship of certain content and individuals. The forms of control have ranged from written memos to verbal directives. One of the most well known cases was the banning of the former Chief GIS officer Gladstone Holder, who was banned 'for life'. According to Holder, now a nationally acclaimed columnist, he received a written notice that banned him for allowing the presentation of views not necessary in favour of the then government's point of view.

In other cases, banning has taken on a more subtle form, especially in the news and public affairs programming, an area in which politicians have taken the most interest. A former television news director at the CBC recalled subtle, informal edicts directed at curtailing the views of individuals considered 'hostile' toward the ruling party's positions.

Another case involved a team of independent producers who produced a pilot programme for a soap opera called 'Shadows in the Sun', and submitted it to the CBC with a proposal for airing it as an ongoing pay per view programme on STV. Under such an arrangement, the CBC would get a percentage of the revenue from the showings and all production expenses were to be handled by the independent team.

The producers met with the CBC managers responsible for programming, marketing, and STV to view the pilot. After screening the pilot, the management team unanimously approved of carrying the programme and instructed the team to proceed with the development of promos for the programme.

However soon afterwards, the board intervened and instructed the deputy general manager to generate a letter to the producers stating that the programme would have to be aired in a 'Heart of the Matter' format to ascertain its 'merits and demerits'. What this means was that the programme would be viewed and evaluated by a group representative of a cross-section of the community. The group would provide feedback to the board about the 'eligibility' of the programme for continuous airing.

Although no foreign-produced soap opera aired on the CBC has been subjected to the same type of scrutiny proposed for the 'Shadows in the Sun' pilot, the board justified its action, stating that it is now more closely reviewing the content of such programmes. With the introduction of midday showings of soap operas in late 1991, a CBC informant confirmed, the board has become increasingly concerned about the morals and lifestyles portrayed in these programmes.

However, one of the co-producers insists that the board's motive was political and attributes the decision to the fact that she ran as a candidate for the newly formed opposition National Democratic Party (NDP) during the last election. The NDP is a splinter group that broke off from the then ruling Democratic Labour Party (DLP). Also, this individual writes a weekly column that is often vitriolic of the current administration, thus earning her the label as 'anti-government' among DLP supporters.

Initially, the board denied any political motive and reaffirmed its commitment to ensuring, when possible, that desirable morals are portrayed in programmes aired by the CBC. However, a division manager who participated in the initial screening and approval of the programme for airing, said emphatically that the board's decision was political. Eventually, a board informant, while maintaining that the board discourages programming with less than desirable lifestyles and practices, conceded that the board did in fact screen the pilot, among other things, 'to make sure that it was not anti-government'.

In another case, the board intervened and declined a request from a non-profit group known as the Caribbean Policy Development Centre (CPDC), which approached the CBC about airing an informational video about economic structural readjustment, and the role that the IMF has played in that process, especially in other Caribbean countries. During that time in 1990, Barbados was involved in negotiations with the IMF to acquire a loan to offset the country's debts.

According to the CPDC director, the management at the CBC was initially enthused about showing the timely video that would further explain the process of structural readjustment to the public. However, after the board reviewed the proposal for the programme (which would be funded by the Centre, not the CBC), the CPDC director was informed that the programming schedule did not have adequate space to accommodate the video. However, that very same week, the CBC showed a one hour documentary provided by the IMF about structural readjustment.

That CBC would turn down a timely, fully paid programme with local and regional focus did not sit well with the CPDC informant, who exclaimed: 'In a financial crisis, how do you reject a $5,000.00 programme?' The CPDC video which deals with debt and structural adjustment, takes a critical look at the impact of such IMF programmes in other developing Caribbean countries. The CPDC informant contends that their video was likely deemed as too critical, and therefore, declined for airing. The informant reasoned that an IMF video, which she described as a 'propaganda documentary' was given precedence in an attempt to appease the IMF. In response to these allegations of censorship, a board informant confirmed, though reluctantly, that the board intervened and 'decided that during such sensitive negotiations, it was not the time to show a documentary critical of the US or the IMF'.

OTHER RELATED FINDINGS

In addition to the problematic practices of undercapitalisation and political influence within the communications sector, fragmentation has influenced the nature of television programming policy in Barbados. Instead of strengthening the endogenous capacity for the development of policy measures to redress some of the most pertinent programming issues, this fragmentation has generally served to weaken such endeavours, resulting in, at best, vaguely defined planning objectives.

The traditional partitioning of the communications sector among Ministers with different objectives has encouraged more of an ad hoc, arbitrary approach to decision making that has not necessarily been in the long term interest of communication planning endeavours. This is evidenced by the current scenario where the BA, CBC and GIS are under the Prime Minister's Office, while telecommunications falls under the aegis of the Minister of Public Works, Communications and Transportation. Despite the diminishing distinctions brought on with the advent of the information age, communication in Barbados is regarded basically as government communications, while telecommunications is seen as encompassing internal and external telephony and aviation types of matters.

The BA, the only entity in Barbados capable of filling a centralised type of role in conjunction with communication and development sector planning, has assumed a passive posture in relation to advancing substantive policy. The Authority has been relatively silent on issues of regulation of foreign programmes, has not generated comprehensive broadcasting proposals, and has often deferred to other government divisions on interrelated issues of broadcasting and culture.[6]

It is evident that external influences stemming mainly from Barbados' affiliation with the United States, and its recent dependence on the US and organisations like the IMF for financial assistance have occasionally influenced management and programming decisions. The board's decision not to air the CPDC's video which takes a critical view of the IMF's role in structural readjustment is an indication of that type of influence. A more apparent example of US influence on programming decisions in Barbados stems from the addendum to the Caribbean Basin Initiative (CBI) bill that threatens economic sanctions for CBI recipients who retransmit unauthorised recorded materials from the US. The addendum has prompted the CBC to move quickly to cooperate with the CBI. Unlike some other stations in the region, the CBC scrupulously adheres to the conditions of the Initiative and pays a fee for retransmissions of programmes like 'CNN News', while the government has cracked down on satellite pirating (Cuthbert and Hoover, 1991).

The proximity of Barbados and other countries of the English-speaking Caribbean to the United States places them in a situation of strategic interest to the US. Indeed the US views trade programmes such as the CBI as contributing to what it defines as the 'economic growth and political stability in a nearby strategically important region', which enhances 'our country's security' (United States Department of Commerce, 1990, p. 1).

Throughout the 20th Century, the United States has expanded its political involvement and commercial interests in the region. Cuthbert (1986) notes that 'the Monroe Doctrine of the US gave way to the Good Neighbour policy of the 30s and 40s which has given way, since the 50s, to the cold war policy of keeping the region free of Soviet influence' (p. 162).

In keeping with this recurrent ideological theme, the US Ambassador to Barbados, Philip Hughes, recently saw fit to remind Barbadians of the importance in maintaining 'friendly' relations with its North American neighbour. Noting his astonishment with Barbados' and some Caribbbean Community (CARICOM) countries records in voting less with the US at the United Nations, the ambassador said that Barbados should better demonstrate its friendship by voting more with the United States at the UN. Hughes said: 'In the international community there is no more valuable commodity than the practical evidence of friendship, based on shared values and common purpose. A historical record of cooperation is a good building block of friendship'.[7]

Such an admonishment, according to a Barbadian newspaper editorial, leaves little 'doubt that successive governments of Barbados are unlikely to discount the weight and importance of the fact that the United States is a super power ... and that Barbados lives within its underbelly'.[8]

POSTCOLONIAL CONTINUITIES

The consideration of the economic, social and political contexts in which a communications system functions, is vital to the analysis of any process which takes place within that system. The confluence of factors that inhibit the full and purportedly desirable use of Barbadian television in development are inextricably related to an identifiable set of circumstances rooted in the country's colonial legacy.

Problems with the television broadcasting system are reflective of the overall system in which most economic resources are controlled by a small minority. In keeping with that tradition, a small interest group, through advertising, directly influences television programme content; content that further cultivates an external orientation said to be debilitating to societal values.

By its constitution, Barbados is a parliamentary democracy patterned after the British system. In fact, it boasts of having the third oldest parliament in the British Commonwealth. Similarly, the CBC is patterned after the BBC model, a design which Barbadian officials promote as the most promising for social development. Yet unlike the BBC and other Commonwealth media systems which receive substantial government subvention, Barbadian television receives at this time no direct government subsidy and has not been able to successfully function as a public service or commercial entity. In their survey of developing world media systems, Katz and Wedell (1977) note that when countries are able to produce most of the programmes they need, then they can become more selective in their import policy. Yet the authors note that the development of human resources for innovation in broadcasting requires more than professional and technical enhancement of broadcasters, there also needs to be an understanding among broadcasters and policy makers of their jobs and functions in relation to the cultural development of their countries. Since a sense of self confidence is needed to undertake this arduous task, broadcasters (including programmers) and policy makers in Barbados must have an informed understanding of the cultural history of their country.

One of Africa's most prolific scholars, Cheikh Anta Diop, has emphasised cultural and historical consciousness as the basis for development. The Senegalese scholar captured this stream of consciousness that permeates all of his work when he wrote that 'profound cultural unity' is still very much 'alive beneath the deceptive appearance of cultural heterogeneity' (1990, p. 7). Diop posits that only limited progress in contemporary development can be made without a holistic understanding of the inherent value of indigenous cultures, languages and social structures. Meaningful progress is dependent on what Diop describes as a resilient 'historical consciousness' that provokes developing societies to '... reject elements of imposed structures which are inimical to their self-assertive development'. (Moore, 1992, p. 276). While speaking largely from an African historical perspective, Diop's postulates also strike a resonant chord among Caribbean practitioners and scholars who emphasise the urgent need for policies which recognise the inherent value of traditional communicative approaches (Simmons and Niles, 1987).

A prevailing ethnocentric bias has informed traditionally Western-based models that tend to emphasise the use of media systems in the developing world for assimilation and social control instead of endogeny and self-reliance. In most Caribbean countries government ownership, control and management of television stations, often via statutory boards has prevailed. Similarly, in sub-Saharan African countries, existing communication policies tend to emphasise the management and control of communications systems, often to disseminate information about government policies and programmes (Boafo, 1987). According to Awa (1982), both African and Caribbean governments have frequently omitted one or more of five necessary stages of planning:

1. identify the problem(s);

2. analyse the problem(s);

3. suggest all possible solutions;

4. select the best possible solution(s);

5. suggest ways in which to implement the solution(s). (p. 19)

Awa's planning design emphasises the importance of continual evaluation and adoption to change, and calls for a new 'typology' of development communication that concentrates on 'the careful and sensitive adoption of Western models' (p. 10) to the cultural and economic priorities of the developing world.

Awa also notes that national plans have often overlooked the complicity of communication channels and ignored the unanticipated hurdles of implementing the plans. Similarly, Ham and Hill (1984) emphasise the need to recognise that implementation of reform plans 'involves a continuation of the complex processes of bargaining, negotiation and interaction which characterise the policy making process' (p. 109). Ideally, the process would cater to the needs of the implementers as well as the communication users.

The inadequate integration of communication into overall national development strategies has served to mitigate against the development and successful implementation of effective programming policy in the Caribbean and the developing world. Within the Barbadian context, the vague definition of the role of television in social development, and the manner in which television and programming have been financed, have largely influenced the nature and direction of programming policy. If the CBC television programming does not reflect the desirable development, social or even moral content and quality, it is partly due to the absence of a stably financed, comprehensive policy designed to redress the imbalance between foreign and local content, and to facilitate the continuous development of alternative local-oriented programmes.

In choosing as its national symbol the broken trident shaft which represents the break from the historical and constitutional ties of the past, Barbados has acknowledged the need for social restitution, so vital to any people seeking to forge national identity in the wake of three centuries of colonial domination. Yet, by perpetuating the wholesale importation of North American lifestyles and values through satellite television, it would seem that in the absence of effective policy measures, Barbados is disparaging the very goal of cultural restitution it seeks to accomplish. In so doing, the country is in danger of fulfilling the worst fears of one of its founding fathers by loitering on 'colonial' premises well after closing time.

NOTES

1. Excerpt from address to the Barbados Constitutional Conference in London, July 1966. As Premier, Errol Barrow headed the Barbados government's delegation.

   This article is based on research conducted as part of the author's doctoral dissertation, and a conference paper presented at the 10th Annual Intercultural/International Communication Conference, Miami, Florida, February 1993.

2. This estimate is from *Television programming trends in the Anglophone Caribbean: the 1980s* (p. 21) by Brown, 1987, Jamaica: CARIMAC , UWI. Barbadian television encapsulates a trend throughout the English-speaking Caribbean where the average amount of imported television material is more than 80 per cent.

   The 1986-87 estimate cited here does not include Subscription Television (STV) which was introduced in late 1987. Also, since 1991, the CBC has reduced its programming hours. CBC sources estimate the percentage of imported content, excluding STC, to be around 75-80 per cent.

3. Interestingly, the ongoing debate about whether or not television in Barbados should be privatised

has called into question not only the benefits that are said to accrue from a publicly owned and operated television system and what function it should serve, but also what function it **actually** serves. By effect, the debate has challenged the heretofore, generally loosely stated 'to inform, educate, and entertain' definition of television used by public officials.

4. In 1992 the then administration announced its intention to partially divest itself of the CBC beginning with a 20% share to be made available to staff.

5. The service turned its first profit in 1991 and has continued to do so.

6. Despite a promise to staff it within six weeks of the May '86 elections it took more than two years for the necessary persons to be named to the Authority.

7. Quoted in *The Nation*, 1992, p. 3.

8. Quoted in *The Nation*, 1992, p. 3.

REFERENCES

Awa, N.E. (1982). Mass Communication and Change in Africa: Implications for the Commonwealth Caribbean. Journal of Black Studies, 13, 1-10.

Boafo, S.T.K. (1987). Africa Must Rethink Its Course in Communication. Media Development, 34 (1), 14-16.

Brown, A. (1987). The electronic recolonialisation of the Caribbean. Media Development, 34 (1), 20-21.

CBC News Broadcasting Policy (1987). Caribbean Broadcasting Corporation publication.

Cuthbert, M. and Emke, I. (1988). Communication policy making in the Caribbean. International Association for Mass Communication Research, (Occasional Papers, 8), 3-11.

Cuthbert, M. and Hoover, S. (1990). Laissez faire Policies, Vcrs and Caribbean Identify. In S.H. Surlin and W.C. Soderland (eds.), Mass media and the Caribbean (pp 287-298) New York: Gordon and Breach.

Cuthbert, M.L. and Hoover S.M. (1991). Video Beachheads: Communication, Culture, and Policy in the Eastern Caribbean. In G. Sussman and J.A. Lent (eds.), Transnational communications: wiring the world (pp 263-278). Newbury Park, Ca: Sage.

Cuthbert, M. (1986). Communication Technology and Culture: Towards West Indian Policies. Gazette, 38, 161-170.

Diop, C.A. (1990). The Cultural Unity of Black Africa. Chicago: Third World Press.

Government of Barbados Development Plan 1988-1993. Communication Services 109-110.

Ham, C. and Hill, M. (1984). The Policy Process in the Modern Capitalist State. New York: St. Martin's Press.

Katz, E. and Wedell, G. (1977). Broadcasting in the Third World. Cambridge: Harvard University Press.

Laws of Barbados (November 11, 1963). Caribbean Broadcasting Corporation Act, 1963, 36, 1-12.

Moore S. (1992). Interview with Cheikh Anta Diop. In I. Van Sertima (ed.), Great African Thinkers: Cheikh Anta Diop (pp 238-283). New Brunswick, N.J.: Transaction Books.

Report of the Caribbean Broadcasting Corporation. (1990, February). Unpublished government document.

Simmons, P. and Niles, B. (1987). State of the Media in Barbados. In A. Brown and R. Sanatan (eds) Talking With Whom?: A Report on the State of the Media in the Caribbean (pp 70-83). Jamaica: CARIMAC, UWI.

United States Department of Commerce (November 1990). 1991 Guidebook: The Caribbean Basin Initiative, Washington, D.C., CBI Centre.

7

BROADCASTING AND THE STRUGGLE FOR CULTURAL AUTONOMY IN CANADA

Robert Martin

INTRODUCTION

We live in a world which is increasingly being homogenised. International airports are virtually identical, each as awful as the next. But homogenisation has gone much further. The world's large cities are sometimes hard to distinguish from each other — they all have too many people, too many cars and too much pollution. The hotels, the restaurants and the signs of poverty look pretty much the same wherever you go.

The most important force driving global homogenisation is the internationalisation of capital. It has both demanded and facilitated a remarkable standardisation of products, tastes and techniques. Going hand in hand with the internationalisation of capital has been the expansion and improvement of means of communication.

The means, and frequency of moving information, goods and human beings have been transformed beyond recognition. The most unimaginative of after-dinner speakers now refer regularly to the 'global village'.

This banal phrase does contain a substantial truth. More and more, human beings tend in whatever part of the world they may live, to watch the same television programmes, see the same movies, listen to the same music, and read the same, or indistinguishable, newspapers and magazines.

There are many who are not enthusiastic about global homogenisation, who do not see the internationalisation, or the standardisation of everything as a desirable result. There are those, further, who do not regard the process as inevitable and wish to see it slowed or stopped.

When arguments are raised against homogenisation they invariably seek to counterpose the virtues of a local or regional 'culture' against the corruption and materialism of international or, as is commonly known, 'Western' 'culture'. Proponents of these arguments seek to protect 'our' culture against the onslaught of 'foreign' culture.

The word 'culture' is, itself, problematic. It is over-used, its incessant repetition being, paradoxically, one of the indicia of global homogenisation. It is also misused, being employed to designate a variety of situations, practices and thoughts far too diverse and contradictory to be embraced by any single word. Finally, the word can be dangerous and divisive. Many who favour it imply that what it denotes is primarily a product of human genes, rather than human history, thereby promoting vast amounts of hostility and suspicion amongst peoples.

Nonetheless, the claim in favour of cultural distinctiveness is made with great vigour in almost all parts of the world. It is based in the understanding that different societies have different institutions, different ways of doing things, in a word, different traditions and, more important, that there is value in these traditions, not simply because they are different, but in and of themselves.

The desire to hold on to national or regional traditions leads to the identification of the mass media as primary bearers of homogenising influences. The most important of these is clearly broadcasting and, more specifically, television.

The usual purpose in resisting the homogenising effects of television is not to achieve cultural autarchy, but to preserve something of the traditional understanding of the nation and the human beings who make it up. The global babel cannot be defeated or held back completely, but in its cacophony a national voice may still be heard. As a Canadian group urged in 1974, 'It should be possible to turn on one's television and know what country one is in'.

It is common that those who would seek to protect 'our' culture against the intrusions of outsiders will turn, almost reflexively, to the state as the proper instrument for the job. A variety of laws may be enacted. There may be a state broadcasting system which is charged with the responsibility of manifesting the national culture. Legally enforceable limits may be created to control the amount of foreign material which is broadcast. The balance selected will vary from state to state, but these two elements are bound to be present. The state will both encourage the production of domestic programming and attempt, to some degree or other, to keep foreign programming out.

This is where the Canadian experience becomes relevant. What has happened in Canada is of interest for two reasons. First, Canada is situated next door to the United States, and secondly no other country, I suspect, has been subjected to as much foreign broadcasting for as long a period as Canada. As a corollary, few countries have had as much experience of trying to deal with foreign broadcasting as Canada.

There is both English-language broadcasting and French-language broadcasting in Canada. This paper will address only English broadcasting, since the audience for french broadcasting is less susceptible to the influence of U.S. broadcasting than is the audience for English broadcasting.

THE CANADIAN EXPERIENCE

The starting point of the Canadian experience has to be the 1929 report of the Aird Commission — the Royal Commission on Radio Broadcasting. The Commission was established in 1928 by the government of Canada to 'examine into the broadcasting system in the Dominion of Canada and to make recommendations to the government as to the future administration, management, control and financing thereof'. It took its informal title from its Chair, Sir John Aird, president of the Canadian Bank of Commerce.

The Commission's report, completed in nine months, was brief and straightforward. The commissioners claimed to have discovered '... unanimity on one fundamental question — Canadian radio listeners want Canadian broadcasting'.

> At present the majority of programs heard are from sources outside Canada [i.e. the U.S.]. It has been emphasised to us that the continued reception of these has a tendency to mould the minds of the young people in the home to ideals and opinions that are not Canadian. In a country of the vast geographical dimensions of Canada, broadcasting will undoubtedly become a great force in fostering a national spirit and interpreting national citizenship.

The answer, clearly, was that broadcasting must be '... carried on in the interests of Canadian listeners and in the national interests of Canada'. This would be achieved through '... some form of public ownership, operation and control behind which is the national power and prestige of the whole public of the Dominion of Canada'. So not only was there to be state control of broadcasting, and direct state involvement in providing programming, but the Aird Commission recommended that there be no private broadcasting. This is important because in the history of Canadian broadcasting, **private** broadcasting and **American** broadcasting have meant in practice very much the same thing.

The Aird Report was, in fact, the high watermark of the related ideas that broadcasting in Canada should be Canadian, national and public. A confusing succession of official reports and legislation followed the Aird Report.

Few subjects have been studied as extensively as broadcasting in Canada. As well as the Aird Report, there were official studies in 1951, 1957, 1965 and 1986. Major national broadcasting legislations were enacted in 1932, 1936, 1958, 1968, 1976, and 1991. Indeed, one of the few constants of Canadian politics is that, with the exception of the short-lived Clark government of 1979, every time there has been a change in the party in power there has been a change in broadcasting legislation. Competing political perspectives have been essential in shaping broadcasting policy.

It will be argued that two threads run throughout the story. The position of private broadcasting has expanded and improved, while the public, or state element has declined in importance. At the same time the emphasis, both rhetorically and in fact, on the **Canadianness** of Canadian broadcasting has been diminished.

The recommendations of the Aird Report were not implemented immediately, but, after intense lobbying by the Canadian Radio League, a group strongly committed to Canadian public broadcasting, legislation was enacted in 1932. This followed the Aird recommendations in broad outline, but with one important exception: provision was made for privately-owned radio stations.

The original legislation was not well thought-out. A House of Commons Special Committee looked into the matter in 1936 and recommended certain changes. The Committee affirmed the '... principle of complete nationalization of radio broadcasting in Canada' and called for the physical extension of broadcasting coverage to ensure that the largest number of Canadians possible would receive programming.

A fresh statute, the Canadian Broadcasting Act, was enacted in 1936. This act established a new body called the Canadian Broadcasting Corporation (CBC). The CBC was to perform a dual role. It was mandated to 'carry on a national broadcasting service' and, at the same time, to issue regulations 'to control the character of any and all programmes broadcast', and to make recommendations on all applications submitted for the licensing of private stations. In other words, it was to be both broadcaster and regulator.

In 1949 an archetypally Canadian project was launched — the Royal Commission on National Development in the Arts, Letters and Science. Inevitably, the enquiry, known popularly as the Massey Commission after its Chair, the diplomat and public servant, Vincent Massey, turned its attention to broadcasting. The Commission's report observed drily, 'We do not wish to suggest that our national system of broadcasting has fulfilled all the hopes of its founders and its supporters'. But, neither apparently, had it failed, for the report went on to state that:

The national system, however, has constantly kept in view its three objectives for broadcasting in Canada: an adequate coverage of the entire population, opportunities for Canadian self-expression generally, and successful resistance to the absorption of Canada into the general cultural pattern of the United States.

So, at least insofar as the Massey Commission was concerned, there was to be no retreat from the fundamental principles set out in the Aird Report.

However, the Massey Report was written just before the dawn of the television age. While it could be argued that, even by 1950, a reasonably distinctive Canadian approach to radio broadcasting was alive and thriving, the same argument cannot be made today about television broadcasting.

Massey had recommended a new major study of broadcasting. In 1955 the Royal Commission on Broadcasting was launched. It became known as the Fowler Commission, after its Chair, Robert M. Fowler, President of the Canadian Pulp and Paper Association.

The Fowler Report and, even more important, its legislative aftermath, the 1958 Broadcasting Act, were turning points in Canadian broadcasting. First, private broadcasting acquired a status, which if not quite equal to that of public broadcasting, was close enough. Section 10 of the new Act spoke of a 'national broadcasting system' which was to have both 'public' and 'private' elements. Private broadcasting had come a long way from the death sentence passed on it in the Aird Report. Second, the CBC, as had long been urged by private broadcasters, lost its regulatory authority. It was to continue to operate broadcasting facilities and to provide programming, but its authority over private broadcasters was taken away and given to a newly-created state agency, the Board of Broadcast Governors. The result was that Canada would henceforth have, in fact, two separate and distinct broadcasting systems — the CBC and the private broadcasters. Third, the new Act made the CBC financially dependent on annual appropriations by Parliament, thus allowing the government in power to restrict the money available to the public broadcaster and, if the government so wished, force it to raise revenues through commercial advertising. Finally, the new Act qualified the national commitment to having broadcasting which was 'Canadian'. The Act spoke, ominously, of a 'broadcasting service' which was to be 'basically Canadian in content and character'. The 1958 legislation laid the foundation for what has occurred since — the ascendancy of private broadcasting and the concomitant decline and commercialisation of public broadcasting.

In 1965 Robert Fowler was asked to look at Canadian broadcasting again, but this time as chair of a ministerial advisory committee, rather than of an independent royal commission.

In retrospect the second Fowler Report can be seen as the last attempt to resuscitate the principle that broadcasting in Canada should be both 'public' and 'Canadian'. It sought to argue that 'private' broadcasters were really 'public' in character in that they made use of a public asset — the airwaves — and were subject to public regulatory control. Fowler also saw the CBC as the 'essential' element in the broadcasting system. He proposed the creation of an agency to regulate all broadcasting and, in the process, promote its Canadianness.

The new Broadcasting Act of 1968 created yet another regulatory authority, the Canadian Radio and Television Commission (CRTC). This body replaced the Board of Broadcast Governors. The CBC and the private broadcasters were put on a formally equal footing, subject only to the convoluted and unclear proviso that

> Where any conflict arises between the objectives of the national broadcasting service [i.e., the C.B.C.] and the interests of the private element of the Canadian broadcasting system, it shall be resolved in the public interest but paramount consideration shall be given to the objectives of the national broadcasting service.

The Act was also unusual for Canadian legislation in that it set out, in section 3, a broad, rambling and wordy statement of 'Broadcasting Policy for Canada'. This affirmed that the airwaves were 'public property' and that broadcasting should 'safeguard, enrich and strengthen the cultural, political, social and economic fabric of Canada. There were also other, more overtly political, goals set out. Broadcasting was to contribute to 'national unity'. One Member of Parliament remarked at the time that this suggested a move from 'public broadcasting' to 'state broadcasting'.

The new Act crowned the complete emancipation of private, commercial broadcasting in Canada. The Canadian broadcasting system had evolved into something vastly different from what Sir John Aird had hoped to create.

ADVENT OF CABLE TV

It is likely nothing has done more to transform Canadian broadcasting than a technological development which began to make itself felt in the 1960s. This was cable television.

Prior to the advent of cable, substantial number of Canadians were too far away from CBC or private transmitters to be able to receive television signals off-air. Cable transmission promised to remedy this. Nevertheless, far more urgent and important to millions of potential Canadian viewers, cable would also bring them American television, clearer and crisper and in greater profusion than could ever be available off-air. This was the real impetus behind the spread of cable television in Canada.

127

Cable was unregulated until 1968 when the new Act expanded the jurisdiction of the regulatory agency to include 'broadcasting receiving undertakings' — cable systems. Now in the early days of cable television, subscribers could only be offered signals on the 12 channels available in the VHF range. The CRTC issued regulations, binding on all cable operators, to establish a system of priorities. The regulations required cable operators to make available all local Canadian signals before channels could be allocated to signals originating from the U.S. This had the result of limiting the number of U.S. stations the ordinary cable subscriber could receive.

The cable operators responded by offering 'augmented' service, providing customers with converters which would allow them to receive additional signals beyond those available in the VHF range. The result was that cable operators could provide the Canadian signals they were required to carry and give their customers all the U.S. signals they wanted. Today standard television receivers have built-in converters which create the potential for cable subscribers to receive a hundred, or more, different signals. The simple fact is that, in the case of cable television, technology allowed the cable operators to more effectively challenge the ability of the Canadian state to limit the amount of U.S. programming directly available to Canadian viewers.

Nonetheless, the dream of Canadian and public broadcasting was not completely dead. The first Chairman of the newly-created CRTC, Pierre Juneau, came into office determined to reverse the direction of the previous decade. Juneau strengthened the 'Canadian content' requirements which had first been introduced in 1959. The purpose of these was to require broadcasters to devote a fixed proportion of their broadcasting time to programming which was 'Canadian'. In 1972 broadcasters were directed to devote 60% of the broadcasting day to Canadian content. But, as one commentator has noted, 'the quotas are not as demanding as they appear'. The period over which the observance of the quotas is to be measured has steadily increased in length. Although there are separate quotas for 'prime time' television programming, the regulations actually define prime time as 6:00 p.m. to midnight, a period which is conveniently wider than the actual peak viewing hours. Finally, the question of what constitutes 'Canadian' programming has been interpreted in an exceedingly formal fashion. Thus, a Canadian network can produce a cop show which it hopes to market in the U.S., fly U.S. flags from all the buildings, dress its police in U.S.-style uniforms and hire American actors for the leading roles, but if the show was actually shot in Canada with Canadian crews and Canadian extras, it will qualify as 'Canadian content'.

Juneau was also determined the CBC should play the role originally intended for it. In 1974 the CRTC renewed the CBC's broadcasting licences. In its formal decision the Commission called the CBC 'the cornerstone of the Canadian broadcasting system' and noted its special responsibilities under the Broadcasting Act. However, the reality, the Commission said, was '... a lack of purpose, determination and vigour in implementing the objectives established by Parliament'. The problem was that the CBC had become too much like a commercial broadcaster. It was too dependent on advertising revenues and had exhibited '... a preoccupation with mass audience concepts, stimulated by the contemporary North American marketing environment (that) is inappropriate for a publicly supported broadcasting service'. As a condition of renewing its licence, the CRTC required that CBC television drastically reduce the amount of commercial advertising it carried and increase its Canadian content.

There is an inescapable reality about state-operated broadcasting, however. If such a broadcasting service is to operate entirely free of commercial constraints, it must be given full financial support. To the extent it is not given sufficient money to discharge its formal mandate, it is obliged to turn to commercial sources for financing. And the more it has to rely on advertising revenues, the more its programming will become indistinguishable from the fare offered by commercial broadcasters.

Pierre Juneau was not successful. The period since the mid-1970s has seen the unrelenting abandonment of the goals of the Aird Report. Indeed, the author of a recent history of Canadian broadcasting entitled his chapter on the 1980s, 'The Eclipse of Public Broadcasting'. More concretely, this period was one of uncertainty and pessimism — uncertainty about what, if anything, 'Canadian' broadcasting meant and pessimism whether there remained any real possibility of maintaining a broadcasting system which was both public and Canadian. A major reason for the abandonment of the goals of the Aird Report was the evaporation of the self-confidence which had originally underlain it. Two official reports are redolent of the confusion of the period.

Louis Applebaum and Jacques Hébert were co-chairs of something called the Federal Cultural Policy Review Committee, which gave its report in 1982. The committee asserted, without much vigour, that there was still a national broadcasting system with a 'privately-owned' and a 'state-owned' component. It went on to note that the CBC was not playing the role envisaged for it. Indeed, it is difficult to think of a harsher criticism than the Committee's assertion that '... we need a better, more vital, more courageous CBC'. Finally, the CRTC had not in fact used its regulatory authority to require that private broadcasters comply with Canadian content rules. The Committee was, if anything, too charitable in its assessment of the CRTC. It was widely apparent by the middle of the 1980s that the CRTC had largely abandoned the attempt to regulate what was being broadcast in Canada.

The last official enquiry to note is that of the Task Force on Broadcasting Policy of 1985-86. This report is a testimony to the degree of confusion which has become endemic in current Canadian public discourse. It talked of 'community' and provincial involvement in broadcasting, repeated shibboleths about 'Canadian' broadcasting, but the committee, in the end, clearly had no concrete idea how to address any of the manifold ills of the national broadcasting system.

The final abandonment of the goals of Canadian broadcasting occurred during the period, 1984-1993, when Brian Mulroney was Prime Minister. Mulroney had two goals while in office. He sought closer integration of Canada with the United States and he wished to reduce the role of the state within Canadian society. The effects of these policy goals on broadcasting were, first, that the CRTC formally embraced the principle of 'self-regulation' on the part of private broadcasters and, second, that funding for the CBC was cut drastically.

The result is what exists in 1994 — a system where the average Canadian television viewer can watch dozens of U.S. signals, where 'Canadian' private programming is indistinguishable from American programming, and where CBC television is indistinguishable from private television. The one exception to this dismal picture is CBC radio, which still manages to be both Canadian and non-commercial.

CONCLUSION

I do not believe the current position to have been inevitable. Many unimaginative Canadian commentators have suggested that the dream of Canadian broadcasting was always unattainable. This is to misunderstand history. We got to where we are through a process, through conscious choices made at a number of key junctures. Had different choices been made, the outcome would also have been different. To take one obvious example, had the CBC been more generously funded over the last decade, the programming it presents today would be very different.

Other countries confronting similar issues also have choices. The range of possible choices may be broad or it may be narrow, but there is always some opportunity to make choices.

With respect to creating a 'national' broadcasting system, it must be remembered that what is involved is not a straightforward conflict between 'us' — nationals — and 'them' — foreigners. The goal of Canadian broadcasting was largely subverted, not by Americans, but by Canadians who were proponents of private broadcasting. The history of Canadian broadcasting is not a history of a united people struggling bravely to resist a hostile cultural invasion from the south. The fact is that substantial numbers of Canadians have for long seen that there was money to be made in supplying U.S. programming to their fellow

Canadians and even more substantial numbers of Canadians have been eager to have as much of that American programming as possible.

The great homogenising power of the contemporary international culture lies in its palpable attractiveness, in its tremendous appeal. No one could force young people all over the world to listen to rock music or wear blue jeans. If nationals were not attracted by foreign broadcasting, erecting barriers against it would not be an issue.

A lesson to be drawn from the Canadian experience is not, and emphatically not, that it is impossible to limit or control national exposure to foreign broadcasting. The primary means through which Canadians today receive American television programmes is Canadian cable television operators who are licensed by the Canadian state. American programming is not an illegal commodity peddled on street corners by criminals. Without the active involvement of Canadian entrepreneurs and the formal blessing of the Canadian state, American programming would not be available in its current abundance.

Nonetheless, as I have argued, technological development does place difficulties in the path of a state which is committed to controlling the reception of foreign broadcasting. This is likely to become even more the case as the distinctions between broadcasting and telecommunications become blurred. Fibre optic transmission will mean that the subscriber, whether through a telephone service or a broadcasting service, will be able to receive a practically unlimited number of signals.

In addition, the use of direct broadcasting satellites will mean the adoption of a technology which will be effectively beyond the capacities of state control. The significance of this development is, however, easily exaggerated. Until a vastly cheaper antenna is marketed, the ability to receive signals from direct broadcasting satellites will be confined to the wealthy.

The simple point is that if the political will and the administrative capacity both exist, it is still possible for states to control foreign broadcasting within their own territory. Technology has not, or at least not yet, eliminated that possibility.

Despite this, I believe the central lesson to be drawn from the Canadian experience is that the most effective means of challenging foreign programming is the creation of national programming. The vigour of CBC Radio is a concrete testament to this truth. The reason for this, which should be evident to the most cursory listener, is that CBC Radio has not attempted to transform itself into an imitation of commercial radio.

Indeed, it may well be that radio is the most practical means through which to promote broadcasting which is both national and public. Producing television programmes is ferociously expensive. Partly, I suspect, this is because we have all come to expect the so-called 'production values' of U.S. network programming. Not only are individual programmes expensive, but so is maintaining the infrastructure necessary to allow the production of programmes. CBC television, for example, despite having received vast amounts of public money, has not kept up with technical innovations. It did not begin transmitting in colour until 1967 and remains the only television network in Canada not to provide stereophonic sound. My instinct is that it will always be difficult for cheaply produced television programmes to win an audience in competition with programmes produced to international standards. All cable operators in Canada are required to provide a 'community channel' which makes homemade programmes available. Few people actually watch this channel. On the other hand, CBC Radio is able, at a comparatively low cost, to provide its own unique programming, programming which is not available from commercial radio broadcasters. What is particularly interesting is that CBC Radio has become one of Canada's significant cultural exports to the U.S. Many of its programmes have attracted large and loyal audiences in that country.

Nonetheless, if the government of a particular state is indeed committed to relying on broadcasting as a means of protecting and affirming the national culture, it seems to make far more sense to invest public money in the production of national programming than to a regime of legislation, regulations, boards and commissions.

REFERENCES

Note: My colleague, Dr. Margaret Ann Wilkinson, provided helpful comments on an earlier draft
1. Quoted in Susan M. Crean, Who's Afraid of Canadian Culture, Don Mills, Ontario, 1976.
2. Royal Commission on Radio Broadcasting, Report, Ottawa, King's Printer, 1929.
3. The classic account remains Margaret Prang, 'The Origins of Public Broadcasting in Canada', (1965), 46. Canadian Historical Review 1. A recent general history is Marc Raboy, Missed Opportunities: The Story of Canada's Broadcasting Policy, McGill-Queen's University Press, Montreal and Kingston, 1990.
4. Canadian Radio Broadcasting Act, Statutes of Canada.
5. Canada, House of Commons, Special Committee to Inquire into the Administration of the Canadian Radio Broadcasting Act, 1932, Report, Official Report of Debates of the House of Commons, volume III, Ottawa, 1936, p. 3077.
6. Statutes of Canada, 1936, chapter 24.
7. See Report, King's Printer, Ottawa, 1951, pp. 38-41.
8. Queen's Printer, Ottawa, 1957.
9. Statutes of Canada, 1958, chapter 22.
10. Canada, Advisory Committee on Broadcasting, Report, Ottawa, Queen's Printer, 1965.
11. Statutes of Canada, 1967-68, chapter 25.
12. In 1975 the Commission's regulatory jurisdiction was expanded to include national telecommunications systems and its name was changed to the Canadian Radio-Television and Telecommunications Commission. See Statutes of Canada, 1974-75-76, chapter 49.
13. Quoted in Raboy, op. cit., p. 178.
14. See Crean, op. cit., p.

15. Bruce Feldthusen, 'Awakening From the National Broadcasting Dream: Rethinking Television Regulation For National Cultural Goals', in David H. Flaherty and Frank E. Manning, eds., The Beaver Bites Back? American Popular Culture in Canada, McGill-Queen's University Press, Montreal and Kingston, 1993, 42 at p. 60.

16. Decision CRTC 74-70, Ottawa, 31 March 1974.

17. Raboy, op. cit., p. 267.

18. Report, Supply and Services Canada, Ottawa, 1982. The careful reader will have noted that the government publications office was no longer called the 'Queen's Printer'. The title of this committee is uniquely Canadian, it being difficult to imagine any other country in the world which would give such a name to an official enquiry.

19. This is made distressingly apparent in a tired and lifeless essay written by the individual who was Chair of the CRTC at the time. See John Meisel, 'Stroking the Airwaves: The Regulation of Broadcasting by the CRTC' in Benjamin D. Singer, ed., Communications in Canadian Society, 3rd ed., Nelson, Scarborough, Ontario, 1991, p. 217.

20. Report, Supply and Services Canada, Ottawa, 1986. By this time changes in fashion had dictated that 'committees' should be styled 'task forces'.

21. CRTC, Annual Report, 1986-87, Supply and Services Canada, Ottawa, 1987.

22. Feldthusen, op. cit., is a typical expression of this hopeless perspective.

23. See Irvin Goldman and James Winter, 'Mass Media and Canadian Identity', in Singer, op. cit., p. 146.

24. The current Broadcasting Act, Statutes of Canada, 1991, chapter 11, states in section 3(1)(b) that the Canadian broadcasting system now has three elements: the 'public' —CBC and the French service, Radio Canada, the 'private', and the 'community'. It is not at all clear what this means and is only mentioned in the Act, I suspect, in order to create the impression that the government listened to the recommendations of the Taskforce.

PART THREE

Globalization and Telecommunications

8

A ONE-WAY STREET JUST OFF THE GLOBAL DIGITAL SUPERHIGHWAY:
DEBATING MONOPOLY CONTROL AND POLICY-MAKING IN CARIBBEAN TELECOMMUNICATIONS.

Hopeton S. Dunn

INTRODUCTION

A protracted public discussion over licensing and regulatory issues in Jamaica has highlighted the deficiencies in telecommunications policy-making among Caribbean governments. The debate focused attention on public dissatisfaction with the extensive monopoly privileges accorded to Cable and Wireless PLC through its local subsidiary companies in the region. This debate in Jamaica forms part of the wider global deliberations on the changing telecommunications environment and its effect on economic and social development. Using the Jamaican debate as a point of departure, this chapter discusses the dominant role of external transnational interests in the Caribbean telecommunications sector and the difficulty faced by small states in the regulation of global companies.

JAMAICA AND THE REGIONAL CONTEXT

Jamaica is the largest of twelve independent, English-speaking territories of the Caribbean, which together with the British colony of Montserrat, make up the membership of the Caribbean Community and Common Market (CARICOM). The collective population of this grouping is just over 5 million and of this number Jamaica's population of close to 2.4 accounts for close to 50 per cent. As a major tourist destination, the Caribbean is the hub of a large volume of international telephone traffic between the region and North America/Europe. This volume is further augmented by a large expatriate Caribbean population, living mainly in the United States, Canada and Britain. Traffic balance figures from the US Federal Communications Commission (FCC) indicate that the US **to** Jamaica route was among the most heavily used, accounting for a higher volume of calls than from the US to Australia, India and Nigeria, respectively. United States telecommunications operators therefore regard Jamaica and the Caribbean as an important and growing telecom market, with strong potential for the development of non-voice services. Proximity to the large United States market has stimulated the establishment of a data processing industry in the region, with export processing zones (EPZs) being located in Montego Bay, Jamaica and in Castries, St Lucia.

The British transnational company Cable and Wireless has been a major operator of telecommunications services in the English-speaking Caribbean for over 125 years. The company initially operated in the service of the British colonial government as the West India and Panama Telegraph Company, starting in 1868. Despite changes, it has remained largely unchallenged by external or local competition over these years. During the first decade of political independence in the Caribbean (1960s), the governments of the more developed territories, in response to the pressure of popular expectation, began to strengthen regional control over national resources. These measures included majority takeover of foreign-owned telecommunications systems. This meant state and local private sector acquisition of a part of the monopoly shareholdings of Cable and Wireless.

Government shareholdings in the profitable overseas networks ranged from 40% in Barbados to over 51% in Jamaica and in Trinidad. Such acquisitions were feasible propositions in the 1960s and even early '70s when the basic technology of telecommunications in use in the region was still a relatively stable body of knowledge which could easily be acquired and managed. But, starting in the early 1980s both global market conditions and technological applications underwent dramatic transformations, leading to major policy changes. In Jamaica for example, Cable and Wireless moved from a shareholding of 9% of the total equity in Telecommunications of Jamaica (TOJ) in 1987 to 79% in the region's largest telecommunications company by 1989.

These acquisitions were also facilitated by a century of traditional ties which left a legacy of loyalty to the company among policy-makers. Particularly in the Eastern Caribbean, many senior civil servants and even political leaders were formerly employed by the company. And important sporting competitions, including West Indies Test cricket and other activities are sponsored by Cable and Wireless. Despite political independence, the region has remained fettered to these old loyalties and dependent on such external capital, technology and corporate direction in telecommunications. This situation has been reinforced within the last decade by the wider, structurally-based economic dependence and indebtedness of many Caribbean countries. The response to this crisis by multilateral lending agencies such as the International Monetary Fund (IMF) and the World Bank has created conditions for even greater dependency. For example, IMF loan conditionalities and its insistence on rapid privatization have facilitated successive increases by Cable and Wireless in the extent of its equity holdings in Caribbean telecom operating companies.

Today, Cable and Wireless has exclusive licences in 15 Caribbean territories. [See Table 1]. It operates data-processing teleport facilities in Jamaica and St Lucia, and controls the international cable and satellite gateway facilities linking the region with the rest of the world.

The company also owns the Digital Eastern Caribbean Microwave System (DECMS) linking most of the region's territories, and is the dominant player in the installation of a new Eastern Caribbean Fibre-optic System (ECFS). Cable and Wireless, therefore, continues to refurbish what may be considered its own one-way Caribbean lane, just off the so-called digital, global information superhighway being built in neighbouring United States. As part of its regional strategy, the company has been consolidating its position and seeking to extend its reach beyond the English speaking Caribbean. In 1993, it contracted the services of former Jamaican prime minister Michael Manley to lead an exploratory delegation to Cuba in an attempt to gain an early foothold in that hitherto closed market ahead of its U.S. competitors.

THE COMPANY: CORPORATE PROFILE AND GLOBAL STRATEGY

The Caribbean region represents just one corner of the extensive global network of this British transnational firm. In all, Cable and Wireless supplies domestic and international telephone services to over 30 countries around the world. An emerging player in the liberalized United States market, the company offers long distance connections to business customers there. In Europe, it is developing joint partnerships in Germany, Italy and Sweden. And in its home market, Britain, it owns 80% of Mercury Communications Limited, the main network

Table I C&W CARIBBEAN OWNERSHIP OF TELECOM

Country	Percentage of C&W Ownership in	
	Local Telco	Overseas Carrier
	%	%
Anguilla	100	100
Bermuda	100	100
Br. Virgin Is.	100	100
Cayman Is.	100	100
Dominica	100	100
Montserrat	100	100
St. Lucia	100	100
St. Vincent	100	100
Turks Is.	100	100
Antigua	0	100
Barbados	85*	85*
St. Kitts	80*	80*
Jamaica	79*	79*
Grenada	70*	70*
Trinidad & Tobago	49*	49*

Compiled by H.S. Dunn, CARIMAC
*Single merged company.

competitor to British Telecom for services to business and residential customers. The company's other operating subsidiaries are distributed in countries of the Indian and Pacific regions, the Middle East and the Caribbean. Hong Kong Telecom, despite the relatively small size of its domestic coverage area, represents the company's most profitable subsidiary — bringing in over 75% of the group's annual revenues each year. C&W's network of fibre-optic cables span the globe, and the company has the world's largest fleet of ships dedicated to the laying and repair of submarine cables.

The maintenance of these worldwide operations by Cable and Wireless forms part of the company's corporate strategy aimed at creating a global network of services available from a single point of contact. By controlling national telephone companies around the world and their international connections, the company plans to provide seamless global services without having to share responsibility, or revenues, with other service providers. Similarly, within countries, domestic markets which were shared between a local telco and an international operator are now being merged to create a more cost effective single entity.

It is within this global corporate framework that the Caribbean subsidiaries of Cable and Wireless operate. Its corporate investments and network planning in the Caribbean area are part of this global strategy. The proposed installation for example, of a new US $60-million digital Eastern Caribbean Fibre System, while beneficial to the region must be seen less as a policy decision to upgrade Caribbean services *per se*, and more as part of the strategic global routing of the corporate digital highway by a competitive 'world telephone company'. The larger such companies become, the more difficult it is for small countries to monitor and regulate them in protection of the public interest.

REGULATION

Regulation in the telecommunications sector presents a daunting set of theoretical and practical challenges. Reflecting on the issue of regulatory policy, the Secretary General of the International Telecommunications Union (ITU), Pekka Tarjanne observed, that the process of 'globalization was changing the basic structure of the telecommunications industry so that it is dominated by a small number of global alliances which extend beyond national boundaries. 'De-regulation', he notes, 'has become the new model for telecommunications development, displacing traditional approaches based on bi-lateral and multi-lateral financial and technical assistance.' In his experience, 'privatization has reduced the competence of ITU member countries in dealing with technical issues.' These developments are among the consequences of a global transformation, the impact of which is being felt not just in the industrialized countries but also throughout the under-developed world.

Referring to the process underway mainly in the industrialized North, the ITU Secretary General noted that 'Competition has reduced the importance of government's traditional regulatory role in controlling the industry and has transferred the power to the marketplace.' [1993: 12]. However, in the Caribbean, it is not competition but monopoly power, a weak state apparatus and the influence of multilateral lending agencies which have contributed to reducing the importance of government's regulatory role and restricted the power of the marketplace. Far from requiring less regulation, an environment dominated by a private monopoly operator requires organized systems and institutions for regulation.

Convergence of technologies also poses important problems for regulation. Policy-makers will not only have to consider how to regulate but also what to regulate, or whether to regulate at all. Writing against the background of the Australian experience, Houghton observes: 'The real value of introducing regulated competition is to move communications sector organizations from an outmoded technology paradigm to a market paradigm. However, this is only the first step. Convergence, including the breakdown of the carriage/content dichotomy is leading us towards an information paradigm. In the not too distant future, access and content will be the focus and competition law will ultimately be marginalized.' [Houghton: 1993 :2] That may be the case in the industrialized, de-regulating societies. However, in many countries of the under-developed world where monopoly operators remain dominant, the struggle for the foreseeable future is for basic level competition and the creation of competition law and adequately resourced regulatory institutions. In many countries, the telecommunications operating companies or oligopolies are so large and powerful that they overwhelm the limited resources of the regulatory agency and dominate its decision-making. This concern with regulatory capture also exists at the global level where the regulatory agency, the International Telecommunications Union (ITU), is regarded as being increasingly influenced by a corporate lobby of equipment manufacturers and service providers, backed by their parent governments.

Writing from a World Bank, economic perspective, Levy and Spiller [1993 : 3-7] advocate a conceptual approach which treats telecommunications regulation as arising from the need to mediate the demands of several divergent interests groups. Three sets of 'contracting problems' are identified as typical of international utility regulatory environments.

1. The Firm/Consumer contracting problem arises when competition is absent, as in market failure scenarios; and there is a strong monopoly operating company facing consumer concerns about tariff levels and systems of control to protect the public.

2. The Firm/Government contracting problem relates to the interests of the investing company to have provisions to protect its profitability and against arbitrary government actions such as expropriation.

3. The Government/Interest Groups contracting problem is one involving contending social views on the distribution of network resources, technical standards and the allocation of returns from state investment.

Levy and Spiller argue that the efficiency of the regulatory mechanism will depend on the extent of commitment and 'institutional endowment' within countries. These are identifiable in the form of legislative, judicial and executive supporting institutions for regulation, and the administrative and financial capacity to operate the system. They also cite the role of ideology and the character of the contending social interests within a society as key factors in regulatory efficiency.

THE DEBATE

Ever since the start of the government's programme of share divestment in Telecommunications of Jamaica, sporadic public commentaries have raised questions about the role of foreign investment in the sector. Most commentators accepted the necessity for foreign equity participation, mainly on the grounds of access to new global technologies. However, the more controversial issue has been the relinquishing of national control over what is seen as a vital sector for trade, commerce and social development. The Opposition Jamaica Labour Party (JLP), which initiated the preliminary equity-transfer to C&W wanted majority control to remain within the country, even if not with government. The party has been a strong critic of the Manley government's decision to give the dominant control to Cable and Wireless. Other analysts have argued in favour of extending local private sector participation in a mix that would retain decisive control within Jamaica.

However, in an article in the *Jamaica Record* of December 2, 1990, economist Wesley Van Riel wrote: 'If the concern is with the fact that government, in selling out to Cable and Wireless, is relinquishing national control of the company, perhaps it is time for us as a nation to have serious dialogue as to what is our attitude towards foreign capital.' He argued that the sale of majority equity control to Cable and Wireless was an economic necessity and was in line with global trends.

In essence, this is the position adopted by the Manley government in its pursuit of telecommunications privatization and liberalization as key elements of a new economic policy. In his controversial letter to TOJ's Chairman Mayer Matalon, dated November 2, 1990, Manley sought to give assurances of legislative reform in order to encourage the company to continue with its investment and capital development programme.

Rejecting this approach and the notion of the 'desirable globalization of monopoly capital', *Gleaner* columnist Dawn Ritch later commented that 'the trend worldwide is for de-regulation away from monopolies and to a competitive regime with multiple providers.' Taking the argument further, she contends: 'It seems we are to be sold into a slavery no different to the days when sugar was king. Jamaica is about to become the telecommunications plantation of Cable and Wireless, and we will owe our souls to that company's store.' [Ritch, *Daily Gleaner* November 14, 1993:8A].

Among these varied viewpoints, the public debate has proceeded, encompassing other critical press commentaries, heated discussions on radio call-in programmes, parliamentary statements, numerous government and company press statements, public panel discussions and television programmes. The most intensive phase of the discussion took off in October 1993 when the

Chairman of the Cable and Wireless subsidiary, Telecommunications of Jamaica (TOJ), announced that the establishment of a Public Utilities Commission to regulate the telecom and other utilities would contravene his licence. The Chairman, Mayer Matalon said the terms of the TOJ licence recognised only the role of the Minister as the main regulatory actor. He also underlined the exclusive nature of the existing licensing arrangements for voice and wire-based services. These declarations opened a floodgate of public criticisms of the restrictive licences and service limitations of the company, with the morning time radio discussion programme Breakfast Club playing a leading role. The debate, which will continue for the foreseeable future, has been significant both for the range of issues raised and for the fact that it was the first of its kind being held in Jamaica. Until then, issues of telecommunications licensing and regulatory concerns were treated mainly as private negotiations between corporate entities, government elites and their advisors.

The debate and the call for the re-establishment of a Public Utilities Commission emerged as part of the growing frustration of both domestic and corporate telecom users with the perceived high cost and restrictive policies offered by Cable and Wireless subsidiaries in the Caribbean. The concerns expressed in Jamaica have given rise to further public debate and policy reflections elsewhere in the Caribbean region. Four main issues emerged among the concerns expressed:

1 Foreign Debt, the IMF and Enforced Privatization

2 Monopoly and the Public Interest

3 The Prospects and Challenges of Competition, and

4 Deficiencies in Regulation and Policy Planning

Debt, the IMF and Enforced Privatization

The high level of government foreign indebtedness has had important implications for control of the asset base in the regional telecom sector. Over the last decade, economic conditions in the Caribbean have been worsened by the accumulation of massive external debts. According to Girvan et al [1989:ii], total CARICOM debt in 1980 was US$4002 million, requiring an annual debt servicing of US$672.3 million. By 1988, however, this level of indebtedness had more than doubled to US$9802 million. This meant a debt per capita in the Caribbean of US$1634 million and an annual debt service of US$1161.8 million. The debt owed by Jamaica loomed largest, totalling 4.5 billion, or more than half the regional total in 1990. By 1992/93, repayment and debt rescheduling had reduced Jamaica's total external indebtedness to US$ 3.7 billion.

While in absolute terms these figures may not appear dramatic on a global scale, they mean annual debt repayment of over forty percent of export earnings for Jamaica. This level of indebtedness, when translated into a national per capita debt, amounts to about US$1,800 owed by each Jamaican, in a situation where annual per capita income is less than US$1100 and where there is an official unemployment level well in excess of 16.3% of the workforce. [Economic and Social Survey 1993:18.9].

In Jamaica, the merger between the largely state-owned Jamaica Telephone Company and the overseas carrier JAMINTEL was initiated in the wake of an IMF mandated re-structuring of public sector companies. The merger negotiations were concluded in July 1987 with the formation of Telecommunications of Jamaica Limited (TOJ), in which government retained 53.1% of the shares. Cable and Wireless later obtained a 39% equity in the merged company, thereby extending its Jamaican holdings beyond its original stake in JAMINTEL. The remaining 7.9% of TOJ shares were owned by employees and members of the public.

In 1989, government sold a further 20% of its holding in TOJ to Cable and Wireless, as a result of which the company became the majority shareholder with 59% of the TOJ equity. This was further extended to 79% by the sale to the company of the remainder of government's holdings of 20% in late 1990. The Jamaican minister responsible for telecommunications, Robert Pickersgill offered the following explanation as the basis for this equity transfer to Cable and Wireless:

> I think it was moreso economic. It had to do with foreign exchange constraints and of course the whole question of these companies being on the budget. The IMF watches these things very zealously. However, if the company is owned 51 % otherwise than government, it is not regarded as a government entity, although you could wield some amount of influence in terms of policy and other things. That was a consideration. So I think it was a mixture of economic and policy. Policy in the sense that you are trying to give yourself more room to do what you want to do, without being a burden on the budget, or without having to answer too many questions to the IMF." [Interview with Robert Pickersgill 26/10/89]

The minister's frank explanation of the major factors then motivating Jamaica's telecommunications decisions, makes it clear that external pressure from the IMF was the decisive influence on divestment policy. These decisions by the Jamaican government, under pressure or direction by the IMF, restored to the British transnational firm both legal and operational control of the region's largest telecommunications network, and over one of the largest companies in the English-speaking Caribbean.

Similar developments took place in Trinidad and Tobago, where foreign exchange deficiencies derived from the overseas indebtedness, helped to create the conditions for this external control. The 1989 acquisition of 49% of the shares of the Trinidad and Tobago Telephone Company (TELCO), at a cost of US$ 85-million, also took place in the face of stringent IMF demands. Part of the money was urgently required to meet external payments in advance of International Monetary Fund (IMF) performance evaluations of the Trinidad economy. The first payment of US$ 50-million was to go directly to government revenues with part paid in U.S. dollars to the account of the government at the Federal Reserve Bank of New York, to fulfil IMF foreign reserves requirements in advance of a performance evaluation. Of the remainder, a sum of US $15-million was also to be paid to the government earlier than its normal due date, in the form of a loan.

Such developments suggest that the historically dominant position of Cable and Wireless in Caribbean telecommunications was immensely strengthened by the powerful external influence of the IMF. In effect, the global lending agencies are mediating on the side of this transnational corporation within two debt-burdened underdeveloped countries. Discussing this dilemma in its macro-economic context, Frobel notes that:

> One tactic among several forced on countries in such straits is to try and transform external debt into foreign-owned equity by selling national assets at cut prices, providing golden opportunities for TNCs to expand in debt-ridden developing countries. In addition, a number of formerly more reluctant Third World (and other) countries are now abolishing many of their remaining restrictions and controls on foreign investment, at the same time increasing other incentives to attract TNCs [Frobel 1988: 64].

It is this process which has been very much in operation in the region. In the field of telecommunications, the industrialized countries of the United States, Britain and Japan have led the way in implementing policies of either divestment or liberalization. But in each case strong regulatory organizations have been established to protect the public interest and ensure fair competition. In the English-speaking region of the Caribbean, divestment policies have entrenched private monopoly control and has not been accompanied by any strengthening of regulatory arrangements.

Monopoly and the Public Interest

In 1988, while still a majority government-owned company, Telecommunications of Jamaica (TOJ) was granted an exclusive 'All-island Telephone Licence'. This licence protected the company's monopoly position over wireline telephone services, and provided that this exclusivity should remain in force for 'a duration of 25 years upon the same terms and conditions', with a renewal clause for a further 25 years enforceable if no notice of change is given 2 years in advance of expiry. Four (4) other exclusive licences granted to the company covered external telecommunications services, wireless telephony, telegraphic services and telex and teleprinter services, all over the same 25 year duration. When Cable and Wireless acquired majority control of the local company a year later, these licensing provisions were inherited, without re-negotiation or modifications and even more importantly without any regulatory re-structuring. Government had not only divested its control of equity, but also its regulatory responsibilities as well.

This situation enabled the company to effectively write its own rules and introduce new services virtually at will. TOJ has been operating a cellular telephone service without a licence while other interested applicants such as the US firm Motorola, were frustrated in their bid to compete. 'TOJ currently has a licence for wire-based telephone only. So cellular is not covered. The only problem is that it would have been pointless for Motorola to invest in Jamaica, unless they could connect with the subscribers held under monopoly to TOJ. The discussion between Matalon and Motorola just went round and round until Motorola got fed up and left.' [Dawn Ritch, *Gleaner* Nov 14, 1993 p 8A]

Another area receiving much attention during the Jamaican media and public discussion has been the matter of the profit levels enjoyed by the monopoly operating company. Because of the absence of competition, Cable and Wireless is awarded a fixed band of profitability, in the form of a guaranteed rate of return on its investment prescribed within the terms of the licence under which the company operates. Section 27:1 of the main Telecommunications of Jamaica (TOJ) licence guarantees the company a rate of return of 'not less than 17.5 % nor more than 20% on revalued assets annually.' In order to achieve this, the 1988 licence further prescribes that 'the rate charged for telephone services shall be adjustable annually as necessary to provide the permitted rate of return.' Thus, the company's rate of return on its investment is not subject to the movement of costs or any specific economic variable. Instead, it is negotiated with the government and the agreed level inserted as a legal guarantee in the overall bi-lateral contractual arrangements.

This guaranteed profit level appears to be unduly generous, particularly since it is not accompanied by any defined performance criteria. A further concern was that this arrangement does not provide the company with any incentive either to improve efficiency or lower rates. And, although the guaranteed rate is based on revalued assets, the government had failed to ensure that they have a role in the verification of the annual asset revaluations. For its part, the company argued that the rate of return clause, though mutually agreed on, also represents a cap on its maximum possible level of profitability. However, the company cannot have it both ways. If it wishes to have limitations on its profitability removed then it should agree to relinquish its monopoly position and allow for competition on a phased basis, starting with customer premises equipment and moving rapidly towards direct competition in network services.

This comprehensive monopoly regime came under strong public criticism, both because of its virtually unregulated operation and because the terms and conditions of the licences were kept secret by successive Jamaican governments. The details were never presented in Parliament or to the public and were only made public 5 years after they were agreed. This attempt to keep the Cable and Wireless deal secret is consistent with the practice elsewhere in the Caribbean. In line with traditions engendered by the British Official Secrets Act, licence documents and other agreements arrived at between governments and the company, and to which the public should have ready access, are often treated throughout the region as secret and confidential documents and arrangements. This has helped to create a policy environment of suspicion and lack of transparency. Important groups affected by these decisions are excluded from direct input, participation and access to relevant information.

All of these factors led to calls for closer scrutiny of the policies governing telecommunications in the country. Reports of technologically-induced reductions in telecommunications charges, and the Jamaican government's establishment of a Fair Trading Commission as part of a new liberalization strategy also contributed to a more critical environment and emboldened the expression of concerns about the monopoly operator in the sector.

From the point of view of the company, it must be acknowledged that the securing of an exclusive licensing arrangement constitutes the legitimate activity of a transnational operating firm, requiring integrated corporate planning to cope with its competitors in a global market. But how are the interests of the Jamaican citizen and the wider Caribbean public to be protected or reconciled with this process of corporate expansion and global interconnectivity? This was one of the points at issue in the debate in the Jamaican mass media. Speaking at a public forum that formed part of this debate, the managing director of a small data processing company viewed the answer as being in the province of competition. He pointed out that while such foreign investments provide the region with some opportunities for commercial development of information-based industries, operating a business within the exclusive corporate framework of one major player created significant dis-economies and constraints in gaining access to the advantages of the global competitive environment.

The Challenges of Competition

There have been some recent indications that the next decade will be a less cosy one for Cable and Wireless in its Caribbean enclave. According to Gregory

Staple, a Washington-based telecommunications attorney and editor of the journal *TeleGeography*, 'the days of monopoly service are numbered.' In an address to a business meeting of the Commonwealth Telecommunications Council, held in Jamaica, he notes that 'where monopolies still exist, the reason usually has less to do with economics than with politics — with the fact that would-be competitors are barred from entering the market by law'. Staple predicts that by the year 2000, 'the most economically efficient and politically defensible structure for the telecommunications sector in most countries is likely to be one which is more plural, with a mix of service providers, private and public, using various technologies, wireline and cellular, to meet the different needs of users.'

Intelligent networks, which have been enabled by software and silicon-based micro-processors together with very large capacity submarine fibre-optic cables have changed international and domestic telecommunication from a supply-constrained to a demand driven business. The result of this, according to Staple is a paradigm shift from monopoly to a competitive structure.

> The current service paradigm for international telecommunications can be characterised as a joint venture among independent national monopolies or oligopolies. This paradigm is nationalistic, monopolistic and hardware intensive. I have therefore called it the 'Heavy Carrier' paradigm. It has two main parts. First, there is a facilities regime based on carrier ownership of half circuits which are interconnected at a midpoint. Second, there is a complementary financial regime: it compensates or settles carriers for interconnecting their half circuits through a 50/50 division of an agreed accounting rate.

This is the regime in force in the Caribbean. Except that instead of nationally owned monopolies, the region has the Cable and Wireless corporate monopoly. The company's own subsidiaries in the region settle interconnection costs among themselves and seek to operate within national jurisdictions. However, it is the parent company which provides the financial, administrative and policy co-ordination for the conglomerate of subsidiary firms. Among similar private operators in the traditional mould are AT&T and British Telecom. The inter-governmental satellite agency INTELSAT, also provides a similar traditional form of service delivery. These 'Heavy Carriers', according to Staple are being challenged by a new breed of global operators:

> The Light Carrier provides international services by re-selling, re-routing, re-packaging or re-programming the offering of heavy carriers. The Light Carrier is primarily software based. It may enter a market without owning a single international cable or satellite circuit (but instead operates) via international 800 (freephone) numbers, calling cards, call-me-back or "boomerang boxes", corporate private lines or mobile satellite services."

Already some of the indicators of this new form of competition are making their appearance in the Caribbean. United States based companies, using digital signal compression technology, have been operating 'Call Back' services to high volume users in the region since 1993. These companies, including International Discount Telecommunications (IDT) Inc., allow potential callers to place multiple overseas calls to an automated re-dialling network without incurring the heavy tariff levels imposed by some of the national subsidiaries of Cable and Wireless. Despite intense pressures from the incumbent C&W subsidiaries, the initial indication was that some governments, particularly those in Trinidad and Tobago and Barbados, were reluctant to take any action against the users or operators of the Call Back facility since this technology, while circumventing monopoly rights, did not appear to be illegal and the operators are outside of the jurisdiction of Caribbean national regimes.

Other developments in the region also suggest a slow but significant diversity away from the Cable and Wireless dominance. The linkage of the University of the West Indies into the INTERNET creates international tele-accessibility by means other than the Cable and Wireless network. In Barbados, both the Caribbean Broadcasting Union (CBU) and the Caribbean News Agency (CANA) have been authorised by the government to establish satellite uplink segments, enabling them to transmit as well as to receive data and programming outside of the usual C&W network. Proposals for closer collaboration between these two agencies or for their eventual merger would provide an even stronger basis to develop an expanded Caribbean-owned communications network.

In the Jamaican debate, relevant developments at the international level have been cited in considering the options faced by the region. It has been noted that the monopoly position of Cable and Wireless outside of the region is also under challenge. Over the last two years, telecommunications authorities in both Hong Kong and the small territory of Bermuda have unveiled plans to diversify their markets by providing some competition for Cable and Wireless. This is despite the fact that both territories are British colonies with strong Cable and Wireless historical dominance. Analysts in Bermuda argue that services could be more than a third cheaper than the tariff levels then in existence under Cable and Wireless. While being a small dependent territory, Bermuda occupies a central position in the international cable communications link, especially at the strategic trans-atlantic mid-point for routing cable traffic to the Caribbean and parts of the United States.

In Hong Kong, a country with a population size just above that of the English-speaking Caribbean, recent policy changes have involved breaking the C&W monopoly. 'Monopolies do get out of hand' says a senior officer of Hong Kong's Hutchinson Whampoa company. Speaking for one of that British colony's largest trading companies, the Hutchinson Whampoa representative was concerned about C&W's 'total control of the external and internal telecommunications business.' in Hong Kong. After exploring several options, the government of Hong Kong established a regulatory Telecommunications Authority (OFTA) in 1993. Since then, OFTA has announced a plan to award three new fixed telecommunications network services (FTNS) licences for competitors to Hong Kong Telecom (HKT). According to OFTA Director General, Alex Arena, 'the three new operators together would provide effective competition across the board for HKT and would stimulate the market..' [Lam: 1994:20-21].

In the past, Cable and Wireless has justified its monopoly position in the Caribbean on arguments of market size and the so-called geographical complexity of the region. A director of the company, Jonathan Solomon, said the region was 'too small' for competition. [Dunn 1991: 30]. Technological developments have clearly overtaken this viewpoint, as the earlier observations by Staple indicated. Several local and overseas companies, have expressed an interest in entering the Caribbean market. US domestic satellite 'footprints', which cover most of the area, could facilitate the rapid growth of data processing and mobile communications businesses. But prospective North American and other investors have been virtually shut out. The interest of Motorola, MCI, AT&T, the American Satellite Corporation (AST), International Discount Telecommunications (IDT), British Telecom International and other companies interested in competing in the region's domestic and international markets have come up squarely against C&W's monopoly licences or its technological hegemony.

Deficiencies in National and Regional Policy Planning

In Jamaica, there are now less than 6 telephones per 100 of the population (Table 2) and a very long waiting list of applicants. According to a former Chief Executive Officer of the Telephone Company, Noel Rickards, while the real waiting list was more than twice the number of telephones in operation in the country, there were still thousands who did not bother to apply because of perceived futility of joining a very long queue. In addition, rising domestic rates for those who have phones was causing public irritation. The automatic rate of return clause in the licence of the company meant periodic upward price adjustments in addition to costly foreign currency adjustments. Despite this tense socio-political situation, the company was visibly increasing its annual profitability. Yearly announcements of close to maximum allowable profit levels by the Cable and Wireless subsidiary, TOJ, has been greeted with demands for more realistic limits on customer charges, for more rapid expansion of the network into rural areas and unserved urban homes as well as for a measure of competition to help put pressure on the cost of services to consumers.

Table 2 TELEPHONE PENETRATION RATES IN CARICOM - 1994

Country	Lines/100 of pop
Guyana	4.0
Jamaica	5.7
St. Lucia	8.3
St. Vincent	9.1
Dominica	9.9
Belize	13.3
Grenada	15.1
Antigua	15.5
St. Kitts	15.7
Trinidad and Tobago	17.5
Bahamas	25.3
Monsterrat	25.9
Barbados	30.6
CARICOM AVERAGE	15.0
USA AVERAGE (1991)	96.5

Sources: Compiled by H. S. Dunn 1994

Even in the face of this conflict situation, Jamaica, like most other English-speaking Caribbean states, does not have formal telecommunications policies in operation. Instead, the unstated policies involve reliance on Cable and Wireless for leadership in network planning, investment and even in regulation. In dealing with a 1993 request by Cable and Wireless for a revised licence, the Jamaican Minister of Public Utilities, Robert Pickersgill admitted that he had invited the company's legal officers to prepare a draft of its own licence. The document was already in circulation as an official blueprint before it was leaked and its provisions exposed. They included further provisions for monopoly control by the company over videophone, cellular radio, mobile radio as well as 'all forms of data transmission services regardless of the transmission media, including, without limitation, telex, facsimile, electronic mail and packet switching and data transmission associated with cable systems.' [Schedule 1 of 1993 Draft Licence].

This regulatory, economic and technological dependence is facilitated by the failure of Caribbean governments, policy-making elites to create adequate regulatory institutions, shape common telecommunications strategies and engage in joint bargaining to deal with internal requirements and external interests. Instead, the approach has been that what is in the regional and global corporate interest of Cable and Wireless, will also redound to the benefit of the Caribbean. The assumption appears to be shared by Cable and Wireless in its close reciprocal arrangements with the governments. In announcing, for example, a 1988 investment programme valued at US $200-million for digital equipment, the company stated: 'As the Group operates in so many locations, it has been possible to co-ordinate centrally all the improvements on a regional basis, so that network flexibility and compatibility are assured. The digitalization of the region will lay the groundwork for the introduction of ISDN (Integrated Services Digital Network)...By the time THE GROUP (my emphasis) introduces ISDN, the Caribbean will have leap-frogged a whole epoch in the evolution of telecommunications technology into the age of information.' [C&W 1988:1].

This scheme, while being well intentioned on the part of the company, was never subject to any long-term evaluation of its overall implications for the region. The proposed system or its configuration were not derived from any regionally defined planning objectives. Its introduction into the region was to be integrated only into the global corporate strategy of the external multinational corporation.

It was not until 1988/89 that the CARICOM governments officially recognised and accepted that the consequence of their continued fragmentation was their own increasing marginalization in policy planning within their countries and region. With the assistance of the CARICOM Secretariat, the Caribbean Telecommunications Union (CTU), began operation from permanent offices in Port of Spain, Trinidad in 1990. The preamble of its charter recognises 'the sovereign right of each state to regulate its telecommunication system', 'the growing importance of telecommunications for the social and economic development of all states', and 'the need to foster international co-operation and economic and social development among peoples by means of efficient telecommunication services.'

It would appear, however, that the CTU as currently funded and structured, is unlikely to provide an adequate long term response to the challenges facing Caribbean telecommunications. Despite its obvious importance and wide ranging remit, the CTU's limited staffing and inadequate resources generally put a major brake on its effectiveness as either an advisory or a regulatory body. The extensive scale of foreign control over the transmission systems and operating companies in the region's telecommunications sector requires stronger and more well resourced national regulatory agencies and a stronger and more stable regional co-ordinating institution. The situation in the region also handsomely makes the case for a more supportive role by the International Telecommunications Union (ITU) and its special bureau for development support.

In the wake of the public controversy, the Jamaican government took the decision in 1993 to set up a regulatory institution for telecommunications. However, it turns out that this body is planned to be a sub-department of an Office of Utilities Regulation (OUR), which would also regulate water, electricity, public transport and aeronautical services. Proceeding on the basis of a top-down policy approach, and arguing cost-limitations, the government has paid little attention to reservations expressed about such an omnibus agency. The OUR is likely to stifle and subsume telecommunications and its emerging potential both as a lucrative sector and an enabling industry capable of helping to re-generate other areas of the national economy. The introduction of realistic, revised licence fees for operating companies in the sector could provide a large portion of the operating cost of a separate telecom regulatory agency.

In any event, even the telecoms division of the proposed Office of Utilities Regulation was not incorporated or even referred to in the draft of a new Telecommunications Act which the Minister of Public Utilities tabled in the House of Representatives in mid 1994. This draft understandably fuelled a further round of public controversy. It was not accompanied by any policy framework for the proposed changes, no analysis of the point and purpose of the provisions as they affect rural people or any other sector of the economy. The draft legislation gave no recognition to the notion of independent regulation, but rather reinforced the dominant control of the Minister of Public Utilities. It was widely perceived as simply fulfilling a promise to TOJ by the government.

Numerous organizations, including the Caribbean Association for Communication Research (CACR), the Jamaican Institution of Engineers (JIE), and sections of the public media called for the draft legislation be re-considered and that the public should be given a specified period for discussion of the bill.

Among the provisions causing public uproar was a waiver of transfer tax and stamp duty amounting to millions of Jamaican dollars on corporate merger transactions by the Cable and Wireless subsidiary. Redundancy payment arrangements for the employees in JAMINTEL and the Jamaica Telephone Company were also among the issues creating further complications in public acceptance of the draft bill. While the bill fulfils the urgent need for updating of the obsolete 1893 Telephone Act, it would also effectively extend the existing Cable and Wireless monopoly licence for wire-based telephone to cover the full range of present and future telecommunications services. While it is unlikely to forestall a growth in alternative telecom services, the law, if passed, could create a deterrent to market competition in the sector. Technological innovations are already circumventing the TOJ licence arrangements which, for the most part, expires in August of the year 2013.

CONCLUSION

In their 1993 study Cronin et al have found that 'investment in telecommunications infrastructure is causally related to total factor productivity in the United States and that contributions to aggregate and sectoral productivity growth rates from telecommunications advancements are both quantifiable and substantial'. [Cronin et al 1993: 677-690]. In another earlier study of telecommunications and rural development, Heather Hudson reported that 'where telecommunication services are available, rural people often use them more heavily and spend more of their disposable income on telephone calls and telegraph that do city dwellers' [1985:198]. She argues that large multinational companies are unwilling to take the risk perceived to be involved in investment in rural telecommunications, preferring instead the relatively well known and lucrative of the urban business users. Although these and other studies have established telecommunications as a catalyst for economic growth and an important interactive link within and between societies and groups, it is not being accorded appropriate priority in national and regional policy planning in most under-developed countries, including those in the Caribbean.

In Jamaica, which formed the focus of this study, the government has been pressured by public opinion into initiating several policy measures. But the approach has largely been a top-down one with policy details emerging from the monopoly company and from tradition-bound bureaucratic and political elites. Many analysts (among them Jonscher (1985) Leff (1984), Maitland (1993) have indicated that the choice faced by planners is not simply between telecommunications and other sectors. Telecommunications as a sector is lucrative in its own right, but is also a vital requirement in improving the efficiency of all other productive and service-based sectors of the economy. This potential can best be derived if the industry develops in an orderly and well-regulated fashion, including regulation of not just rate levels but the quality of service provision to consumers, technical standards and environmental protection measures.

Telecommunications policy in Jamaica and the region should also allow for the phased introduction of competition at two levels: The first is at the level of customer premises equipment (CPE), under which businesses and consumers would be entitled to buy and maintain their own domestic and office equipment, from basic telephone set or fax machine to the equipment requirements to establish a local area networks (LAN). Provided these equipment conform with a publicly available set of technical standards and are compatible with the national network, purchasers should not be required to buy them through the TOJ or to pay any fees to the company for installation, as now applies. Such a change would set the stage for the development of an independent sub-sector in the provision of equipment, maintenance and in a body of expertise outside the immediate staffing of the transnational provider.

The second more complex and long term aspect of competition is in the area of network service provision. This is the area which is even more substantially blocked by the existing TOJ licence, and involves direct competition in the provision of local and international telephone and data services. While the economics of the industry is increasingly undermining concerns about the size of the market, the main obstacle is a legal one relating to connectivity into the established national network. This issue of connectivity is an important one because no competitor would be expected to establish and operate a new or parallel transmission system. The incumbent operator would have to be required by law to share the network with a competitor, with the relevant payment arrangements being worked out and monitored by the national regulatory agency. Variations of this system operates in several other countries, including the United Kingdom and in parts of Latin America and Asia.

This approach recognises that the main responsibility for development planning, using telecommunications, belongs to the governments and citizens of the region. The company can play an important contributory role, but its main responsibility is to its shareholders and their legitimate profit-taking objective. Effective utilization of global telecommunications potential in the interest of the wider public involves re-structuring away from the existing monopoly arrangement where possible. The recent developments discussed here suggest that sections of the public understand this need more sharply than many government policy-makers do. Ongoing public debate and discussions represent important challenges to these bureaucratic stakeholders and political elites as it does to the protracted monopoly control by companies such as Cable and Wireless.

Without national and regional strategies for the incorporation of telecommunications into Caribbean industrial planning, any additional competition and externally-generated policy initiatives could further enmesh the region in a wider net of dependency. Both in the existing scenario of monopoly control in a more competitive environment, the regulatory responsibilities of governments are vital. Ultimately, the competitive scenario envisaged by the critics is what will enable Jamaica and the Caribbean region to join a global tele-environment, offering cheaper and more reliable telecommunications services for businesses, household clients and to enhance regional economic development.

POSTSCRIPT

Seemingly in response to months of sustained public pressure, Telecommunications of Jamaica yielded some ground at the end of 1994 by agreeing to modify its Customer Premises Interconnection Policy. The agreement was arrived at after negotiations with the Fair Trading Commission (FTC) of the Ministry of Industry and Commerce.

The concession was in direct response to a formal challenge by computing specialist and writer, Mr Jens Wynton. It followed an undertaking given by then executive director of the FTC, Mr Philip Paulwell, that his department would be "examining the operations of TOJ to see if that entity was in breach of the Fair Competition Act". (*The Gleaner*, November 24, 1993:1 - "TOJ May Come Under Probe"). The undertaking was given at a public forum on telecommunications and national policy planning hosted jointly by the Caribbean Association for Communication Research (CACR) and the Jamaica Institution of Engineers (JIEJ) at the Jamaica Pegasus Hotel in Kingston on November 22, 1993.

The statement issued by the FTC and TOJ in December 1994 is reproduced below, together with the full text of the Agreement:

Statement - Fair Trading Commission, December 22, 1994

1. The Fair Trading Commission (FTC) has arrived at an agreement with Telecommunications of Jamaica (TOJ) concerning modification of its inter-connection policy. The new policy will, to the extent stated herein, modify the current inter-connection policy which was introduced in 1986. Under the 1986 policy, the instruments numbered 1 to 10 on the following list could be connected to the network. (Items 11-14 newly agreed)

    1. Answering Machines

    2. Facsimile Machines

    3. Auto Dialers and Emergency Dialers

    4. Caller Sequencers

    5. Personal Computers with Inherent Modems

    6. Teleconferencing Systems

    7. Announcement Machines and Hands Free/Loud Speaker Units

    8. All Telephone Devices for the Deaf

    9. Alarm/Control Supervisory Systems

    10. Automatic Paging Systems – (One way special path only)

    11. Telephone Handsets

    12. Cordless Telephones

    13. Modems

    14. Credit Authorization Machines

2. The new policy will be introduced on a phased basis commencing January 1, 1995 with full implementation by April 1, 1995. During the implementation phase, TOJ will, inter alia,

(a)   undertake staff training to familiarize counter-service personnel with the new policy;

(b)   install into the network appropriate equipment to facilitate the new policy; and

(c)   introduce new forms and administrative procedures consistent with the policy.

3. The new policy will now permit the use and/or connection to the network of telephone hand-sets, cordless phones, modems and credit authorization machines subject to certain conditions including technical compatibility. With respect to the connection of telephone hand-sets, under the 1986 policy, at least one telephone instrument on the service premises had to be a TOJ-owned instrument, which incorporated an inherent network termination testing apparatus (NTTA) thereby enabling TOJ to undertake remote line testing to the point of interface.

4. Under the new policy, a customer may elect not to rent any telephone instrument from TOJ. In that situation:

(a)   the customer will be responsible for maintenance of his own instrument and for any damage which may be done by him to TOJ's network;

(b)   TOJ will have the right to install a separate network termination testing apparatus (NTTA);

(c)   the instrument must comply with quality standards and criteria established by the US Federal Communications Commission (FCC) and the Canadian Department of Communication (CDC) as well as TOJ's own technical standards;

(d)   where TOJ, at the request of a customer, makes a service call and discovers that the customer's equipment is defective, the customer will be obliged to pay visit charges based on rates to be agreed with the Minister of Public Utilities, Mining and Energy.

5. Permission will not be granted for any equipment if such equipment:

   (a)   would degrade any service being provided by TOJ; and

   (b)   could be used to by-pass the network or for the purpose of evading legitimate charges payable to TOJ.

6. The new policy will provide opportunities for entrepreneurs who may wish to enter the telephone equipment market.

7. With regard to value-added services, competition has also been enhanced in that area. Value-added services are computer-controlled operations such as message handling, internet services and alarm monitoring. They do not include call-back services or any other service designed to evade or by-pass the network or evade legitimate charges or to utilize the network without charge.

8. TOJ will provide circuits on commercial terms to person wishing to provide value-added services subject to the following conditions:

   (a)   the service must be properly licensed under existing legislation and regulations.

   (b)   basic telecommunication services will have priority over value-added services and, therefore, TOJ's ability to provide circuits for value-added services will depend upon the availability of circuits.

   (c)   the service must be such that it will not degrade the basic telecommunication service provided by TOJ or cause damage to the network.

   (d)   the equipment must be approved by TOJ.

   (e)   the service must not be used for the transmission of indecent, immoral, abusive, defamatory, offensive, profane, obscene or menacing messages or signals. If so used, the service may be withdrawn and/or terminated.

The following is the full text of the agreement:

1. IT IS HEREBY AGREED between TOJ and the FTC with the concurrence of the Minister of Public Utilities, Mining and Energy that the parties in this issue have agreed to have any further procedural steps in this matter as follows:

   1.1   This Agreement is for settlement purposes only and does not constitute an admission by TOJ that the Law has been violated, as may be alleged in any complaint under the Fair Competition Act.

1.2   This Agreement shall not become part of the public record of the proceedings unless and until it is accepted by the FTC and becomes binding upon the parties hereto and upon such acceptance, it shall be available for public access at the offices of the FTC.

1.3   If TOJ fails to implement the agreed policy, the FTC may thereafter either withdraw its acceptance of this Agreement and take such action as it considers appropriate and so notify TOJ, or issue and serve a complaint in such form as the circumstances may require.

1.4   TOJ understands that after this Agreement becomes effective, it will be required to file as requested by the FTC one or more compliance reports to show that it has fully complied with the Agreement.

1.5   TOJ understands and accepts that formal proceedings may be instituted if it fails to abide by this Agreement.

2.   2.1   IT IS AGREED THAT TOJ shall amend its policy guidelines regarding Customer Premises Equipment ('CPE') to permit customers to connect their own equipment itemized at 11 to 14 inclusive of the Appendix without prior approval subject to the following terms and conditions which shall also apply to equipment which were previously within TOJ's policy guidelines.

(a)   Such equipment may be installed by the consumer through qualified contractors or by engaging TOJ to do so.

(b)   At the point of interface with customer's equipment, TOJ may install or require the installation of a network termination testing apparatus (NTTA) at the customer's expense to permit remote testing of the lines.

(c)   Each equipment must comply with:

   (i)   quality standards and criteria established by the US Federal Communication Commission (FCC) and the Canadian Department of Communication; and

   (ii)   TOJ's own quality and technical standards prescribed from time to time.

(d)   Equipment not satisfying condition (c) above must be submitted to TOJ for testing and evaluation. Such testing shall be undertaken by TOJ and the evaluation of the testing result shall be done by a committee comprising representatives of TOJ and Government. The cost of testing and evaluation will be borne by the customer.

(e)   A customer whose equipment damages the network or who, in the course of installation, damages the network will be liable for such damage and will be required to cover the cost of repairs and consequential losses.

(f)   Each customer will be responsible for the maintenance of his own equipment while TOJ will continue to be responsible for the transmission line up to the NTTA.

(g)   Permission shall not be granted for the connection of any equipment if such equipment

  (i)   would cause degradation of any service being provided by TOJ; *and*

  (ii)   could be used to bypass the network or, result in the avoidance of evasion of any legitimate charge payable to TOJ.

(h)   Where TOJ visits the customer's premises in response to a repair by the customer call and TOJ discovers that the fault does not lie in their line or equipment the customer must be informed of this and will be required to pay visit charges which will be published after consultation with the Minister of Public Utilities, Mining and Energy.

2.2   IT IS AGREED that TOJ shall amend its "Terms an Conditions of Service" by deleting Part II 1.8 and by adding a new clause in the terms stated at 2.1 of this Agreement.

2.3   In pursuance of the foregoing, the new inter-connection policy shall permit the inter-connection of the equipment set forth in the Appendix hereto. It being understood that equipment numbered 1 to 10 were previously approved for inter-connection as from 1986.

2.4   Subject to the conditions stated below TOJ will provide circuits on commercial terms to persons wishing to provide value-added service ("VADs"). VADs are computer-controlled operations such as message handling, Internet services and alarm monitoring. VADs does not include call-back services or any other service designed to evade or bypass the network or evade legitimate charges or to utilize the network without charge. The relevant conditions are as follows:

(a)   The service must be properly licensed under existing legislation and regulations.

(b)   Basic telecommunication services will have priority over VADs and,

(b)   Basic telecommunication services will have priority over VADs and, therefore, the availability of circuits of the provision of VADs will depend upon the availability of circuits.

(c)   The service must be such that it will not degrade the basic telecommunication service provided by the Company or damage the network.

(d)   Equipment must be approved by TOJ.

(e)   The service must not be used for the transmission of indecent, immoral, abusive, defamatory, offensive, profane, obscene or menacing messages or signals. If so used, the service may be withdrawn and/or terminated.

2.5   The implementation of the new policy will commence on January 1, 1995.

3. IT IS FURTHER AGREED THAT:

(a)   TOJ shall duly inform its officers, or representatives having responsibility with respect to implementation of the policy of the subject matter of this Agreement;

(b)   TOJ shall notify the FTC at least thirty (30) days prior to any proposed change in its structure or operations which may affect compliance with this Agreement;

(c)   TOJ shall, within sixty (60) days after the date of this Agreement file with the FTC a report detailing the manner and form in which it has complied with this Agreement.

DATED THE 21st day of December 1994.

CACR RESPONSE

In responding to the Agreement, the CACR noted that it represented a step in the right direction. However, the Association said it remained concerned that the company retains its monopoly control over certain categories of customer premises equipment (CPE) and over the network as a whole.

The Association called for the new modifications in CPE policy to be recognized in the proposed Telecommunications Law alongside stable, institutional arrangements for regulating and monitoring their implementation.

It said the next major stage is a strategy and timetable for the introduction of direct network competition. The Association noted that the 7-year monopoly period for the Montego Bay-based Jamaican Digiport International (JDI) will come to an end in April 1995, opening the way for more substantive competition in international data traffic under the Radio and Telegraph Control Act.

It also noted that no official licences currently exist for the operation of cellular telephone services, although TOJ continues to provide the service.

REFERENCES

Amin, Samir - Imperialism and Unequal Development, Harvester Press, Sussex England, 1977

Barty-King, Hugh - Girdle Round the Earth — The Story of Cable and Wireless, London, 1979

Budhoo, Davidson L. - Enough is Enough — New Horizons Press, New York, 1990.

Cable and Wireless PLC - Communications For the Caribbean, London, 1988.

CANTO, - Caribbean Association of National Telecommunications Organizations: 1989 Conference Proceedings, CANTO, Dominican Republic, 1989.

Caribbean Telecommunications Union - Draft Agreement for the Establishment of the CTU, mimeo, Georgetown, Guyana, 1988.

Commonwealth Secretariat - Technological Change: Enhancing the Benefits Vols 1 & 2, Report by a Commonwealth Working Group, Commonwealth Secretariat, London, 1985.

Commonwealth Secretariat and CARICOM Secretariat - Caribbean Development to the Year 2000, Commonwealth Secretariat, Georgetown, Guyana, 1988.

Demac, Donna A and Morrison, Ruth J. - U.S. Caribbean Telecommunications: Making Great Strides in Development — Telecommunications Policy, March 1989, pp 51- 59.

Dunn, H.S. - Caribbean Telecoms — A Call for Competition: A Call for Regulation — Intermedia, Vol 22 No 2, April/May 1994 IIC, London, pp 23-26.

Dunn, H.S. - Telecommunications and Underdevelopment: A Policy Analysis of the Historical Role of Cable and Wireless in the Caribbean [PhD Thesis], City University, London, 1991.

Frobel, Folker - Perspectives on the International Division of Labour — In The Future of the Caribbean in the World System: Two Contributions — FES/UWI, Kingston 1988, pp 47-67.

Galtung, Johan - A Structural Theory of Imperialism — In: Smith, M; Little, R and Shackleton, M - Perspectives on World Development, Croom Helm, London, 1981, pp 301-303.

Girvan, Norman -The Debt Problem of Small Peripheral Economies — Association of Caribbean Economists (ACE), Kingston, 1989.

Hills, Jill - The Telecommunications Rich and Poor- Third World Quarterly, Vol 12 No 2, April 1990, pp 71-90.

Houghton, John - Shaping The Network Resource - CIRCIT Newsletter, Vol 5 No 1, 1993

Hudson, H.E. - When Telephones Reach the Village: The Role of Telecommunications in Rural Development, Norwood, Ablex, 1984.

International Commission for Worldwide Telecommunications Development (ICWTD, Maitland Commission), ITU, Geneva, 1985.

Lam, Vincent - Hong Kong Telecoms Relaunches Competition — China Willing — Intermedia Vol 22 No 2 April May 1994 pp 20-22.

Leff, Nathaniel - Social Benefit Cost Analysis and Telecommunications Investment in Developing Countries — Information Economics and Policy Vol 1, 1984, pp 217-227

Levy, Brian and Spiller, Pablo - Regulation, Institutions and Commitment in Telecommunications: A Comparative Analysis of Five Country Studies — The World Bank, Washington, 1993

Petras, J and Brill H - The IMF, Austerity and the State in Latin America, Third World Quarterly Vol 8 No 2 1986 pp 425-48.

Spiller, Pablo and Sampson, Cezley - Regulation, Institutions and Commitment: The Jamaican Telecommunications Sector — World Bank, Washington, 1992.

Staple, Gregory C - International Services Competition: Challenges and Opportunities for Small Carriers — Unpublished address to the Commonwealth Telecommunications Council 33rd Meeting, Ocho Rios Jamaica, July 7-13, 1993.

Tarjanne, Pekka - New Concepts for Public Communication Policies- Media Development Vol XL No 2, 1993 p 12.

9

TELECOMMUNICATIONS RESTRUCTURING AND THE DEVELOPMENT OF EXPORT INFORMATION PROCESSING SERVICES IN JAMAICA

Beverley Mullings

Introduction

As world markets become transformed into integrated global information systems based on electronic media, many developing countries have found that a modern telecommunications infrastructure is necessary if domestic industries are to effectively compete in world markets. As part of its programme of structural adjustment, Jamaica has significantly restructured its telecommunications industry by transferring its ownership from the public to the private sector. By transferring ownership of the telecommunications network to Telecommunications of Jamaica (TOJ), the government anticipated that large investments would be made in modernising Jamaican telecommunications capabilities. With this step, the foundations were to have been laid for new industries to develop based on information technology. In 1986, the government sought to promote this new industry, based on the export of information processing services. It was envisaged that export information processing in Jamaica could contribute significantly to foreign exchange earnings and savings.

This chapter examines the extent to which the export information processing industry has become the growth catalyst that was envisaged in 1986. Drawing upon extensive interview data, it argues that a combination of inadequate financial support, marketing and technical skills, has limited the potential of the sector to become a growth catalyst. Instead of becoming an industry that provides foreign exchange earnings, jobs and technical skills, export information processing in Jamaica remains at the low end of the information processing industry, reliant on 'text down' data-entry and part time, female, low cost labour. While there is some movement towards developing higher value added export information processing services, most provide employment and skill upgrading opportunities for men rather than women. It is argued further that the monopoly privilege accorded to TOJ in the delivery of the telecommunications service has contributed to the limited growth of the export information processing industry. Finally, it is argued that in order for the export information processing industry to positively contribute to the development process in Jamaica, a mutually supportive environment will need to be created. In such an environment, the government, TOJ and firms involved in information services would devise strategies that enabled the local information processing industry to become globally competitive in factors other than the sale of cheap female labour.

OVERVIEW

Since the introduction of electronic switching in the early 1970s, telecommunications have continued to attract new customers and suppliers, new services and new ways of delivering old services. As telecommunications technology has advanced, the cost of acquiring basic network components such as electronic switches, cables, microwave links and exchange terminal assemblies has also fallen. Nulty (1991, 8) estimates that in 1983 it cost US$12,000 — $14,000 per month to lease a private half-channel for voice communication from the USA. By 1991 Nulty estimated that cost to have fallen to US$4,000-$5,000. In addition to these technological advances in the basic public packet-switched telephone network, new information technologies such as cellular radio, small satellite terminals and phone patches for simplex radio have provided alternative communication facilities.

  The advances in telecommunications technology and the reduction in the relative cost of acquiring the technology have provided a number of developing countries with opportunities to 'leap-frog' over the more expensive phases of telecommunications development. As a result, a number of new services have emerged that are bounded by neither time nor space. Thus U.S. judicial opinions can be abstracted and entered into electronic data bases by clerical workers in Jamaica, stored in central computers in the USA and accessed by lawyers worldwide. Similarly, modern switching and signaling technologies allow voice services such as those used for airline bookings to be provided by agents at any geographical area in an airline's network (Nulty, 1989).

The convergence of telecommunications, information technologies and electronics has not only given rise to new services and products of greater reliability, capacity, speed and compatibility, but it has also generated new levels of demand from consumers. As argued by Exton (1992), it appears that technology has finally caught up with the market, because the marketplace has accepted all of these advances and continues to demand more. Thus the potential of a modern telecommunications infrastructure to promote the process of development lies in its ability to make existing industries more competitive in their delivery of old goods and services, and to create demand for entirely new products and services. There are potential advantages for those countries that are able to develop or attract industries dependent on telecommunication services. Such advantages include greater access to knowledge at a lower cost and lower barriers to entry than most conventional industries and long term competitive advantages. This point has been forcefully made by UNIDO, who state that:

> 'Any development strategy which in anyway is dependent on international linkages for finance, technology, goods and services and/or involves the local participation of foreign firms in any sector of the economy will face considerable and growing difficulties in the future if an adequate, modern, digital-based telecommunications system is not in place' (UNIDO 1989, 41).

The ability of a modern telecommunication infrastructure to act as a catalyst for the growth of both manufacturing and service industries, however, is heavily dependent on the economic and regulatory environment in which the infrastructure is developed. In Jamaica the government sought to modernize the telecommunications infrastructure by turning ownership over to the private sector. By transferring ownership of the telecommunications network to TOJ, the government anticipated that large investments would be made in modernizing Jamaican telecommunications capabilities. In making this step, the grounds were laid for new industries based on information technology to develop. In 1986, the government took the first steps towards developing a new export oriented industry, based on the export of information processing services. This was achieved by the provision of fiscal incentives for both domestic and foreign investors and infrastructural support in the form of a teleport: Jamaica Digiport International.

THE RESTRUCTURING OF
THE TELECOMMUNICATION INDUSTRY IN JAMAICA

The government took the first step towards restructuring the telecommunications sector in 1987 when a holding company, TOJ was created and two previously separate government owned companies, the Jamaica Telephone Company Limited (JTC) and Jamaica International Telecommunications (JAMINTEL) became its wholly owned subsidiaries. Through five separate transactions over a period of four years the government disposed of its shares in TOJ and in so doing made the British telecommunications company Cable and Wireless, the holder of 79 per cent of the shares. [Dunn 1991: 353]

At the outset Cable and Wireless was identified as a potential buyer for TOJ. Cable and Wireless was already a shareholder in JAMINTEL, the more profitable part of TOJ and it was hoped that through ownership, the telephone company operations would substantially improve. In addition to creating TOJ, the government set up a regulatory structure that would determine access, exit, and pricing, once the sector became private. Adam et al. (1992) point out that the regulatory structure set up, was unusual because instead of focusing on measures to protect the consumer from excess profits, it had the additional objective of enticing Cable and Wireless to commit substantial investment resources with guarantees on the security of such investments. This is evident from the liberal regulatory framework in which TOJ operates its service. In 1988 the government granted TOJ a twenty-five year licence for the exclusive provision of both domestic and international telecommunication services. The licence which is renewable for a further twenty-five years specifies that TOJ is entitled to charge rates sufficient to result in post-tax consolidated earnings of no less than 17.5 per cent and no more than 20 per cent in consolidated shareholders' equity at the end of the preceding financial year. In 1993, the government sought to institute new legislation on the provision of telephone services and at the same time amend the licence issued to TOJ in 1988. The prime motivation was to update the 1893 Telephone Act so that it would take into account the technological advances in the provision of telephone services that have occurred since then. In so doing, the exclusiveness of the licence granted to TOJ in 1988 would be maintained.

In allowing TOJ to become an unconstrained monopolist, incentives for efficiency improvements such as competition with other firms or the contracting out of particular services have been lost. This is particularly clear where issues of connectivity and telephone rates are concerned. Until recently, individuals who wanted to connect to the telecommunications network with instruments that were not issued through TOJ, were unable to do without the permission of the company. TOJ claimed that it had the right to do so under the terms of its licence. While government representatives and TOJ are in the process of negotiating the issue of inter-connectivity, its impact has been to limit access to technologies that would make the production of many information processing services more cost efficient. The impact of this limitation on the competitiveness of local businesses was made clear in this interview with the manager of a local data-entry firm:

> 'You now have the technology of dealing with a single .... 56KB line where you get instruments on it to break up the line and get multiple phone lines out of one line...[but] they (TOJ) also have a licence on telephony in Jamaica which says that you cannot attach gadgets like that to the phone line. Now for domestic consumption of phone lines they can't stop that .... in a business environment, however, they can do that, so I can't in my shop attach the new devices that give me multiple uses from one phone line.' (*Interview Data, 1994*).[4]

With pricing, the current limitations placed on the rate of TOJ's return on investment are not adequate in providing government with sufficient incentives for TOJ to effect efficiency improvements. Under the current rate of return regulatory mechanism for example, TOJ is free to set its own prices on selected services within the telecommunications system, so long as its overall return constraint is met. This will have the effect of introducing additional constraints on the efficient allocation of resources.

While the dangers of stifled local industrial development are a real possibility given TOJs present monopoly position, it is fair to say that to date the company has introduced a wide range of advanced telecommunications services to the island. Cable and Wireless has invested heavily in the development of a range of telecommunications innovations throughout the region including the provision of a microwave radio relay system (DECMS) connecting the islands of the Eastern Caribbean, the British Virgin Islands and Trinidad (Demac and Morrison 1989) and a Trans-Caribbean Cable System (TCS-1) using fibre optics linking Jamaica to the US, Florida, Puerto Rico, the Dominican Republic and Colombia. In addition, since privatisation substantial sections of Jamaica's transmission system have been digitised, and in 1992/93 35,740 additional telephone lines were provided (TOJ 1993).

CREATING A NEW INDUSTRY: THE DEVELOPMENT OF AN INFORMATION PROCESSING INDUSTRY

The government's participation in the development of an export oriented information processing industry began in the mid 1980s as part of its structural adjustment programme. Under this programme, the government sought to increase the number of foreign exchange earning industries on the island. In its 1990-1995 development plan the Jamaican government outlined its commitment to the development of an information processing industry. In the plan the government stated that:

'The Government is committed to the provision of development support for information in a timely manner to both individuals and sector interests within the society. The Government will, therefore, give special priority to the development of the information industry. ...An operational plan has been formulated for each sub-sector and reconciled to ensure consistency and economy of policy objectives throughout the sector. The overall strategies to ensure attainment of sub-sector objectives involve: ...developing export markets for locally produced information services, products and skills'(PIOJ 1990, 52-53)

and

The export of information services is seen as an area for immediate action by Government. In the last 5 years the industry has grown from 2 to 29 companies, 25 of which are Jamaican owned and operated and located outside the Free Zones. The United States possesses a large and growing market for these services, with revenue from data processing totalling some US$27.1 billion in 1989, an increase of 13 per cent over 1988' (PIOJ 1990, 84).

In the five year development plan the government's belief in the developmental potential of an export information processing industry was clear. They suggested that, in keeping with the growing contribution of services to Gross Domestic Product world-wide, export information processing in Jamaica could rapidly increase foreign exchange earnings and savings. Jamaican services, the government argued, grew in its contribution to GDP between 1984 and 1989 from 67 per cent to 69 percent and the foreign exchange earnings from information services in particular averaged US$10 million annually. A number of additional reasons were given for targeting the information processing industry as a growth industry. First, Jamaica's proximity to the North American market and the fact that the island was English speaking was seen as an advantage for ensuring rapid turnaround times. Second, proposed improvements to the telecommunications infrastructure and air transportation links would facilitate greater efficiency in the speed with which data could be transferred from the United States to Jamaica. Third, the government indicated that the potential strength of the sector rested on the fact that there was an easily trained work-force. It was envisaged that given government assistance, the sector had the capacity to generate US$200 million in foreign exchange earnings over the 1990-1995 period (PIOJ 1990 p.84).

In developing the export information processing sector, the government outlined two major objectives: to attract local and overseas firms to set up operations in Jamaica, and to secure profitable long term contracts with foreign data-entry and other information service companies. The government planned to attract major data-entry, telemarketing and desktop publishing firms in the United States to locate in Jamaica or subcontract work to Jamaican firms through a number of incentives.

Fiscal Incentives

Fiscal incentives for local private sector investors in the export information processing industry were provided through three pieces of legislation: the Export Industry Encouragement Act, the Industrial Incentives Act and the Jamaica Export Free Zone Act. Under the Industrial Incentives Act, and in 1990 the amended Export Industry Encouragement Act, investors in export information processing could benefit from tax holidays, and customs and excise duty remissions for periods between three and ten years. These incentives have since been modified. Local information processing operations no longer benefit from the incentives outlined in either the Industrial Incentives Act or the Export Industry Encouragement Act and the moratorium on duties has been discontinued (JAMPRO 1993).

Much wider incentives were provided for foreign investors who located in the free zone areas. Investors who located in the Jamaica Digiport International (JDI) were provided with a number of concessions under the Jamaica Export Free Zone Act. Concessions included 100 per cent tax holidays on profits in perpetuity, duty free imports of capital and consumer goods, raw materials and articles imported for the construction, alteration or repair of premises within the free zone, unlimited repatriation of profits and permission to operate foreign currency accounts. In addition, the free zone assured minimal customs procedures with a permanent customs office located on the site.

Technological Support

For investors with foreign currency, the fiscal incentives provided through the Jamaica Export Free Zone Act were complemented by the telecommunications services provided by the JDI. Located in the Montego Bay Free Zone, the JDI was built in 1989 as part of a joint venture among Telecommunications of Jamaica (TOJ), American Telephone and Telegraph (AT&T) and Cable and Wireless. The digiport offers services such as International Long Distance, advanced 800 services, switched 56 kilo bits per second lines (KBPS) and dedicated private line services from 56 KBPS to 1.5MBPS. Supported by a satellite earth station located in the Montego Bay Free Zone, the digiport uses a 15 metre 125 watt, C-band antenna, INTELSATs network and an AT&T 5ESS switch as its main technology.

The establishment of the JDI in the Montego Bay Free Zone was therefore seen as a direct commitment by government to the long term development of export information processing. The expectation behind the development of the teleport facility was primarily that of attracting foreign investment and creating employment. Potential investors were expected to provide foreign exchange to the government in the form of rental, leases and concessions related to activities carried out in the free zone as well as local employment. In exchange, the fiscal incentives outlined in the Jamaica Export Free Zones Act were made available to foreign investors by virtue of the fact that the digiport was located in a Free Zone Area.

Marketing

In addition to the fiscal and technological incentives provided, the government planned to embark upon a marketing programme to attract investors. In the 1990-1995 development plan, it was stated that JAMPRO and a major telecommunication company in North America would undertake a programme to market Jamaica's geographical and labour advantages as well as its technologically advanced digiport located in the Montego Bay Free Zone. Plans were also made to lobby for the establishment of a consultancy and engineering desk within CARICOM which would be responsible for preparing projects before they were tendered out, and promoting joint ventures for regional consultancy and engineering firms.

THE STRUCTURE OF THE EXPORT INFORMATION PROCESSING INDUSTRY IN JAMAICA

The outcome of the government's incentives and support to the industry can be seen in the current structure of the industry. In 1993, there were 49 firms involved in the export of information services from Jamaica. The majority (76%) of the companies in export information processing were engaged in a range of data-entry services such as text-entry and Geographic Information Systems (GIS), and a tenth provided sales, training and marketing services (Table 1). Only four companies were engaged in telemarketing services, and all were located at the JDI. In 1993 over one half of the information processing industry was located in Kingston and the majority (21), of the companies there were engaged in activities related to data-entry. Of those companies in Kingston engaged in services related to data-entry, eleven were involved in text-entry operations. In this section, various structural features of the industry, such as its use of advanced telecommunications technology, labour requirements and technology transfer, and competitiveness in global markets will be looked at. Initial focus will be on the data-entry sector because it represents the largest and oldest form of export information processing on the island. Later some of the more recent

Table 1 Export Information Processing Services in Jamaica 1993

	Companies		Regional Distribution		
	Number	%	Kingston	Montego Bay	Other
Data entry & related services	37	76	21	11	5
Telemarketing	4	8	0	4	0
GIS	3	6	2	1	0
Sales, training & marketing	5	10	3	0	2
Total	49	100	26	16	7
% of total			53	33	14

information processing services will be examined, with a view to assessing their potential contribution to the development of the industry.

Data-Entry

Data-entry is the process of capturing data by keying in, scanning or digitising information, and converting it into computer readable files. Increasingly it is becoming an essential part of the storage and processing of information normally held in paper form. It is an expanding service because the conversion of paper-based to computer-based information not only ensures the easy retrieval of archived information, it also reduces the costs associated with the storage and preservation of paper-based data. Some of the paper-based documents which are converted into machine readable form include internal company data such as personnel and pay-roll records, inter-firm transactions such as sales records and orders, consumer-firm transactions such as credit card transaction records and insurance applications, and customised services such as publisher's manuscript typesetting and legal and court records.

Data-entry is not a new service to Jamaica. As early as the 1960s, Jamaica housed firms involved in the importation, processing and export of information from the United States. Information processing at that time was largely confined to data-entry. Data held on card files would be shipped to Jamaica by the trailer load, where local key punch operators would enter the data onto magnetic tapes and send them back to the United States. The process was described by an ex-employee of one of these firms:

'.... I remember we were doing [work] for the Wall Street stock exchange, all those cards that they used to turn out ... if you see any of those old movies or anything like that where you see all those cards ... we would do some of those here. And Value line is still in business ... they're a big catalogue warehouse and they evaluate other people's books and that sort of thing ... we would have like a trailer load of their things on card' (*Interview data, 1994*).

The structure of the overall data-entry service has remained remarkably unchanged over the past twenty years, although admittedly access to high speed telecommunications facilities provide opportunities for much faster turnaround times. Most of the current data-entry operations in Jamaica involve the importation by air freight or courier of data in the form of paper documents, magnetic tapes, cards, discs or audio recordings. Using computers, data is processed into a machine readable format and then sent back to North America in the form of discs or magnetic tapes. For a minority of the data-entry companies in Jamaica, data is imported and exported directly in the form of digitised data, from one computer terminal to another.

Under the current licencing agreement between the government and JDI, only investors located inside the Montego Bay Free Zone can have access to the switched digital telecommunications service. Firms outside the digiport, however, can gain access to the high speed digital services of the JDI in two ways. Firms outside of the Montego Bay Free Zone have the option to connect to the digiport via the JTC lines using a high speed microwave link between Kingston and Montego Bay. Few outside of the free zone, however, make use of this facility. Most companies continue to receive paper-based data which are processed and exported by air freight or courier on discs or magnetic tapes. Some of the companies outside the free zone transmit data through the TOJ telephone lines, and only two of the data-entry companies in Kingston relay processed information directly to off-shore computers using the Kingston-based JDI facility.

The reliance of firms outside the digiport on seemingly antiquated methods of information transmission is largely cost related. Transmitting data through the existing telephone lines provided by TOJ is not only slow but costly, because rates are priced at the same level as that of domestic users. While the JDI's dedicated private line facility exists, only large volume users could profitably utilise them. The cost in 1994 of procuring a 56 KBPS half-channel service was US$1,750 per month, a cost that most of the companies outside of the JDI found prohibitive given the scale of their operations. As stated by the owner of a Kingston based data-entry firm:

> 'we do do some transmitting of data but we do it with the local telephone lines....we don't have high volumes of transmitting and we are not linked into the overseas computers on a steady basis. For those purposes it suits you to use that facility because it is clean, dedicated only to the data, and the transmission should be faster. But for what we do, we are doing [it at] certain times of the day and not necessarily every day of the week' (Interview data, 1994).

Labour Requirements and Technology Transfer

The availability of cheap, skilled labour is a major component of Jamaica's comparative advantage as an off-shore data processing location. The industry mainly employs secondary and commercial high school graduates between the ages of 17 and 20. Presently women comprise approximately 90 percent of the data-entry labour force. In interviews, managers felt that in order to perform at close to the 99.8% accuracy levels that they promised, workers needed to be particularly focussed and patient. Women, they felt, were more likely to display these characteristics than men. While most firms do not specifically target women for employment, most firms prefer to recruit individuals with typing skills, which is a decidedly female dominated skill in Jamaica. Most new entrants to the industry are trained for a period of two weeks to three months, during which time they receive a training allowance to cover transport and subsistence costs. After this period of training workers are usually employed as temporary staff for an average period of three months. During this period, if an individual is unable to key at the required speed and accuracy, or if the company is unable to provide work for all of its staff, he/she will be laid off. In 1993, JAMPRO reported that within the industry the average number of key strokes entered per hour was 12,000 with top performers regularly achieving 15,000 keystrokes per hour.

Most of the workers in the industry receive formal benefits such as health insurance under a group scheme, transportation allowances and subsidized meals. Most firms also provide transportation for workers who work on late shifts. Benefits inside the free zone in Montego Bay are generally considered to be higher than those offered by firms in Kingston (Barnes, 1989). This, however, is contested by Pearson (1993) who states that the belief that the firms located in the Montego Bay Free Zone offer superior worker benefits, may be related more to the type of work undertaken at the JDI than to any intrinsic difference between local and foreign owned firms.

Most data-entry companies maintain a very small group of 'core' workers, largely supervisors, some keying staff and staff involved in data quality control. These employees are full time workers and they are assured a basic wage even when there are no jobs to be done. Most firms also employ a number of part-time/temporary workers who are taken on when the number of jobs cannot be managed in the required turnaround time by the core group. These part time workers are usually laid off when the work load is small. Most companies pay a basic wage with a variety of performance related bonuses. The basic wage, in most of the interviews conducted was $400-$550 per week for a 40 hour work week (US$13-$18 at January 1994 exchange rates). This was slightly above the minimum wage of $300 (US$10) for a 40 hour work week. Above this basic wage, the average data-entry keyer's take-home wage is directly related to the number of keystroke inputs per week. In comparison to the United States, the labour costs associated with data-entry services in Jamaica are very low. Basic key operators in Jamaica earn on average between $1,200-$2,000 per week (equivalent to US$1–1.67 per hour at January 1994 exchange rates). This is far less than the earnings of workers doing similar jobs in the United States who receive on average between US$7-10 per hour (Wilson 1994, 7).

Labour turnover in the industry is very high, with the longest standing workers averaging two or three years within any one firm. Typically most workers remain in the industry for periods between four and six months, before moving into clerical and secretarial positions in private sector companies. Managers explained the high level of turnover in the industry as largely due to the factor that data-entry work is relatively low paying and is perceived by workers as less prestigious and secure than jobs in the private sector, particularly those in the larger insurance and manufacturing companies. As one manager that was interviewed explained:

> '... we have been training school leavers coming in and moving on..this is an entry level job, you do not generally wish somebody to retire as a data-entry operator' (Interview data, 1994).

Although there is a high level of worker turnover in the industry, most workers do receive valuable computing related experience. During the period spent in the industry most would have learnt how to quickly adapt to a variety of computer systems, ranging from those on PCs and Apple Macintoshes to NCR Towers. Most also learn how to manipulate simple computer programs, and in a few cases write programs to enable paper-based data to be keyed.

The extent to which data-entry activities have resulted in the transfer of skills or technology is an important question in the assessment of the overall contribution of the information processing industry to the island's development. The issue of technology transfer is one that has been also researched extensively by Pearson in her examination of the internationalisation of office work and its impact on conditions for women's employment. Pearson (1991, 1992) argues that in order to assess whether data-entry is an activity that transfers a skill, the whole issue of what constitutes a 'skill' needs to be re-assessed. She argues that in Jamaica, there is a great variety of activities involved in data-entry work, which suggest that the industry is more involved in data processing than high volume/high speed data-entry. While many women in the industry do not progress from key punch operator to computer programmer, Pearson argues that many do learn valuable skills. She states:

'It is a damning reflection on the evaluation of women's skills that workers who have been able to adapt to considerable pressures at work, who have shown flexibility of response to frequently changing programmes on an ad hoc basis and have organized speedy through put of data-entry at a guaranteed level of accuracy and quality, should be considered no more qualified than school leavers with basic typing skills' (Pearson 1993, 294).

While it is clear that the data-entry industry does transfer valuable and competitive skills to the many women who enter into it, few are provided with opportunities to further enhance these skills particularly in the higher end of the information processing industry. The lack of incentives to develop a career in information processing remains one of the main obstacles to the industry's development. The current organisation and instability of work, the low levels of pay and the absence of any prospects for occupational mobility all result in low levels of motivation among workers. In interviews many managers complained about worker attitudes. They felt that most workers had no enthusiasm or loyalty to the work-place, and that this placed a strain on their operations.

Whether the data-entry industry in Jamaica has contributed positively to the island's development process cannot be solely assessed on the basis of the skills that it has transferred to workers. An important contribution lies in the extent to which the industry has been able to establish a foothold in the global market. In order to assess this contribution, it is necessary to look at the extent to which Jamaican owned firms in the industry have performed.

Performance of the Data-entry Industry 1986-1990

The performance of the data-entry service in Jamaica between 1986 and 1993 demonstrates the importance of complementarity in government policy objectives. From the beginning, the data-entry industry in Jamaica was comprised of more Jamaican owned than foreign owned firms. The industry was unusual, because it had attracted a new breed of Jamaican entrepreneur, the middle class professional, who traditionally would not have become an owner of the means of production. The potential for local industrial development demonstrated by this sector was, however, shortlived. A combination of inadequate and differential access to technological and marketing support as well as the removal of fiscal incentives led to an early decline in the data-entry sector. Differences between the supports and incentives offered to local and foreign investors led to the creation of a dual information processing industry.

In the mid 1980s when the government first announced its commitment to the development of the export information processing industry, a number of firms, ranging from the representatives of large manufacturing and insurance companies such as Grace Kennedy and the Insurance Company of the West

Indies Limited (ICWI) to small family operations, responded to the governments promotions. In 1986, there were three data-entry firms employing approximately three hundred people and generating US$1.5 million. By 1991, the number of firms had increased to twenty, employing over three thousand people and generating approximately US$17 million from the export of data-entry services (JAMPRO 1993). This positive growth in the number of data-entry firms masks a number of difficulties that faced the sector. Between 1986 and 1990 the industry experienced a 'shake-out' as many of the locally owned firms that had responded to the promotional programme closed down.

'Shake-out' in the local Data-Entry Industry

Between 1986 and 1989 the data-entry industry grew rapidly from two firms to twenty nine, the majority of which were locally owned concerns (PIOJ 1990, p.84). The tax holidays offered under the Industrial Incentives Act, and the promised access to the rapid transmission technologies of the proposed Teleport, were crucial elements in the rapid growth of the local industry. These supports and incentives, however, were short-lived. As more and more local firms entered the industry the fiscal incentives such as tax holidays offered under the Industrial Incentives Act, were withdrawn. In addition, when the teleport became operational after a three year delay, only investors located there could gain access to the superior telecommunications facilities. This immediately created a dual industry. Investors with foreign currency gained access to the benefits of a cheaper, more technologically advanced telecommunication system, as well as the financial benefits of locating in the free zone. Local firms on the other hand, had no access to the telecommunications technology of the digiport, and the fiscal incentives that they had received under the Industrial Incentives Act were now withdrawn. The impact of these two developments on the growth of the local data-entry industry was devastating. As the owner of one of the early data-entry companies explained:

> 'At that time, we had two main incentives, one was a ten year tax holiday where we could bring computers in and computer related equipment or maybe I should say specific equipment for the business. You could bring [it] into the country duty free. They had another incentive where they negotiated with the customs department that some of the time sensitive documents that [needed to] come into and get back out of the country fast, would'nt go through the normal customs clearing procedures. ....They also attempted at that time to erect a teleport to handle high speed transmission between mainly the United States and Jamaica. The teleport never really came into being and then through a series of negotiations and the redrawing of the whole plan it ended up being called a digiport.... a number of companies came in and then for some strange unknown reason the government at the time withdrew its incentive... I think...they

withdrew the incentive because they figured that the industry was just mind bogglingly profitable and then because of that they withdrew the incentives .... and the industry began to stumble, really stumble. I think there were some 28 firms that got in the business some of the large Jamaican firms got in the business like Wray and Nephew, ICWI and they all lost money and closed down and some who entered the business lost everything. ..'(Interview Data 1994).

Many of the new entrants to the industry were unable to remain profitable without the fiscal incentives, and an environment of cut-throat competition and inefficiency developed. This further jeopardised the industry as foreign firms began to perceive the Jamaican information processing industry as inefficient and untrustworthy. As another data-entry Firm Manager explained:

'In 1986/7 we got in or it appeared that we got in [to the market] .... people who wanted to get in were rather suspicious of each other and at that time we were competing against each other. So you'd find that if a guy had a job and [if] he'd speak to three different shops he would get three different quotes because everybody was trying to under-cut to get the job and it wasn't really doing Jamaica any good.. The industry and the people were getting a bad name abroad because overnight lots of big companies sprang up didn't know what they were doing and just messed up jobs..'(Interview Data).

The 'shake-out' in the industry at the end of the 1980s, however, was not only attributable to the removal of the fiscal incentives and technological supports. Many of the entrant firms were insufficiently prepared for the large financial commitment that was required for them to adequately compete with local and international data-entry firms for contracts. Although the government provided some amount of marketing support, few of the entrants to the industry had active marketing programmes. Many firms relied upon time consuming, weakly effective marketing strategies. One of the data-entry firm owners described how markets were acquired in those early days. She states:

'I used the United States Information Service and Library quite a bit, They have books on industries and so on....I did a lot of 'door to door', phoning, sending out brochures, letters... that was the sort of marketing [done]' (Interview data).

Few of the early entrants seemed prepared for the level of competition that came from countries like the Philippines, India, China and Bangladesh. There seemed to be a false sense of security in the fact that Jamaica was an English Speaking country whose geographical proximity to the United States could provide quick turnaround times for processed work. As the manager of another data-entry company states:

Just about 1985 or 1986, the Philippines also started to promote the industry .....and their costs were lower than our costs...... Also at the time in America, ... there was a large explosion in the construction of databases, ... all the current data bases [such as] encyclopaedias began in America, which demanded a lot of keyers work for conversion.......Now we thought we would get all of that work and a lot of that work went to the Philippines. ...The industry never understood that you have to market your service. So I guess most companies basically thought that we could just sit down in the office and the work would just come. It never happened that way....' (Interview data 1994).

The problem of marketing was not solely a result of the failure of local companies to adequately find clients. For any data-entry company to remain profitable there needs to be a constant flow of contracted work to be processed. This constant flow could come from a single large company contracting the data conversion of particular parts of its operations to a specific data-entry operation. This type of contract would be similar to that which exists in data-entry firms that are subsidiaries of large US based service companies. More typically, local data-entry firms in Jamaica received jobs from a range of companies seeking to contract out one-off, specific data conversion jobs. The resulting situation was, as one data-entry company manager described, that of 'hills and valleys'. He states:

'there is a hill and valley situation that I haven't yet found the answer to. It has to do with the nature of the contracts which we land. The ideal situation is to get a contract where work is generated every day throughout the year, and perhaps several such contracts if you had a long term situation, I have been fortunate enough to land a few of those contracts, but I have never been able to have enough of those long term contracts to keep the companies stable So then you end up with short term contracts. Short term contracts mean that if you are doing a project for three months you will have to staff up to deal with that. At the end of three months if you do not have another contract starting exactly behind that one, then you're back down to a valley situation. Perhaps just dealing with the long term contracts [is better] and then you might have a gap of about a month, one month, two months, three months who knows, it depends on how the marketing activities work out. Theoretically I live for the day when I can have a number of steady long term contracts, ... a number of short term contracts which will come in and ... a non time-sensitive job which I will probably ... as an incentive to the customer, charge at cost, which I can use to fill in the gaps ...'(Interview Data, 1994)

Today there are signs that the local segment of the industry is beginning to recognise the benefits of joint collaboration particularly in regards to marketing. Seven local data-entry companies have recently formed a marketing and work distribution company which operates out of Florida. Through the company, work is distributed to its members and this has helped to maintain regularity of work. The group has also instituted a training programme for prospective data-entry operators in conjunction with the Human Employment and Resource Training trust/National Training Agency (HEART/NTA) and USAID.

In 1989 a group representing local information processing firms, The Exporters of Information Processing Services (EXIS), prepared a document highlighting the differentials between the incentives provided for information service companies inside and outside of the JDI. In this document it was argued that the local investors situated outside the digiport had contributed significantly to the development of the sector, employing approximately 2,000 persons and contributing US$10 million per year to the local economy. They argued that despite these contributions, the government continued to provide the industry with very little support.

Since those claims were made in 1989 the industry has undergone a number of changes. In 1990, investors outside the digiport did receive importation and customs duty concessions under the Export Industry Encouragement Act, which previously had been only open to manufacturing firms. These concessions, however, have since been phased out and information processing firms outside of the free zone areas are no longer eligible for moratoriums on duties or incentives under the Export Industry Encouragement Act (JAMPRO 1993). A more significant change, however, is the fact that the technological improvements to the TOJ infrastructure have provided firms outside the free zone areas with access to the same high speed telecommunications services as the JDI albeit at a higher cost.

The local companies outside the digiport that survived the industry shakeout in the late 1980s, did so largely by minimising their variable costs. Many of the entrants who had fallen out of the market had invested heavily in expensive computer hardware, and could minimise costs only by reducing their demand for labour. As previously described, this has been achieved by maintaining flexible contracts with workers and tying wages closely to output. Most of the local companies attempted to find niches in the data-entry market, which allowed them to remain globally competitive. Many attempted to remain competitive by bidding for jobs where a quick turnaround of processed data was required. Generally jobs with over 500 keystrokes per page with a turnaround time of one or two days attract the highest rates, and Jamaica's proximity to the United States allowed them to have a comparative advantage. Given this advantage it was very easy for documents to be flown in in the morning, keyed, and the processed tapes flown out by night.

The advantages of spatial proximity, however, have since been overtaken by technology. The development of technologies such as Optical Character Recognition (OCR), Bar Code Systems (BCS), and Online Transaction Processing (OLTP), and the cheaper telecommunications costs of competitors have significantly eroded the advantages offered by cheap labour and quick turnaround times. The impact that these developments have had on the local information industry are described clearly by this manager who states:

'I decided to move into an area of fast turnaround and I approached companies..... to do the kind of data-entry work that required a quick turnaround and that decision was probably the best one I [could have] made. That one paid off for me because then the Philippines could not compete with that, because they couldn't get the documents over to the Philippines and back because it [mine] was a next day operation. I had a couple of contracts like those and I was able to survive during that period....I really went down a lot after that [however] because of the massive revolution now happening in America in telecommunications and capturing data at source....Four years ago you would sign those slips and ... that little slip of paper with those 16 keystrokes on it would be key-punched..They used to send out about 250,000 per day to be key-punched in Jamaica. ...Now you can just swipe it and it can go into the computer, the whole thing! (Interview Data, 1994).

The threat that recent advances in data processing technology and the general lowering of global telecommunications costs pose to the future of the Jamaican data-entry industry is recognised by most of the data-entry firms. Firms located in the digiport still maintain an international comparative advantage, given their access to a cheap source of labour, advanced telecommunications technology and generous tax and duty concessions. Interestingly, since the shake-out in the local data-entry industry there has been a constant growth in the number of data-entry firms entering the Montego Bay Free Zone. Between 1989 and 1993 for example, the number of information processing companies located at the JDI grew from three to sixteen, resulting in the almost complete occupancy of the digiport's rental space. The extent to which the advantages provided by cheap labour and free zone incentives will continue to attract foreign investors is unknown. For data-entry firms located outside the digiport, there are even fewer comparative advantages. The lack of a domestic market for data processing services and the relatively small supply of labour trained in the higher end of the information processing sector e.g. programmers and engineers, together with a lack of enthusiasm on the part of government and larger local capitalists, all threaten the prospects for the industry's growth in the future.

NEW SERVICES AND TRENDS FOR THE FUTURE: THE EXPORT INFORMATION SERVICES 1991-1994

While data-entry remains the oldest and largest of the information processing services exported from Jamaica, a number of other services are being offered. Telemarketing and GIS are two such services that are currently in operation. In 1993, there were four Telemarketing operations in Jamaica, all of which were located in the JDI. Only three companies currently operate GIS services in Jamaica, two in Kingston and one in the JDI.

Telemarketing

Telemarketing is a service which uses telephone communication to sell products and maintain existing customers. It is used in diverse operations such as surveying potential customers, providing answers to questions about particular products and retail distribution points, and selling products and services to groups that are identified as potential customers. The growth of services such as home buying in the United States makes this a lucrative sector, and the potential for expansion once the planned Information Super Highway becomes a reality is very positive. Telemarketing can be segmented into two main types of operations: Inbound and Outbound. Inbound operations refer to telephone transactions initiated by a customer who makes a call because he/she is already interested in a particular product or service. This form of telemarketing is generally less difficult to perform as the element of interest is already established. Outbound telemarketing on the other hand involves a telemarketing operator initiating the mart ing transaction. This form of telemarketing is generally more difficult as the telemarketer usually has to quickly develop a potential customer's interest and trust before a sale transaction can be successfully completed. Outbound and Inbound services may both involve transactions between one business and another, or between a business and consumer. Most telemarketing is weighted towards outbound services, as this is the segment that generates new consumers. This segment, however, is the most difficult to establish because success is easily influenced by factors such a caller's gender, accent or marketing style. A recent report by JAMPRO estimated that the revenue projections from outbound telemarketing services in the United States in 1991 were worth US$50 billion, and this represented a third of the entire global telemarketing market (JAMPRO, 1993).

Considerable labour cost differentials make the telemarketing service in Jamaica attractive to potential investors. In 1993, the average telemarketer in Jamaica earned between US$0.70 and $1.19 per hour, while her/his counterpart in the United States earned between US$6.00 and $14.00 per hour. While the Telemarketing firms that locate in Jamaica are also attracted to the island's advanced telecommunications infrastructure, it is not a major pull factor. In fact, on the basis of cost alone, the telephone service in Jamaica in far more expensive than the United States. In 1993 the minimum cost of a telephone line in Jamaica was US$0.22 per minute. This was more than twice the cost of the cheapest telephone line service in the United States (US$0.09 per minute) (JAMPRO 1993). Two years ago when the cost of a telephone line in the United States was higher, the advantages gained from access to low cost labour would have outweighed the relatively higher cost of the telecommunication service in Jamaica. This advantage has now been eroded and with continued competition among the deregulated telecommunications companies in the United States, there is likely to be even more reductions in the cost of telephone communication.

Access to cheap telecommunication lines, is not the only factor that has limited the sector's expansion. The larger corporations in the United States have been reluctant to locate their services in Jamaica because of the sensitivity of the service to perceived cultural differences. In the case of one of the United States largest telemarketing agencies that recently closed its operations in Jamaica, there were concerns that characteristics of the Jamaican work-force such as accent, and the reluctance of large corporations to conduct business off-shore limited the number of contracts that were received. In its policy guidelines to the government, JAMPRO has stated that telemarketing services can be successfully exported from Jamaica if emphasis is placed on the inbound business-to-business segment of the market. While in theory this appears to be the least risky segment of the market (the inbound caller has already expressed interest in the product or service), its success is highly dependent on the extent to which potential clients feel that quality of service can be maintained.

Geographic Information Services (GIS)

This is one of the newest export information service sectors in Jamaica, with only two firms currently in operation. GIS like text-entry involves the capture of data by digitising information and converting it into computer readable formats. Unlike text-entry, however, GIS converts paper drawings into computer readable formats and allows data to be organised, analysed and modelled spatially. While GIS is relatively underdeveloped as an export information service, it is one of the fastest growing niche markets, and is currently valued at $5 billion in the US alone with an annual growth rate of 22 per cent (JAMPRO, 1993). GIS constitutes an interesting niche market because it requires technical expertise at both the low paying and high paying ends of the market. In terms of providing employment, GIS is unlikely to make a significant contribution. In fact it is likely to result in the transfer of labour from under-resourced sectors, because the workers that are selected to do GIS are generally trained draftsmen and technical drawers. It is also to be noted that this sector, which is generally higher paying than text-entry (in interviews, managers suggested figures of US$3.40 per hour), is unlikely to provide employment opportunities for women because of the skill specifications required.

CONCLUSION

The export information processing industry has not become the dynamic foreign exchange earner and development catalyst that was envisaged in 1986 when the first steps to promote the sector were taken. This has not occurred for a number of reasons. First, in giving preferential treatment to investors with foreign currency, the government created a dual industry characterised by a growing enclave sector with access to financial incentives and technological supports, and a stagnating local sector with no financial incentives and more expensive technological supports. For local information processing firms, the relatively high cost of gaining access to efficient telecommunications services has forced most to rely on less efficient and expensive methods of information transfer such as courier services and modem transfers. Second, the inadequate attention paid to marketing, cost the industry dearly in its early years. Neither government nor industry members anticipated the large amount of investment that was required to market the industry and as a result most of the local operations have remained very small and in some cases unprofitable. Third, the comparative advantage gained from a supply of cheap labour and spatial proximity gave the industry a false sense of security. Technological advances are rapidly eroding these advantages and the industry is likely to suffer from the fact that there is not a large technically skilled labour force capable of providing services at the higher end of the information processing service.

In spite of these failings, the export information processing industry continues to be an attractive potential source of foreign exchange earnings and technology transfer. In order for the export information processing industry to positively contribute to the development process in Jamaica, a mutually supportive environment will need to be created. In such an environment, the government, TOJ and firms involved in information services will need to devise strategies that enable the local information processing industry to become globally competitive in factors other than the sale of cheap female labour. Thus for example, the current differentials in the cost of access to telecommunications facilities between firms inside and outside of free zone areas, will need to be removed. Strategies that will aid the industry's growth, however, must go beyond establishing equal competition within national boundaries. As information services become increasingly dependent on the high speed transmission of data, international comparative advantages will become largely dependent on the cost of telecommunications services.

REFERENCES

Adam, C., W. Cavendish and P. Mistry. 1992. *Adjusting Privatization: Case Studies from Developing Countries* . Kingston: Ian Randle Publishers.

Antonelli, C. 1991. *The Diffusion of Advanced Telecommunications in Developing Countries.* Development Centre Studies. Paris: OECD.

Barnes, C. 1989. Data Entry Demands. *Sistren Magazine* 11 (3), 18-20.

Dunn, H. S. 1991. Telecommunications and Underdevelopment: A Policy Analysis of the Historical Role of Cable and Wireless in the Caribbean. City University PhD Thesis (unpublished) London.

Elbert, B. 1989. *Private Telecommunications Networks.* Massachusetts: Artech House Inc.

EXIS. 1989. *'Going for the Iceberg: A Blueprint for Growth and Development in the Export of Information Services'.* Unpublished Report prepared by the Jamaica Exporters of Information Services Group, a sub-group of the Jamaica Exporters Association.

JAMPRO, 1993. *Framework Paper of Determining Guidelines for Industrial Policy in the Jamaican Information Processing Industry.* Prepared and compiled by the Information Processing Unit. October. Unpublished Draft document of the Jamaican Promotions Organisation.

Nulty, T. 1991. Emerging Issues in World Telecommunications. In

Restructuring and Managing the Telecommunications Sector. Wellenius, B., P. Stern, T. Nulty, and R.Stern (eds), 7-18. A World Bank Symposium. Washington: World Bank.

Pearson, R. 1991. *New Technology and the Internationalisation of Office Work: Prospects and Conditions for Women's Employment in LDC's.* Gender Analysis in Development, Sub Series April Norwich: School of Development Studies.

Pearson, R. 1993. Gender & New Technology in the Caribbean: New Work for Women. In Momsen, J. (ed) *Women and Change in the Caribbean.*, 287-295. Kingston: Ian Randle Publishers.

PIOJ. 1990. *Jamaica Five Year Development Plan 1990-1995.* Kingston: Planning Institute of Jamaica.

TOJ. 1993. 'Telecommunications of Jamaica...on the Record. In the Public Interest'. *The Sunday Gleaner* Nov. 28, 16A-17A.

UNIDO. 1989. *New Technologies and Global Industrialization: Prospects for Developing Countries.* Prepared by the Regional and Country Studies Branch Industrial Policy and Perspectives Division. Vienna: United Nations Industrial Development Organization.

Wilson, M. 1994. *Jamaica's Back Offices: Direct Dial Dependency?* Paper Presented to the Association of American Geographers, March 29-April 2, San Francisco, California.

FOOTNOTES

1. The licence could be revoked if the government having given two and a half years notice, decided to acquire at an independently assessed fair market value, the telephone undertakings of either the JTC or JAMINTEL. The licence could also be revoked if the Minister of Public Utilities determined that TOJ had failed to comply with its terms after a reasonable opportunity had been given for the failure of the remedied.

2. Digital Eastern Caribbean Microwave System.

3. The data-entry operations described here use Pearson's (1991, 16) classification of data entry jobs currently undertaken in off-shore sites.

4. In December 1995 TOJ and the government's Fair Trading Commission (FTC) agreed on revisions to the Company's policy on connectivity. However, equipment regarded as "by-passing the network" were excluded. See text of agreement in foregoing chapter.

10

CUBAN TELECOMMUNICATIONS SYSTEMS:
CONFRONTED BY GLOBAL POLITICAL AND TECHNOLOGICAL CHANGE

Hopeton S. Dunn and Felipe Noguera

Introduction

Although Cuba sits in the geographical centre of the Caribbean basin, it remains a country about which little is known in the region. Most analysts agree that ignorance, rather than knowledge is what characterizes the relationship between Cuba and most of its neighbours. In an article assessing Cuba's problems and possibilities, Saunders notes that information sharing would figure quite high on the agenda of a renewed phase of regional dialogue with Cuba. He adds that 'it is also readily apparent in Cuba that there is little information about the Caribbean'. (CANABUSINESS September 1993: 11). The major factors determining Caribbean and global information levels about Cuba are the continuing hostile relationship between that country and the United States, and the related limitation in reach of the Cuban telecommunication system itself.

This paper seeks to provide information and analysis on the structures, technologies and policies which constitute the Cuban telecommunications system, and the global factors which affect it in the first half of the 1990s. It is argued that recent changes in the regulations governing telecommunication between Cuba and the United States are motivated by economic necessity on both sides. Strong corporate pressures are emanating from US telecom conglomerates worried that European rivals could preempt their control of a telecom market on the US doorstep. In Cuba acute economic and social pressures are converging to pry open the hitherto closed Cuban telecommunications market.

This study draws on information from the Cuban Ministry of Communication, from the US State Department, Congressional and private sector sources. The specifics of the Cuban telecom industry are provided as a basis for understanding the significance of political and economic developments which are occurring within Cuba itself, as well as in the United States.

US EMBARGO AND BLOCKADE

One major reason for the paucity of information about Cuba is the lack of reliable, direct telephone communication between Cuba and the rest of the world, including among its Caribbean and American neighbours. Severe tele-communications restrictions, as well as the political and diplomatic isolation of Cuba in the wider international community were imposed by the United States after the triumph of the 1959 Cuban revolution. Direct links between Cuba and the English-speaking Caribbean, already limited before 1959, were further restricted because most calls to Cuba were routed via the United States. With direct telephone links barred, contact between the US and Cuba took place only by routing calls via third countries, particularly through Canada. This resulted in a very low success rate in the placement of calls to Cuba. According to the *Wall Street Journal*, of 60-million attempted calls to Cuba annually, only 500,000 or less than one per cent, were successful. (*Wall Street Journal*, October 26, 1993: 2)

The American Telephone and Telegraph Company (AT & T), the only US telecom operator authorized to relay indirect calls to Cuba, has been barred by US regulations from sharing the proceeds from these calls with the Cuban telecommunications authorities. As a result, since 1966, Cuba's share of revenue from calls with the US has been deposited into a US escrow account, the balance of which exceeded US$ 85-million in 1994.

In response to intense lobbying by American telecommunications companies, the US State Department issued new guidelines in July 1993 liberalizing previous regulations on telephone contact with Cuba. These rules enabled US companies to provide a new, if still limited, range of international telecom services in co-operation with Cuba. The new regulations also allowed Cuba access for the first time in 28 years to profits generated by calls between the two countries, though not to the accumulated sum in the sequestered US escrow account. In March 1994, eight months after the issuing of the new regulations, the Cuban government signed a series of agreements with three United States telephone companies, MCI, Wiltel and LDDS, aimed at re-establishing direct telephone links between Cuba and the US.

However, many of the restrictions remain in force. There is still very little reliable information becoming available about important aspects of Cuban life. Basic data about Cuba's communications and information infrastructure have also been quite rare, including details about the technological advances and deficiencies. For the English-speaking world, the situation is compounded by language differences. Yet, information on Cuba is increasingly being regarded as important given the growing interest on the part of global telecommunications and other companies as well as by CARICOM for greater collaboration with Cuba, and in light of the new opportunities and challenges which are emerging in that country.

CUBA: THE CONTEXT

In population terms, Cuba is the largest territory in the Caribbean basin area. With a population of 10.4 million people, it is twice the size of all CARICOM member countries combined, although its physical size is only half that of Guyana. Most Cubans (73%) live in urban areas, including the capital, Havana, and in 14 provincial capitals. Havana alone accounts for 2.1 million or nearly 20% of the total population. Besides being the seat of government, Havana city is also the country's main industrial and commercial zone, and has the highest concentration of telephones. The 27% of dwellers in Cuba's rural areas are mainly subsistence farmers and agricultural workers.

Cuba has a male-dominated labour force, with 60% of the employed population being men and just under 40% women. Services, including education, commerce, health, transport and tourism accounted for close to 50% of the employed labour force in 1988. An industrial sector of mainly mining and manufacturing accounted for 22%, with agriculture and fishery being the next largest employer at 18%. According to the 1981 Census, two thirds of the Cuban population was of a European ethnic origin, 12% was of African stock and 22% of mixed ethnic background. (Stubs 1989:v) A history of Iberian colonization has left Spanish as the main language, although both Russian and English are in use among sections of the population.

The triumph of the Cuban revolution under the military leadership of Fidel Castro in January 1959, led to the exodus of a large section of the technical, industrial and commercial elite to the United States. Strained relations with the United States and the establishment of diplomatic ties with the Soviet Union characterized the immediate aftermath of the Revolution. The US severed diplomatic relations with Cuba in January 1961, and backed an unsuccessful mercenary invasion of the country in that same year. Cuba moved closer to the Soviet Union and the socialist bloc in the face of an economic embargo, and following the 'missiles crisis' and short-lived naval blockade in October 1962. Among the sectors affected by the trade embargo was telecommunications, particularly with the United States.

Despite hardships, Cuba recorded impressive growth in its main social sectors, particularly health and education throughout the decade of the 1970s. However, a high level of military expenditure, a single dominant export crop, lack of industrial and ideological renewal, as well as heavy reliance on Soviet trade and grant funding all helped to create special vulnerabilities within the country's economy and society. By the mid 1980s, with instability in Eastern Europe and the former USSR, these factors began to make a decisive impact on Cuba's day to day life.

According to a 1994 US Agency for International Development (USAID) report to the American Congress 'Cuba is in the midst of an unparalleled economic crisis precipitated by the break-up of the Soviet Union. The Soviet bloc accounted for 85% of Cuba's foreign trade until 1989. Between 1989 and 1993, Cuba's Gross Social Product (GSP= GDP minus services and salaries) declined by between 50-60 per cent; imports declined from US$ 8.1 billion to US$ 1.7 billion; and from 1989 to 1992 oil imports dropped from 13.3 million tons to 6 million tons. In 1993, Cuba had an external debt of US$ 7.8 billion with exports registered at $2.8 billion and is in default on most of its debt obligations. Shrinking foreign exchange and dramatic reductions in investment have squeezed production and capital formation.' (Extracts from a statement to the US Congress by Mark Schneider, US AID official in March 1994. Reported in the *Jamaica Herald*, April 3, 1994, page 2B)

The statement to the US Congress, presented by USAID official noted further that shortages of fuel and other inputs had led to a complete or partial shutdown of numerous plants, that drastic reductions had taken place in commercial and passenger transport and that open unemployment, which was recorded at 6 per cent in 1988, increased in 1992 to somewhere between 10 and 18 per cent. The absence of major political reform in Cuba was also noted, including prohibitions against pluralistic democratic institutions.

To the extent that this account by the US administration may be regarded as emanating from an implacable enemy of the Fidel Castro government in Cuba, the emphases should be regarded cautiously. However, the overall indication of severe economic and social problems related to the sudden collapse of the Soviet

Union in 1989 is nowhere being contested. Other analysts, from a different perspective take a more long term, geo-political view of Cuba's dilemma. The Deputy Director of Cuba's Centro de Investigaciones de la Economia Mundial, Jose Luis Rodriguez, observes that 'the economic blockade imposed by the United States since 1961 forced Cuba to re-orient abruptly its foreign trade and financial relations, and (thus) limited the policy options within the development strategy. The cost to the Cuban economy of the hostile actions by the United States...amounts to about \$38-billion. Only the socialist countries, and especially the Soviet Union, were able to guarantee the delivery of goods and services essential to the development of the Cuban economy while offering preferential and stable markets for Cuban exports.' (Rodriguez, Jose Luis, 1993)

Rodriguez noted that in 1989, 83.1 per cent of Cuba's trade was with the socialist countries, 9.9 per cent with developed capitalist countries and 7 per cent with developing countries. The new found pro-western trade orientation of several of its Eastern European trading partners as well as Cuba's inability to meet debt commitments among these former socialist allies meant that these trading relations 'practically vanished in 1992'. In the case of the Soviet Union, imports fell by 50 % between 1989 and 1991 and 73 per cent lower in 1992 compared with 1989. According to Rodriguez, the result of these and other developments was that Cuba has had to 'implement a new set of restrictive economic measures that corresponded to the second phase of the emergency programme known as the Special Period in Peacetime that had begun in September of 1990.'

Among the measures adopted by the Fourth Congress of the Cuban Communist Party in October 1991 to help alleviate the crisis was the promotion of joint ventures with foreign investors, greater flexibility regarding economic organization and a more flexible approach towards managing trade. (*Granma* Newspaper, October 17, 1991 p 3). Under Cuban law, first promulgated in 1983 and revalidated more recently, government departments were authorized to create mixed enterprises with participation of up to 49 per cent foreign capital to government's 51 per cent. (Act Number 50 of the Cuban Parliament 1983]. Saunders points out that 'Non-US companies, particularly European ones, have not been slow to grasp the opportunities of over 100 successful joint ventures with the government of Cuba.' (CANABUSINESS Sept 1993:10). He notes that an estimated US\$ 500-million had already been invested, including ventures with Canadian and other companies for nickel mining, oil exploration and tourism.

Telecommunications Liberalization

The telecommunications and information technology areas, also severely hit by the economic crisis, are among those in which this policy of joint ventures is being implemented. According to the Ministry of Communications which oversees the telecom sector in Cuba, most joint ventures operate under an autonomous, privatised framework, allowing profits to shareholders. The ministry recently established a self-financing mechanism to ensure that external resources can earn a profitable annual return on investments. The largest joint venture arrangement in the sector relates to Cuba's International Telecommunications service provider INTERTEL, which is 50 per cent owned by the government and the other 50 per cent by private overseas joint venture partners.

Other joint ventures in the sector include a contract with the private firm ITALcable for the development and installation of five satellite earth stations, with an agreement that on completion the stations will be 100% owned by ITALcable. Telefonica of Spain also operates a small Vista satellite earth station in Havana, providing an alternative transmission path for international traffic between Spain and Cuba. In the newly developing area of cellular telephone services, the Mexican and Cuban governments recently established a new company CUBACEL as a joint venture operating within the city of Havana.

Telecom Structures and Institutions

Cuba's main overseas communications linkages, administered by INTERTEL, are carried out via both INTERSPUTNIK and INTELSAT. Messages are transmitted and received by a Standard A satellite earth station, one dedicated Vista earth station and 5 smaller earth stations linking locations in such major cities as Havana, Veradero, Cayo Largo, Guardalavaca and Santiago de Cuba. There is also one digital international gateway switch, an electronic telex switch, digital microwave radio and recently installed fibre-optic systems. A long-distance analogue cable system linking Moscow and Havana which was completed in February 1975, is now due for replacement. It provides submarine interconnectivity not just to the Russian republic but also to many other countries in Eastern and central Europe.

At the end of 1958, before the triumph of the Cuban Revolution, Cuba was served by a submarine cable link to the United States and a tropospheric scatter system of the kind which also existed in the Eastern Caribbean up to the early 1970s. The Cuban Ministry of Communication notes that this external system was a monopoly controlled by a large United States company, leaving very little scope for national policy planning. In 1958 international telephone traffic reached 301,000 overseas calls, directed mostly at the USA. In 1990, overseas calls had increased to nearly 2-million, with 1.2 million to the United States. Income convertible from international calls in 1992-93 was US$ 26.3 million. In addition, revenue from hotel-based international telecourier service amounted to

US $1.9-million. A digital international telephone switch which has been installed is capable of providing service to subscribers off remote switches, a central office telex switch and a fibre optic network which is linked to the switching hubs in Havana. The digital central office switching capacity is 510 international trunk lines and 5000 country subscribers. The digital telegraph switching capacity is 320 international trunks, 1070 national trunks and 3048 telex subscribers.

Internal Systems

A microwave system, inaugurated in 1977, constitutes the main artery for national long distance transmission. The system covers the entire island between the cities of Pinar Del Rio and Guantanamo, with two bi-directional channels for television and one broadband telephone channel (960 telephone channels in the Havana to Santiago link). The microwave system greatly improved the quality of television transmission for the entire island, as well as for internal long distance telephone traffic. There is also a communication link by coaxial cable from the city of Pinar Del Rio in the eastern extreme of the island to the city of Guantanamo in the extreme west. This incorporates the 14 provincial capitals and important municipalities of the country. It serves as a long distance data transmission link as well as provides a back-up to the microwave system. At present there are 25,000 long-distance telephone channels, representing a 20-fold increase since 1958.

The internal telecommunication system is Cuba, which is mostly owned and operated by the government's Ministry of Communications, suffers from ageing equipment and inadequate capacity. Figures available for Havana indicate that there are 220,898 installed lines, giving the city a teledensity of 13.3 telephones for each 100 of population in 1992. However close to 30% of these lines were out of service, and customer premises equipment was averaging 35 years of age, with a quarter exceeding 50 years old. However there has been modest growth in teledensity and the national spread of access to the phone. National figures for 1958 indicate an 8.9 penetration rate or 124,660 telephone lines. At that time the telephone set count in Havana alone represented 73% of the national total.

Even within a framework of economic hardship, the Cuban government has been attempting to maintain a programme of network replacement. Between 1987 and 1988, a total of 27.7 million pesos were invested in the Havana network. The money was used mainly for the installation of new cables, totalling 1655 kilometres. In 1989 and 1990, a further 1003 kilometres of cable were installed along with 47,260 new lines. A modest but significant 70 kilometres of fibre optic cable was also installed for more efficient transmission between Havana's central office switches.

In order to accommodate the new digital technology alongside the old analogue (Strowger) step by step system of transmission, the Cubans have developed what their technicians call the digi-step system. This involves a digital central office system linked to remote subscribers using the old step by step technique on the periphery of the system. In order to achieve compatibility, the Cuban technicians have modified available software and added special circuits constructed by an indigenous Research and Development (R&D) Centre.

While the pre-revolutionary pattern of concentrating development of the network around the capital city continues, major efforts have been made by the Castro government to improve tele-accessibility by rural citizens and mountain dwellers. Eight of Cuba's provinces range over mountainous territory: Pinar Del Rio, Villa Clara, Sancti Spiritus, Cienfuegos, Holguin, Santiago de Cuba, Granma and Guantanamo. For a long time, the mountain dwellers in these regions were isolated from the rest of the population. Very poor peasants and agricultural workers were often out of touch with the social, political and mainstream economic life of the country.

Local Telecom Centres

Over the last two decades, a concept referred to as *Centres for Community Communications* was put into practice, to help meet the communication needs of both this rural agrarian population as well as poor inner city dwellers. To offer this service, shared utilization of a particular dwelling unit was implemented, bringing together conditions which permit the provision of telephone, telegraph, postal services, and mass media. All of this is controlled and administered by the community communication centres. Community shareholders receive a commission, based on the performance and profitability of the Centres which operate as family co-operative concerns. These Centres are linked by telephone lines with a central office switch within each rural or urban locality. Among the services offered in the Centres are telephone calls from the localities to any part of the national territory, reception of personal calls, pre-arranged calls, messaging, call forwarding, retrieval and referral of faxes, sending and receiving telegrams, sale of newspapers and magazines etc.

The Cuban authorities indicate that there are more than 1700 of these Centres throughout the country, with positive results for the population. According to an official of the Cuban ministry, 'although Cuba's capacity indicators do not illustrate spectacular statistics, its achievements in social communication and tele-accessibility are impressive. Today, telephone, mail and telegram services are well within easy reach of the entire Cuban population, transforming the quality of life of its inhabitants'.

Local Equipment Production And Import Substitution

Unlike most other Caribbean territories, Cuba has an industrial plant for the manufacture of telephone sets, outside plant equipment, specialized tools; the assembly of cable-laying vehicles, the design and the manufacture of cross connection cabinets and associated circuits for telephone plant. Earnings from telephone production in 1992-93 reached 195.2 million pesos. Other services provided by this industrial unit includes repair and recovery of communication equipment, manufacture of terminal boxes, cables, reels, postal equipment, climate control equipment and electronic covers.

The communication ministry's activities are supported by a number of other specialized state-owned companies. One of these, Empresa de Proyectos de Communicaciones (EPROTEL) provides project management and engineering services to the sector. Another firm, United Techniques, undertakes engineering and construction work for transmission systems, radio communications networks, data processing establishments and special services in energy conservation and climatization.

The human resource development, technical expertise and capacity to carry out these and other functions within the telecom sector have been nurtured by a Cuban Research and Development Institute — The Instituto de Investagicion y Desarrollo de Telecom. This agency deals with the development of both hardware and software systems for production, switching and transmission. According to the Ministry, the main focus of the R and D section is import substitution for the telecom sector. The Institute has developed a system for rural, multi-access analogue or digital switching, known as Systema Satel. Working closely with the Cuban Institute of Sciences, the telecom R&D agency has also developed a 30-channel multiplex system (PCM) and a 2 mgb digital radio network.

National television covers 85% of Cuban territory, despite the overall mountainous character of much of the country. A system of tropospheric defraction propagation is used to determine the zones and microzones not receiving adequate signals. A nationally designed and manufactured network of TV signal repeaters is used, with each carrying 1 to 4 watts of power generated by solar panels. On the software side, the Cubans report that approximately 80% of their television programmes is locally produced and that there is advanced experimentation with a locally designed prototype for a High Definition Television (HDTV) system.

PROSPECTS

It is clear from the available data that the telecommunications system in Cuba is struggling against the formidable odds of a crippling US trade embargo and from the collapse of the main alternative source of supply for equipment and capital. Within its own meagre resources, the Cuban industry has displayed remarkable innovation in the use of local technology and resources. The combination of old and new technology, the manufacture of telephone sets, cables, switches, the systematic use of solar energy and the establishment of the multi-purpose community centres for rural and inner-city communication services are as much signs of creativity and commitment as they are indicators of economic deprivation and pressure. Much of the network is between 30 and 50 years old, with a high proportion of defective equipment and a level of demand for service which outstrips supply many times over.

It is a recognition of these constraints which has contributed to the Cuban government policy of opening up for joint venture participation with private foreign capital. In telecom, as in other sectors, pressures are mounting for the re-integration of Cuba into the economy of the Western world. Former U.S. Diplomat Wayne Smith, who has led exploratory delegations to Cuba against the wishes of the State Department, has been among many American leaders advocating improved relationships with Cuba in all spheres.

European and American telecom conglomerates have also been demanding greater flexibility to permit them to establish platforms from which to compete in the future. Many such companies are beating a path to Cuba to bid for a foothold in what they expect will be a lucrative market in the post communist era.

Among these is Cable and Wireless. Fresh from its most recent conquests in the English-speaking region, the British-based transnational firm attempted to enter the Cuban market in 1993. Former Jamaican Prime Minister, Michael Manley, in private practice as a consultant, was engaged to provide introductions to a team of Cable and Wireless executives, led by Mayer Matalon, Chairman of the company's Jamaican subsidiary, Telecommunications of Jamaica (TOJ). Although the visit does not appear to have borne much fruit, it indicates the global vision of Cable and Wireless and its willingness to use its anglophone Caribbean base as a springboard for expansion into Latin America.

The Cuban authorities have reacted more favourably to overtures from the American carrier MCI Communications Corporation and at least two smaller operating companies. Under the memorandum of understanding with MCI, LDDS and Wiltel, revenues from long-distance calls between the two countries will be shared 50-50 on a US prescribed tariff of US$1.20 a minute. Within months of signing the memorandum, MCI announced direct long distance service to Cuba. It said such calls would generate an estimated US$ 60-million annually. Before approaching the Cuban Ministry of Communications, these US companies had to negotiate several barriers erected by the 1992 Cuban Democracy Act. In a 1993 memorandum to the Chairman of the US Federal Communications Commission (FCC), the State Department set out the following 'policy guidelines for approving proposals for telecommunications between the United States and Cuba:

1. Proposals must have the potential to be operational within a year.

2. Proposals must be limited to equipment and services necessary to deliver a signal to an international telecommunications gateway in Cuba.

3. Settlements more favourable to Cuba than the current 50/50 split of the $1.20 per minute accounting rate shall not be permitted. In addition, Cuba shall cover half the cost of construction, maintenance and/or lease of transmission facilities, consistent with standard FCC practice.

4. Proposals utilizing modes of communication already in place between the US and Cuba (eg satellite, the undersea cable) will be approved. Proposals involving new modes of communications (eg fibre optic cable) will be reviewed by the appropriate agencies on a case by case basis.

5. All circuits to Cuba must be specifically authorized. Carriers shall report the number of circuits activated by facility on June 30 and December 31 of each year, and on the one-year anniversary of the notification by FCC in the Federal Register.

6. Treasury (Department) will license each US company or US subsidiary to remit to Cuba the full share of Cuba's earnings from the service approved by FCC. State (Department) will explore with Treasury and Commerce the possibility of licensing payment-in-kind (e.g., earth stations, satellite equipment etc.) on a case by case basis.

7. There will be no access to Cuba's blocked account of AT&T's past remittances.

8. All applications approved by FCC must also be licensed as appropriate by Treasury and Commerce in consultation with State'. (US Department of State, letter to James H. Quello, Chairman FCC, July 22, 1993)

These regulations form part of the unfolding scenario involving adjustments by the governments of both Cuba and the US to a rapidly changing political, economic and technological environment. However, such detailed rule-making is increasingly being confronted by technological methods which threaten to undermine the regulations. Several telecommunications companies located in Miami are attempting to use data-compression technology to establish 'call-back' services to Cuba, circumventing AT&T, Cuba and the State Department rules. 'People on both sides need and want to make a connection', Jacob Solan told the *Wall Street Journal* after announcing his own call back facility. Using the '800' prefixes, callers dial a number which registers in a computer in London. The machine can automatically switch hundreds of calls between any two destinations. 'We do not believe anybody can block anybody from calling London', Solan has declared, 'but I'm ready to fight'. (*Wall Street Journal* October 26, 1993 p 2) The Israeli entrepreneur is reflecting the aggressive spirit which now marks the effort for alternative means of telecommunication linkages beyond large conglomerates. At the same time, as we have observed, it is the large conglomerates on the US side which are acting as the main motive force for change in American policy towards Cuban telecom. They are intent on securing a place in the Cuban telecommunications market for the future. In the case of the Cuban government, it is economic necessity of a different kind which is playing the central role in achieving a measure of accommodation with US capital. The need for hard currency, for new technology and for spare parts provides an overwhelming pressure for change. In both cases, there is a strongly shared need for global reach and an effective presence in the regional and global communications environment.

There are many lessons which the Cuban authorities can learn from the experience of the English-speaking Caribbean region. Among the more salutary would be that irrespective of the extent of equity divestment by the Cuban government, it cannot afford to divest regulatory responsibility, as many of its counterpart governments in the English-speaking Caribbean have done. For Cuba such a course of action would represent an untypical capitulation to tele-colonialism.

REFERENCES

Budhoo, Ken - 'Cuba Going for the Gold' — *Caribbean Contact*, January/February 1994 P 11.

Call, Mark - Competition for the Phone: The Path from Duopoly to Competition in Telecommunications — Adam Smith Institute, London, 1990.

Cuban Ministry of Communications - General Structure of Telecommunication System in Cuba — A Report to CANTO (unpublished), 1993.

Rodriguez, Jose Luis - The Cuban Economy in a Changing World, Paper presented to a Conference of the Association of Caribbean Economists (ACE), Kingston Jamaica, March 27, 1993.

Saunders, Ron - 'Cuba: Ripe for Caribbean Community Joint Ventures' — *CANABUSINESS*, September 1993 p 10-11.

Stubbs, Jean - Cuba: The Test of Time — Latin American Bureau, London 1989.

The Gleaner - 'Cable and Wireless has Eyes on Cuba' — November 23, 1993, p 1.

The Gleaner - 'US Phone Firms to Get Cuban Business' — March 14, 1994, p 3.

The Gleaner - 'US Backs Improved Telephone links to Cuba' — July 24, 1993 p 4.

The Jamaica Herald - 'The Cuban Dilemma' — April 3, 1994 p 2b.

The Wall Street Journal - 'Cuba Miami Phone Service Slated, Forcing US Trade Embargo Issue' — October 26, 1994 p 2.

United States Department of State - Memorandum to James H. Quello, Chairman, FCC, July 22, 1993 (unpublished).

PART FOUR

Regulatory and Ethical Implications

▌▌

STATE POLICY, GLOBAL TRENDS AND REGULATION IN BROADCASTING:
THE CASE OF JAMAICA

Martin Mordecai

INTRODUCTION

From its earliest beginnings governments have regarded broadcasting as different from the print media. One reason for this may be simply that in several countries the institution of the press was well established before, and in some cases helped to create, the nation state: the First Amendment to the United States Constitution, much celebrated by journalists and publishers, may not have been enacted, or at least so soon after the main document, if so many of the early American nationalists had not been printers and pamphleteers. Differences between the media themselves also account for the difference in treatment.

Printing makes use of privately-owned resources: equipment, paper and ink, usually paid for with private capital (and where paid for with government funds utilised very differently) brought together by human effort and human intelligence. The final product of all of these is, so to speak, in the gift of one individual to another: the production, distribution and consumption of printed matter are entirely private arrangements, or can be.

This is not so with broadcasting, at least as we have known it up to the ninth decade of this century. Bearing in mind its etymological roots in primitive agriculture, broadcasting must be a very public activity; and even if there is only one listener to a particular programme it reaches that listener through the use of the electro-magnetic spectrum, which is a publicly-owned and state-managed resource. That ownership and management of that resource is a universal legal principle, re-inforced by international treaties to which all countries adhere by signature and/or practice. The principle of public ownership and management is not challenged in its basic assumptions because the certain consequence of an unregulated environment is obvious to all: chaos and anarchy, possibly beyond the airwaves.

In its infancy broadcasting was something of a conundrum to its potential regulators, the governments. It had a familial relationship with telegraphy and telephony; and there were obvious similarities with the print media. But it differed from telegraphy/telephony in its ability to reach up to millions of people simultaneously, and from the press because in its final 'product' it was insubstantial.

Early broadcasters of the 1920s and 1930s, led the way out of the tangle of precepts according to the uses to which the new technology was put. In the United States the commercial potential of the new medium was quickly appreciated by private entrepreneurs who concentrated on providing a conduit for advertisements and sponsored entertainment. Thus broadcasting came first within the purview of the Federal Trade Commission — where indeed the regulation of advertising remains, even though broadcasting has been regulated since 1935 by the Federal Communications Commission. In Britain and much of Europe governments saw it as a public duty to harness broadcasting as a channel for the promotion by dissemination of the national culture (in as many forms as were susceptible to radio) and pertinent information, including but not limited to news. The regulatory forms devised were several: from the Royal Charter of the British Broadcasting Corporation (BBC) in Britain to the placement of control (technical and programming) within a cabinet ministry of the government, usually in the same department that controlled postal, telegraphic and telephone services, also usually owned by the state. European broadcasting was, in its early days, resolutely non-commercial and was supported by taxation of one form or another. Canada, befitting its character as a European-ised country next door to the United States — with a small population scattered over enormous distances and a difficult topography — developed a hybrid regulatory/programming framework with elements of both 'systems'.

REGULATORY CONUNDRUM

One of the intriguing aspects of the current discussion on appropriate regulatory structures for the information age is that, after decades of operating various 'definitions', 'solutions' and 'systems', governments once more find themselves faced with the same regulatory conundrum as their predecessors, created by the convergence of the technologies of telecommunications, broadcasting and the computer. Before tomorrow's putative regulators ask themselves the question how do I regulate they must answer the question: What am I seeking to regulate?

As the instruments of regulation are largely state instruments, they can tell us something of what the state wishes to accomplish, or to have accomplished, through the use of regulation. The convergence over the past two decades of the technologies of broadcasting and telecommunications has not only widened the landscape which regulators must address but transformed the substance of regulation. This is no less true in developing countries as in the more advanced, because convergence has had, as one of its *raisons d'etre*, its own internationalisation. The choices made by countries in the next few years, will have a crucial effect on their economic, and to some extent social and political, development in the next several decades; indeed the choices made in some countries will significantly affect those developments in others.

We shall look at regulation, therefore, from other than a conventional perspective: technical nature and extent; rather in terms of purpose: what does the regulator hope to achieve? What is the policy content of the regulation? Regulation will be examined as (positive) enabler/promoter rather than as (negative) definer. The possible consequences of choices made, and not made, in Jamaica over the past several years will be examined, and the issues facing the country articulated in the context of present global trends toward de-regulation and expansion of services and service areas.

EARLY JAMAICAN EXPERIENCE

Jamaican regulators did not need to ask themselves either question in 1939 when a private transceiver was pressed into service by the British authorities in order to broadcast information relating to the Second World War which had just begun in Europe. Using 'ham' radio equipment handed over to the government in compliance with war-time regulations, broadcasting was originally for one hour per week from the home of the owner of the equipment — which indeed remained the 'home' of Jamaican broadcasting until 1951. Daily broadcasts began, with the aid of a small staff, in May, 1940. There were very few sets which could receive the broadcasts at first, but this changed as the war continued, and especially afterwards when programming expanded to include interviews, music (both live and recorded) and even cricket from Sabina Park. The station, with the call sign *ZQI Jamaica*, was government-owned and operated as a section of the Department of Education; no commercials were permitted.

So popular did the service of *ZQI Jamaica* become that the government responded to public desire and gave a licence for commercial broadcasting to the Jamaica Broadcasting Company, a wholly-owned subsidiary of the Rediffusion Group of London, in 1950. The licence, issued under the Commercial Broadcasting and Re-diffusion Act of 1949, was signed by the Colonial Secretary, the top colonial civil servant. After a slow start (apart from the technical difficulties there was some initial resistance to the commercials, which were read in the studio and seen as interruptions) the new service became extremely popular and quickly linked various parts of Jamaica in a embryonic national service.

The expansion of service was not merely a commercial response to popular demand. The government required the licensee 'at his own expense (to) supply.....and install....upon such premises as may be specified by the government the appropriate number of wireless receiving sets......to enable such premises to be used as communal listening centres'. [MacGillivary/Judah, 1949: 3.] Similarly, the licensee was required to 'connect and keep connected (to the radio re-diffusion system) all Government or grant-aided secondary or elementary schools in such area'. Thus, by deliberate policy, was the attempt made to use radio (and rediffusion — crucial in an age before transistor radios) as a force for national cohesion; for identity or at least participation, by contact and simultaneity.

While these requirements were made by the colonial administration it must be remembered that by 1949 the relationship between governor and governed was changing: Jamaicans were playing an increasingly important role in the legislative and administrative arms of government. Two years before India had emerged from the crucible of the anti-colonial struggle to become a beacon for that two-thirds of the world not represented at the still-new United Nations. The very radio service which brought news of such titanic events into homes in remote parts of Jamaica (and of scores of other countries around the world) would have planted the seeds of self-awareness and possibility in the minds of at least some listeners.

What is now routinely referred to as the rising tide of nationalism had increasing influence on broadcasting policy as on other areas during the 1950s. As people became accustomed to the station, which called itself Radio Jamaica, its very popularity encouraged those, like Norman Manley, the Premier from 1955 to 1962, who felt that 'there are definite limitations to the service that can be rendered by a privately owned broadcasting company operating primarily as a profitable enterprise and depending entirely on commercial revenue to finance its operation.' [Norman Manley, 1958: 1] Mr. Manley felt that there were 'special needs...in the fields of self-expression, culture, information and entertainment' which fully commercial broadcasting could not fulfill. The government of 1958, which enjoyed full autonomy on internal matters, argued that 'unless specific measures are taken to guide the development and use of broadcasting in such a way as to maximize its contribution to the fulfilment of Jamaica's special needs and aspirations, the natural commercial pressures may result in its being developed along lines detrimental to those interests.' Mr. Manley was reporting to the House of Representatives on the report made to the government by Mr A.D. Dunton, Chairman of the Board of Governors of the Canadian Broadcasting Corporation, 'on all questions of broadcasting policy in Jamaica'. Dunton's recommendation, which Manley enthusiastically endorsed, was for

> 'a statutory broadcasting corporation.....and.....a public broadcasting service under that corporation, operating on semi-commercial lines.....The Corporation will be concerned with broadcasting 'for entertainment and relaxation; imparting objective news and information; the vitality of democratic institutions and values, free speech, the rule of law, respect for the individual, freedom of worship, freedom of enquiry; the health of the community, the efficiency of its economy, and its good repute abroad; the education of youth; sport; and the creative arts.'

That was the official unveiling of the idea for the Jamaica Broadcasting Corporation (JBC), the adoption of whose name required a change (by negotiation) in the name of the original operating company to Radio Jamaica Ltd, the name by which it is known today, still probably the country's most popular station.

The instruments of regulation saw parallel transformation during this period from 1939 to 1959. *ZQI Jamaica* operated under the Telegraph Control Law, which regulated the government-run telegraphic service and the operations of amateur radio. It is in the genesis of radio broadcasting in Jamaica, as an off-shoot of something that wasn't broadcasting, that a dichotomy was created which still distorts the regulatory landscape, and to which we will return.

With the introduction of commercial broadcasting, new structures had to be created. The Commercial Broadcasting and Radio Rediffusion Law was passed in 1949, under which the licence for Jamaica Broadcasting Company was issued by the aforementioned Colonial Secretary. A Broadcasting Authority was created, whose members were to be appointed by the Governor. Both in terms and precedence and practicality, it could not be any other way in 1949: there was no other locus of power which could have either issued the licence or appointed the Authority. What is more interesting is the changes that have taken place — or **not** taken place — in the issuing and regulation of licenses over the subsequent 45 years, for 32 of which Jamaica has been an independent country.

The Authority was created under the Broadcasting Rules, made as one of two Schedules to the Law, the other being the operating licence. Among the duties of the Authority were: 'to afford guidance to the Licensee as to the opinion of the Government upon the interpretation' of Rules about which the licensee may be in doubt; and 'to grant or refuse to grant ....permission to do any act in respect of which the consent of the Authority is required to be obtained under these Rules' — but not one of the Rules pertains to a matter on which that consent is required. It is difficult not to conclude that the only real role of the Authority was, in the absence of administrative structures like Ministries, purely to 'act as a channel of liaison between the government and the Licensee', as the Schedule says. Nowhere is the real relationship between the Licensee, the Authority and the Government set out more clearly than in the final Rule, number 8, which permits the changing of the rules by the Authority, but 'with the consent of the Licensee and the approval of the government in Council' (my emphasis). [CBRRL, 1949: 7]

Being unsure as to exactly what the new station intended to broadcast, the government set out comprehensive guidelines as to what may *not* be broadcast: from 'any abusive comment upon any race, creed or religion' to 'any matter which describes repellantly any function or symptomatic results of disturbances of the human body or relief granted in such disturbances through the use of any appliance or medicament' — the latter of which, almost verbatim ('repellantly' replaced by 'offensively') is still part of the Broadcasting Regulations!

The licensee had, with regard to news broadcasts, 'a duty.....to regard the fundamental purpose of such broadcasts as being to afford to the public an opportunity of knowing what is happening and of understanding the meaning of what is happening so as to form their own conclusions upon matters of public interest.' To help the public in forming those conclusions the licensee was required, under the terms of his licence, to 'transmit matter emanating from the British Broadcasting Corporation (BBC) or from any British Regional Caribbean Broadcasting Station (all owned by the respective civil authorities).....for such periods as shall amount to not less than thirty minutes on each day and to not less than than ten hours in each week.' No advertisement or commercial could be associated in any way with such broadcasts.

That 'belt and braces' approach was reinforced further in the licence, under which the governor in Executive Council could require 'a written statement of the general nature and source of all matter or of any class of matter (which the licensee) may propose to transmit;' the licensee could then be required by the governor not to broadcast such matter.

All these powers were vested in the governor in Executive Council; the Authority had no status in the 1949 Law, so could not enforce any of the Rules by which it was set up. Ten years later, the Broadcasting Authority was given statutory identity in the amended Act; from the title of which the word 'commercial' had been removed. Consequent on the assumption of full internal self government, the Authority (there were to be 'five or three members') was to be appointed by the Minister, who also named the Chairman and Deputy Chairman.

The role of the Authority was refined in one area: it became 'the duty of the Authority....to advise the Minister on any matter within its knowledge or on which the Minister may seek its advice; and (in particular) to advise in relation to —

(a) the terms and conditions on which the licences are to be granted; *and*

(b) the frequencies, call signs and power to be used by licensees.' [BRRA, 1959: 10]

This obligation was, in the event, an empty device: only one new broadcasting licence was issued in 30 years, in 1963 to JBC for television service, and until the late 1980s no other application for either radio or television was seriously considered. And while the Authority may advise the Minister about frequencies, call signs and output power, it had no power to set those standards, only to enforce them at second-hand as among the terms of the licence. The establishment and monitoring of technical standards was done by the Post and Telegraph Department of the Ministry of Public Utilities and Works.

INDEPENDENCE AND BEYOND

A more significant change was made in 1962, when the law was revised to accommodate JBC's television service and the possibility of closed-circuit television. This gave the Authority the power, after consultation with the licensees and with the approval of the Minister, to make regulations; this indicated at least an awareness of a possibly semi-autonomous regulatory body. Such regulations could, inter alia, 'control the character and standards of programmes broadcast by licensees, and to provide for the allocation of time to the broadcasting of programmes which are of Jamaican origin or performed by Jamaicans'. Jamaica was by then an independent country, a new member of the United Nations; the nationalist concerns of the fifties were articulated in a new flag and, other symbols of nationhood and a public pre-occupation, at least among the intelligentsia, with the defining of a Jamaican 'identity'. The electronic media was perceived by policy makers as a place where such an identity could be both forged and reflected.

That regulatory notion itself has become an index of identity. The idea of a central authority setting necessarily subjective standards is a thoroughly European one. However, among that same articulate minority of Jamaicans who formed the body politic and opinion-shapers, there was also a strong awareness of the other, closer tradition of the United States and the (apparent) absence of statutory controls there. The argument continues to this day, and we will return to it in this paper; suffice to say at this point that such regulations still have not yet been made, more than 30 years after the power was bestowed on the regulatory body to make them; and that that power is still on the books.

No attempt was made in the revised (1962) Act to give the Authority, beyond advice to the Minister, any power to set the technical parameters of broadcasting; that remained where it had been from the beginning of broadcasting, with the Post and Telegraphs Department.

It should not however be thought that successive Broadcasting Authorities did nothing. The files might suggest that the archetypal man-in-the-street of the fifties and sixties took a keener interest in what the media offered him than does his contemporary counterpart. Some of the concerns about a Jamaican identity were indeed expressed to the Authority and the stations by disgruntled or approving listeners and viewers, along with complaints and comments about news and politics. On occasion the Authority, on its own initiative, required responses from the licensees, including the JBC, on matters of taste and accuracy, and regarding possible breaches of licences or the regulations.

On the other hand it would be an exaggeration to characterize the Authority as pro-active in its general demeanour. For one thing its members, all professionals in other areas or retired civil servants, met as was necessary; and the body was serviced by a part-time secretary in the relevant Ministry. So that when the term of the Authority appointed in 1974 ran out in 1977 and a new body was not appointed, it is fair to surmise that hardly anyone except perhaps a few persons in the Ministry and the two electronic media houses would have noticed. It is ironic, though, and not necessarily accidental (nor unfortunate, in the event) that during a period when the Jamaican media found itself not only the reporter of issues and news, but as news itself, and a contentious issue in the day-to-day politics of the country -— and even of its relations with other countries — there was no body that could play the role of arbiter, or 'referee'.

The reasons for this, the history of the period, and the issues themselves, are not appropriate fodder for this discussion. However, it is important to note that between 1977 and 1986, a period of the most profound changes in modern Jamaican political, social and economic life, a period moreover when all radio and television outlets were owned or controlled by the Jamaican government, there was no regulatory body for the electronic media —- only the government itself! At the same time the media continued to function, in general falling no further short of its responsibilities than before. News and public information were reported, national and community events were covered to the limit of available resources, programming reflected resources and perceived markets for the most part. Life, in and with the media, somehow proceeded.

THE 1980S — THE BROADCASTING COMMISSION

A new regulatory body, the Broadcasting Commission , was finally established in 1986, by amendment to Part IV of the Broadcasting and Radio ReDiffusion Act. The changes were more than cosmetic. The authority to appoint members was removed from the minister and given to the Governor General, who 'after consultation with the Prime Minister and the Leader of the Opposition' appoints 'not less than three nor more than five' persons. (The same method of appointment is applied with respect to the Electoral Advisory Commission, a product of the turbulent Seventies.) Commissioners can only be removed by vote of two-thirds of both Houses of Parliament.

The other major change relates to 'impartiality in political broadcasts', built around provisions to prevent the abuse for party political purposes of time 'allocated to the government for broadcasts for reasons of emergency or in the national interest', including 'to attack the policies, plans or programmes of any political party or parties' or to broadcast 'information which is inaccurate'. This cluster of issues was at the heart of the political struggles of the 1980s as played out in the press and electronic media, prompting the Jamaica Labour Party's 1980 election manifesto to call for the establishment of a 'media commission' to regulate all media. The Commission was given the authority, after investigation, to prescribe remedies for the offended party to the extent of being able to dictate the form and content of those remedies.

The statutory autonomy of the Commission was established in another important respect. In the making of regulations, it no longer needed the approval of the minister; and needed only to 'consult' (but not necessarily to accept the views of) the licensees. These regulations could, as previously, control the character and standards of programmes; but now they could also control their technical quality. For the first time, they could also prescribe the frequencies, call signs and output power at which the broadcasting stations could operate. The latter provision gave the regulatory body, for the first time, control of some of the technical aspect of broadcasting. [BRRA, 1986: 23.]

Two things, however, were not done. In 1972, in light of modern realities, the Telegraph Control Law which had been on the books since the early years of the century was updated and re-named the Radio and Telegraph Control Act. Its effect — there is no need for details here — was to strengthen the control of the Post and Telegraph Department over all aspects of wired and wireless communication. No change was made to this piece of legislation in 1986 (or thereafter) to take account of the proposed new powers of the Commission. The result of this has been to create and sustain confusion in the minds of present and potential broadcasters (and of some other spectrum users) as to the locus of authority in things technical; confusion was created and exists, indeed, in the minds of the regulators themselves!

The second omission, if it can be so termed, also affects the work of both regulatory agencies, and relates to resources. Both bodies are woefully understaffed, though for different reasons. The Commission began life with two administrative staff positions on its books, to establish itself, and one of those was not filled for the first two years. At that time there were four radio stations and one television station. Six years on from that, when there are now ten radio and two television stations, there have been no additions to the Commission's establishment; and, in dollar value terms, the Commission's very modest budget has been steadily pared away year by year. Much of its statutory authority, therefore, has been in abeyance since its creation due to lack of resources, and the electronic media has been quick to appreciate and exploit this fact.

The Post and Telecommunications Department, as it came to be called after 1986, operates in equally straightened circumstances. Of twelve posts on its establishment, a small number to begin with, only four are for university-level engineers, and there have not been more than three of these actually on staff for the past several years. It relies on international agencies like the International Telecommunications Union for much of its equipment. Attendance at crucial overseas planning and policy meetings is occasional, and often has to be sponsored.

Much of this deprivation is common to almost all government departments and agencies, and has been a general condition of administrative life in Jamaica — and in other developing countries — over the past decade and more. It is arguable that the adoption of 'free market' policies in these countries during these years is as much from necessity as from conviction — governments simply cannot afford pro-active governance. Other regulatory agencies, some of them established long after the Commission, have begun life with realistic staff compliments and budgets. It is reasonable to argue that telecommunications in general, and in particular broadcasting, has occupied a low place in the political concerns of successive Jamaican governments — except, of course, in relation to the reporting of government and party political activity. The result is a regulatory regime — and a government — completely unprepared for the realities which are already upon the country.

THE 1990s

Jamaicans have not been slow to adopt (and adapt, as we shall shortly note) the latest technology in satellite television. There were TVRO 'dishes' in private homes by the end of the 1970s, and the first commercial one was established for a capital city hotel in 1980 — and quickly confiscated by administrative fiat for JBC-TV. There are now probably 40,000 TVRO installations; hundreds of these, by some estimates, are *de facto* subscriber systems, varying in the number of connections from a few dozen to over four thousand in one case. The socio-economic context in which these systems operate vary from peasant/rural, through working class urban, to upper class enclave; condominiums and apartment buildings — including at least one put on the market by a government housing corporation — boast of having the appropriate wiring to connect each dwelling to a central antennae as part of their structural design.

All of this is unauthorised activity. At time of writing there is no *de jure* regime in Jamaica for licensing and regulating these systems. The operators have no legal entitlement to the programming, predominantly USA domestic cable channels, which they on-sell to their subscribers. No royalties or other fees are paid to the copyright holders of the programming. Without permission the operators routinely drape their co-axial cables on the utility poles of the power and telephone companies, ignoring warnings of prosecution from these entities; if necessary they use trees and the rooftops of non-subscribers as supports. There are reports of turf wars and cable cutting among rivals.

The government recently published 'Proposals for the introduction of subscriber (cable) television' in a Green Paper (by convention, a provisional policy document inviting comment before preparation of final proposals for the Cabinet). To this was attached a document on the subject from the Commission originally directed to the Prime Minister (who has responsibility for broadcasting) in fulfillment of their advisory responsibility. The paper sets the proposals against 'decisions taken in respect of legally liberalising further the whole media landscape'. This is a reference to the burst of activity in policy and implementation between 1988 and 1991, when seven operating licences were issued — three for regional radio, one for islandwide radio, one for islandwide television, all privately owned, and two for special interest groups, the University of the West Indies and the churches.

Significant changes in the policy framework and in conditions of licence were made to accommodate this revolutionary development. Due to the difficulty of enforcement, a veto on cross ownership — for example, a newspaper having equity in a radio station — was abandoned, although collaboration between media in news gathering and certain other activities was carefully proscribed. Total Jamaican ownership — defined as inclusive of nationals of Caribbean Community countries — was insisted upon; within that proviso formulae were set out to avoid equity control by one person or group. For the first time, public hearings were held by the Commission to determine the awardees in the case of one radio and one television islandwide licence, the government having pledged beforehand to accept the recommendation. The right of the government or the Commission to exercise prior restraint on matter to be broadcast was abolished.

Most significantly, the concept of term licences, in place since broadcasting began even with the JBC, was abandoned. Licences are now open-ended, requiring only that a licensee not be adjudged by the minister to be in breach for him to enjoy his grant unencumbered. It was thought by the Commission, at the time that they made this proposal to the government, that they would soon have the resources to actively monitor the activities and output of the stations so as to form the public interest counterweight which is the underlying motivation and rationale for regulatory activity in other societies. In the event, for reasons already mentioned, the operators are virtually unregulated. This situation of *laissez faire* in the extreme is the matrix upon which the government appears ready to lay the tangle of unauthorised subscriber systems.

TELECOMMUNICATIONS

In another channel of the convergence stream, telecommunications, an equally unregulated regime operates, with unequally empowered players posturing in their assigned roles. Ironically, a similar set of policies in the United Kingdom and Jamaica converged in their own way to bring about this situation.

The Jamaican government came out of the colonial experience with a publicly-owned external telecommunications system in which the former colonial operator, Cable & Wireless, was a minority (and largely silent) partner in the company, Jamaica International Telecommunications Limited (JAMINTEL); a technically strong and economically profitable company was built up. The local operating monopoly, which went through two changes of private ownership before ending up as almost entirely government-owned, while profitable on the books, was unable to achieve anything close to an acceptable level of service, whether in terms of reliability, phones per head of population (4.75 : 100 in 1990) or customer service.

In Britain, meanwhile, the Conservative government led by Margaret Thatcher had vigorously pursued a policy of privatisation, abolished its own monopoly in telecommunication services through British Telecom, and sold most of its stake in the company which had linked the empire, Cable & Wireless. The old warhorse has taken on a new lease on life since its manumission. One area of heightened activity has been the English-speaking Caribbean, and this was co-incident with a region-wide foreign exchange crunch among governments. In Jamaica in 1987 the decision was taken to merge the two operating companies into a single entity, the first stage of which was to establish a holding company, Telecommunications of Jamaica (TOJ). Cable & Wireless, a 49% shareholder in JAMINTEL, injected fresh capital in the new venture and was assigned 20% of the equity in TOJ. Government held the rest of the shares, with an intention to sell some to the Jamaican public but to remain, so everyone was led to believe, the majority partner in the single operating company. By 1989, the government had sold the promised 19% to the public, but it had also sold all its own shares — to Cable & Wireless, which then had 79%, its present shareholding.

In the final analysis the real disadvantages to foreign control of a national telecoms company in today's world of convergence devolve from the relative regulatory strength of the government in question. The advantages, in the economic reality of Jamaica of the mid-1990s, are several. And realistic alternatives to foreign control are, for the forseeable future, non-existent.

The advantages have not been long in showing themselves: more than 30,000 new lines installed each year of the past three, as against an average of 3,000 to 4,000 installations for several years before that; digital switches installed at all exchanges; optical fibre trunk lines in the capital city and eventually in the larger rural centres; installation of a virtually islandwide cellular network which has quickly become, as elsewhere, a boon to the serious businessperson and a chic prop to the compulsively fashionable. These improvements are part of a J$30 billion dollar development programme planned for the decade, financed by funds which, guaranteed by the Jamaican government by resolution in Parliament, could probably not have been mobilized by the pre-1987 operating companies on their own.

The disadvantages have surfaced almost as quickly as the benefits. TOJ enjoys a licensed monopoly on internal telephone service, and shares the right to external communications only with a special-purpose digiport company in which it is a minority partner, the majority equity holders being Cable & Wireless and AT&T of the United States. The licensing regime created in 1988, when a number of special licences had to be issued to accommodate the changes in structure, is for 25 years, and is automatically renewed on the same terms unless, two and one half years before the expiry of the present licence, the government gives notice of intention to acquire the company. During the currency of the licence the company will be entitled to profits, after taxes and dividends paid on preference shares, 'of not less than 17 1/2% nor more than 20%'. [All Island Telephone Licence 1988, 27.(1)] This level of profit is necessary, company apologists argue, to sustain its development programme.

The licenses are replete with references to the obligation on the company to 'co-operate with the Minister on programmes to achieve' this or that objective, which 'shall be determined by the Minister'. The ability of the Minister — not personally, as part of a structure — to assert his authority in terms meaningful to the public trust that he holds must be questioned. In a situation such as this, authority must be based on rough parity in information — quality more than quantity. The cozy relationship which existed between utility company and regulator when both were the government had undoubted drawbacks, but it also afforded the government routine access to the considerable theoretical and practical experience of the professionals within the companies. This is no longer routinely the case, precisely when that expertise is most needed.

The traditional role of the government did not require the development of high levels of expertise at the centre, and the present financial resources of the government do not allow for the employment of persons with the expertise necessary to mount a review of the company's performance of a thoroughness commensurate to such a major enterprise. There must, therefore, be an element of faith present in the new relationship between a large player on the global field and an under-resourced regulator in a tiny corner of that field.

THE NEW (DIGITAL) 'JERUSALEM'

Convergence in the technologies of broadcasting, telecommunications and the computer is bringing about another convergence, that between academic research and the boardroom. Billions of dollars have been spent, and billions more will be, in trying to apply the technology of convergence to the exigencies of everyday life. The prophesies tantalize. We are told that the humble television set, linked by optical fibre and microwave to numberless data banks and services, to each other, will become an 'information appliance'; the telephone set will be indistinguishable from a computer. Words and phrases move almost with the speed of — well, light, from dreamtalk to cliche. And for as many as pronounce the imminence of the new 'Jerusalem' of 'the interactive future', 'information superhighways', 'multimedia' and the like, there are the doubters and naysayers pointing to the 'highways of hype', as one American newspaper headlined.

For most of the people currently alive on planet earth the likely reality will lie somewhere between Jerusalem and Babel. Most of the prophesies will be realized — at some time, for some people, somewhere. A complex set of economic, social, cultural and political factors will actually determine what, when, who, and where. But the alacrity and passion with which the dream technologies of just a few years ago — personal computers, VCRs, camcorders, compact discs — have been clasped to the collective bosom of mankind should make us all thoughtful of the future which is now.

'In a digital world, the medium is no longer the message — the message is the message.' So says Nicolas Negroponte, director of the Media Laboratory at the Massachusetts Institute of Technology, a high-tech research centre dedicated to inventing the future. [Heilemann, p 5]. The differences between media, with which we began this discussion, are already beginning to blur. If analysts like Negroponte are correct in their estimation of where technology is taking us, those differences will, for most practical purposes, disappear. Apparently, the message of the future is 'bits', the smallest unit (at present) of electronic information. The evening news (on radio and television), video games, shopping arcades, a best selling book, 'Lawrence of Arabia', money transfers, Bob Marley's 'Redemption Song': all will become compressed, digitalized bits on the 'highways of glass' which academics like Negroponte and businessmen like Ray Smith, president of Bell Atlantic, a large U.S. telecoms company, expect to carry the bulk of our intellectual stimulation, entertainment and, eventually, workplace output in the new century of unimaginable service choices.

In Jamaica, the coincidence in timing between the spectacular growth of an un-authorized subscriber television system, changes in the ownership structure of TOJ, and the company's ambitious development programme, bring the issues of the future to a present and urgent reality. The actions (or lack of) of the government in the short term will have a considerable influence on the shape of future reality.

The history of the past forty years, since broadcasting began in earnest, does not give comfort to the impatient heart. The legislation governing broadcasting and telecommunications does not reflect the changes in technology and governmental precept that have taken place over the past several decades; the Telephone Act still in force, under which TOJ was granted its licences, dates from 1893! A new Telecommunications Act is in the final stages of drafting and should be tabled in Parliament during 1994. However that act deals only with telecommunications services. Use of equipment and services like citizen's band and amateur radio, will still be regulated by the Post and Telecommunications Department under the (1972) Radio and Telegraph Control Act — still so named though TOJ has had a licence to operate the island's telegraphic service since the mid-1980s. No attempt was made to consult broadcasters or the Commission in developing the new Telecommunications Act; only notional attempts have been made, (except by the Commission itself), to address the archaic provisions of the Broadcasting and Radio Rediffusion Act, most of which date from 1962. The Commission has taken, as its central policy assumption, the creation of a single body with extensive authority to regulate (including the issuing of licences for) *all* aspects of telecommunications, except consumer-user rates. It appears to be the only governmental body to adopt that position.

In the event, the *status quo* must prevail. Proposals made for the creation of a proper subscriber television system are predicated, of necessity, on the availability of resources far greater than experience gives any basis for expecting. Given those resources, the job of regulation could begin, based on somewhat of a sleight-of-hand interpretation of the law which would shoe-horn modern systems into a 1962 definition of closed-circuit television which speaks of 'pictures, images and sounds' being transmitted 'over a wired network' (emphasis mine). [BRRA, 1962. Clause 2] A further assumption must be that new legislation will be in place when what is termed 'wireless cable' comes (legally) to Jamaica; there isn't a lot of time.

In the still new era of liberalization, two (contradictory?) issues should be addressed. Convergence is creating a technology of liberation. The question is liberation for whom? With or without the authority of the government — or the permission of TOJ — Jamaicans who see profit or enjoyment in the new digital technology will manipulate the system (or lack of it) and exploit the technology. True democratization of media, with anarchic potential, is becoming possible. Those who can afford it will be offered choices beyond their needs for entertainment. Properly utilized, digital technology will give them opportunities in education, business and commerce which may further enrich and empower them.

What about the entertainment needs of those who can't afford digital access, and the broader needs of the society which telecommunications can help to address: rural development, manufacturing, education, delivery of health care, among others. One thinks of the colonial requirement for radio stations to run wires to and install radios in schools, and wonders if the government — any government, in other countries also — has the *cojones* to insist that schools and colleges be wired and programming made for them, as a condition for enjoying the right to entertain, inform and make money.

The traffic in bits can transcend trade — in entertainment, information, whatever — and become part of the definition of a society. However, to achieve that would require a greater awareness of the importance of telecommunications, at the level where policy is made and implemented, than is exhibited at the moment in Jamaica, and indeed in many other countries.

NOTES

1. It would be impossible to accomplish after all this time, but in the same way that dozens of research projects are no doubt currently underway studying the effect of the electronic media on the collapse of the Soviet empire and its aftermath, it would be fascinating to have a study of the effect of radio on the colonial retreat from empire that characterized the 1950s and 1960s.
2. In 1977 all the shares in Radio Jamaica — majority owned by the Rediffusion Group in the U.K., with local minority shareholding — passed to the government. In 1979, 74.9% of the shares were divested to 'people-based' organizations, and the staff; but the 25.1% which government retained effectively blocked any change in structure or function.
3. Intelligently, the Broadcasting Commissioners appointed the Chief Telecommunications Engineer, who heads what is now the Post & Telecommunications Department, as Technical Advisor to the Commission.
4. There are stories for the accuracy of which many Jamaicans will vouch, of persons in separate rural locations communicating timely information through intermediaries in North American and European cities, because of the impossibility of contacting each other directly.
5. Source: *The World Best Book 1991*, published annually for the United States government by the Central Intelligence Agency.
6. This is a complex issue of economics and politics which still occasionally surfaces in public discussion. Some protagonists of the 'nationalist' position argue that with the inherent profitability of efficiently run monopolies, adequate financing could have been raised perhaps from the World Bank or from a mixture of such agencies, and the expertise needed for implementation hired for specific

tasks, leaving Jamaicans, by definition more responsive to Jamaican needs, in control. Quite apart from the changes which will forever make this argument moot, the fact is that very little expansion of any sort took place, especially in local services in the decades when the operating companies were under national ownership and control.

REFERENCES

AGREEMENT between the Colonial Secretary of Jamaica and Jamaica Broadcasting Company Limited, November 12, 1949.

Commercial Broadcasting (Jamaica Broadcasting Company Limited) Licence, 1949.

The Commercial Broadcasting and Radio Rediffusion Law, 1949.

The Broadcasting and Radio Rediffusion Act 1959, 1962, 1986.

The Radio and Telegraph Control Act 1972.

Commercial Broadcasting Licence, Broadcasting Rules, 1949.

The Sound Broadcasting and Radio Rediffusion Regulations, 1962.

The Television Broadcasting and Radio Rediffusion Regulations, 1962.

The Television and Sound Broadcasting Regulations, 1991.

MINISTRY PAPER No. 5, 1959: Broadcasting: Proposals for Establishment of a Public Broadcasting Corporation and for the Extension of a Licence Held by the Jamaica Broadcasting Company Limited.

John Heilemann, *Feeling for the Future: A Survey of Television*, The Economist, February 12, 1994.

FURTHER READING (Recommended)

Newsweek, *Wiring The World*, April 5, 1993, pp. 26-33.

The Economist, *MULTIMEDIA* — The Tangled Webs they Weave, October 16, 1993.

C. Wishnu Mohan and John Vogler: *Sharing the Spectrum in the Digital Age - WARCF-92*, International Institute of Communications (London), Freidrich-Ebert-Stiftung (Germany), London 1991.

Roger E. Fidler: *'Mediamorphosis' Heralds the Digital Newspaper*, Intermedia, Volume 20/No. 6, Nov-Dec. 1992.

James D. Halloran: *'What We Urgently Require is a Globalization of Moral Responsibility'*, Intermedia, Volume 21/No. 2, March-April, 1993.

Shehina Fazal: *Consumer-driven TV and the Re-definition of 'Public Service'*, Intermedia, Volume 21/No. 4-5, Aug-Sept. 1993.

Martin Mordecai: *Regulating Broadcasting in Jamaica in the 1990s*, COMBROAD (Journal of the Commonwealth Broadcasting Association) No. 92, July-September 1991.

12

COMMUNICATIONS ETHICS AND THE NEW GLOBAL ORDER

Dr Pradip N. Thomas

INTRODUCTION

Ethical standards evolve out of a tryst with tradition. Never conceived in a vacuum, such norms are invariably bounded by a civilisation's dominant imperatives, be they of a social, economic or political kind. Any attempt to evolve a coherent framework for communication ethics must necessarily spring from or at least relate to existing ethical frameworks that provide the tacit ground-rules for interpersonal, intraregional and international relationships in any given society.

It is not at all surprising, therefore, that some of the central tenets of Western civilisation may be traced back to Greek metaphysics and to the philosophical traditions associated with Plato and Aristotle. Similar foundations are the basis for Eastern ways of living and dealing with contemporary reality. The Vedic-Upanishadic, Buddhist, Confucian and Taoist philosophies of life are living traditions that continue to shed light on contemporary problems in the East, be they of a technological, political, economic or social kind. The 'technological apparatus' of an age does as well reflect 'ethical' choices, priorities and values based on a vision of progress. Progress, however, is never unidirectional. Both correspondences and non-correspondences are a fact of life.

ETHICS IN AN INFORMATION AGE

Ethics, unlike 'law', consists of a received as well as cultivated corpus of normative ideals that govern human relationships and that animate 'root-metaphors' in any given society. Taken in this sense, ethical thinking stems from a learning process. Law, unlike ethics, usually refers to a tradition or state-sanctioned body of rules and regulations that govern the basis for contractual rights and obligations.

Ethical standards in any given society tend to reflect as well as complement the dominant discourse of knowledge. By that is meant both the content of knowledge as well as the rules and values that govern knowledge-generation. For instance, in contemporary society, efficiency, productivity and marketability are the dominant values that underpin knowledge-generation, and the content of knowledge is judged according to its easy translatability into a digital bit-stream. In an era dominated by the politics of globalisation, privatisation and deregulation and which is characterised by rampant forms of consumerism, instrumental rationality has become a pre-eminent value, the means-end of life. This situation stands in stark contrast to the still-existing but less-dominant traditions of knowledge that are based on value systems that privilege mutuality and the making of community. The closely intertwined relationship between information technology and contemporary ethics reflects, as Steurman (1988, pp. 57-58) has observed,

> '...the status of knowledge in contemporary society. This change has been brought about mainly by the impact of technology and information technology in knowledge research and knowledge transmission. Knowledge is no longer associated with **Bildung**, with "the formation of spirits". Rather, knowledge has become technically useful knowledge. The criterion of technically useful knowledge is its efficiency and translatability into information (computer) knowledge. Therefore the questions: "Is it true?", "Is it just?", "Is it morally important?" become reduced to: "Is it efficient?", "Is it marketable?", "Is it sellable?", "Is it translatable into informational quantities?'

Historically, ethical systems have kept pace with the 'normative' needs of evolving societies. Increasing complexity in economic and societal structures have given rise to both new interpretations of old norms as well as to the universalisation of certain fundamental norms, particularly as they apply to the questions of truth in the context of rights, peace and justice. This is as well the case with communication ethics. For example, in former times as well as in some societies today characterised by oral, face-to-face means of communication, the norms of interpersonal communications were/are subsumed under a more general ethical framework that gave/gives due place to hierarchy and authority. In caste-based societies, for instance, the rules that govern both inter-caste as well as intra-caste communications are elaborately defined and are the basis for both ritual and daily interaction. Also, experiential forms of communication that are relatively self-contained as in the case of indigenous peoples, are inscribed within a framework of norms, circumscribed by a local-specific ethos.

A HISTORICAL PERSPECTIVE

The advent of printing technology enabled, for the first time, the mass production of books and the dissemination of knowledge through 'tangible' means. Initially, though, books were monopolised by religious orders and ordinary people were proscribed from any form of learning. The power of book-based knowledge was jealously guarded until the Reformation and the first stirrings of liberal thought in the 17th Century. To a large extent, the press played an important role in disseminating the ideals of democracy. Freedom struggles in both the West as well as anti-colonial struggles in the South were built on the mass platform provided by the press and the ideals that they helped disseminate. Habermas (1989) has suggested that the rise of the public sphere in the West was to a large measure due to the growth of a press-fed reading public.

The power of the free press soon became apparent to governments. Both in the metropolitan centres as well as in the colonies, new laws were enacted to curtail the publication of 'scurrilous' prose, 'seditious' material or tracts that preached 'revolution', advocated local-rule or encouraged parochial moralities. This tradition of curbing the power of the press is as manifest today as it was at any other time. Before the advent of the mass press in the early years of this century, ethical considerations were not a given that affected the ground rules of journalism. However, with the recognition of the power of journalism to mould and sway public opinion, there arose attempts to define the ethical parameters of journalism as a discourse. Truth and responsibility became the twin principles of journalism ethics, and to this was added the principle of the free flow of information as enshrined in the First Amendment of the US Constitution.

With the development of cinema and broadcasting — two powerful means of mass communication — ethical frameworks were established to protect the public interest. The increasing sophistication of mass communication led to the formulation of codes of professional media ethics, and to the teaching of journalism ethics. Legal statutes on media responsibility were made public. However, given the overarching influence of market rationality, within a bureaucratised State, the values of pragmatism and instrumentalism prevailed, and ethical standards have been consistently breached by media owners and practitioners. Clifford Christian (1977, p. 22), in an analysis of the teaching of media ethics in the USA, has this to say on the state of the art: '*Objectivity has not achieved full status as an ethical standard, while social responsibility remains ethically inchoate and undeveloped'* (author's emphasise).

The role played by UNESCO in creating a platform for the advocacy of a universal ethics of communications based on reciprocity, cultural sovereignty and truth-building, considerably advanced the agenda of a universal ethic of communication. In spite of the demise of the UNESCO-inspired movement towards the democratisation of the world's communication structures, its residual impact has influenced the development of a multitude of fora, alternative media programmes and media democracy initiatives, particularly in the developing world.

ETHICS AND TECHNOLOGICAL CONVERGENCE

This relatively discrete approach to dealing with communications ethics was sufficient in so far as the existing technologies of mass communication were function-specific. There were clear boundaries and parameters of operations, say, between the telegraph and telephone systems that were in the business of transmission; press and broadcasting — in media production; and computers in the business of information manipulation. With the emergence of synergistic systems, the convergence of computers and telecommunications, creative integration of multimedia technologies, and sophisticated networks such as ISDN (integrated services digital network) that are capable of transmitting both voice and text, image and data in a digital bit-stream, once clear boundaries have become blurred. Functions have become indistinguishable, as interdependence and interconnectivity have become the norm. Information processes today are the life-blood of the service economy, with information fast becoming the dominant episteme of life. As a process, it is geared towards the ends of productivity, efficiency, order and analysis. Its use is pervasive in manufacturing, management, leisure, production, in banking and trade, in the sciences and arts. In fact, one could say that information generation and processing are the dominant processes today, as were the innovations of steam and electricity in earlier eras.

The steady effacement of distinctions between technology, product and process is a characteristic of information in today's society. The ill-starred merger which was attempted in the United States between Bell Atlantic and Tele-Communications Inc., for example, held out the prospect, institutionally, of a convergence of switching technology, computers and the co-axial cable. The venture would have enabled, on a large scale, the transmission of digitalised video, audio and data information to homes, offices, businesses and mobile telephones. Mega-mergers of this kind are the order of the day, as transnational

IT companies as well as national Public Telecommunications Operations (PTOs) gravitate towards controlling a share of future 'communicopias'. Digital technology, for example, allows photographs to be digitally mastered, hence bypassing the traditional space of the press photographer, his/her immediate working environment, i.e., the dark room as well as his/her autonomy and 'traditional' control over the representation of the image. Geoffrey Craig (1993, p. 2) has observed that new technology has not only made it possible for control to shift from the photographer to the picture-editors, but that it

> '...now makes possible to enhance and change the colour of photographs, dissect and rearrange elements within the image, produce or clone elements within the photograph, introduce elements from other photographs, and ultimately with electronic still cameras create photographic images without an original negative.'

Given this situation, the casual reader will increasingly not be able to discriminate between the source of the image or for that matter between image and reality. A situation similar to that of the ordinary television viewer who has no idea of the source of programmes — cable based?, micro-wave-based?, satellite-based? This multitude of sources is difficult to unravel and even more difficult to police. When entertainment, trade, financial transfers and businesses are transmitted/carried out/conducted along electronic highways, we do need an ethical framework that can respond to the challenges posed by information as the primary logic underlying life and work today.

CONTEXT AND OTHER UNACKNOWLEDGED REALITIES OF THE INFORMATION REVOLUTION

It would not be too far from the truth to assume that we live in a historical era characterised by the shifting standards of provisional ethics. The West believes implicitly in the doctrine of the 'free flow of information' but as the controlled media reportage of the Gulf War suggests, this standard is contextually defined. The implications for the developing world of the inclusion of trade in services, trade-related investment as well as matters related to intellectual property rights — in the 1994 GATT treaty — are quite serious. This development is yet another example of the doctrine of the 'free flow' being used to further the power of the industrialised countries, particularly the USA vis-a-vis the developing world. This fragmented, at times tenuous, ordering of rules is reflected in the state of society today, characterised by ebbs and flows, disjunctures as well as discontinuities. The interrogation of received/inherited forms of knowledge, the rise in new, local-specific emancipatory discourses, the emergence of the politics of identity, often expressed through movements for nationalism, the politics of fundamentalism and revivalism as well as regional and linguistic autonomy, are some of the more obvious, visible aspects of a crisis that has affected the status of global and national politics. Underlying this condition is 'information' as the determinant social logic, a dominant constitutive 'knowledge' incorporating all other forms of knowledge and discourses in its image.

The symbiotic relationship between technology and society is expressed in/through the social logic of information. Frederic Jameson (1991, p. 48) links, in no uncertain terms, this dominant 'cultural' logic to the interests of multinational capitalism. He states the need for a new cognitive map for both social theory and politics so that people may be equipped to understand and so come to collective decisions with respect to curtailing the power of information in the interests of the social. There is, as he notes, a need to proactively understand this '... prodigious expansion of culture throughout the social realm' and to realise its influence on 'social life ... economic value and state power to practices and to the very structure of the psyche itself.' An ethical framework for information would, therefore, be contingent on a reasoned, comprehensive understanding of the nature of this paradigm shift.

One way to begin this exercise would be to start from a position that recognises the dual nature of technology in its relationship to society. It is often the case that technology is theorised as a discrete entity, as an object with specific dimensions and functions and/or as a tool or machine. This type of interpretation is essentially limited, for no technology is the result of a dispassionate exercise in invention, design or manufacturing. Values are in-built in technology, and as such, technology is a form of knowledge that incorporates thought processes oriented towards its production, its use, its relationship with other objects, systems, processes and values. However, the crucial distinction between 'information' technology and other technologies is that its product has 'exchange', symbolic', as well as 'constitutive' value in modern society. Its 'dual' existence as a symbolic commodity has hitherto unresolved implications with respect to its regulation. Yet there are other distinctions as well — its tangible and intangible nature, its somewhat ethereal manifestation through time and space, and its primary constitution as a process make it a unique, multi-dimensional, multi-functional entity.

While the positive applications of IT are patently obvious today in a wide variety of fields, perhaps this very obviousness disallows a rational interrogation of its social logic, particularly with respect to the universal claims of its benefits — for example, increased customer choice, diversity, 'access' and 'participation'. Information-based growth is, as the cliche claims, the 'engine of the global economy', yet growth for whom, is a question that is rarely posed, let alone answered. In fact, given capitalism's economic basis in a production-consumption logic, new technologies are strategically suited to maximising this system through applications that allow rationality, efficiency, management and order. Marike Finlay (1987, p. 55), in a powerful critique of new technologies, makes the point that their development and use are conditioned by the needs of social context. As Finlay observes,

> The social context conditions what technology becomes, including its structures and values. The social context is oriented towards the protection of private property, the division of labour, competitiveness, the need for surveillance and testing which are the social conditions of possibility of the way that new communications technology will be conceived, designed, structured, built and used.

When that context is late capitalism, characterised by the politics of globalisation, privatisation, concentration and deregulation, the retreat of the State and the triumph of transnational capital, the changes for the equitable uses of new technologies is essentially limited. Its primary use in rationalising efficiency and maximising growth has enabled new technologies to becoming allies of global entrepreneurs in the pursuit of profits at the expense of labour, cultural and economic sovereignty and equitable growth. Given the power that transnational information corporations already exert, deregulation has merely allowed a number of large corporations, both transnational as well as regional, to take advantage of their already powerful position in the market, and thus reap cumulative advantages. (Murdock, 1990).

In fact, one could reasonably assume that the cumulative advantages of information technology have been enjoyed by a small coterie of privileged sectors consisting of the corporate enterprise, the government, and the upper-income bracket in countries around the world. While 'choice' and 'equal access' have been touted as the 'human face' of new technologies, in reality their diffusion has followed predictable patterns. Murdock and Golding (1986), in a study of the diffusion of new technologies in the UK have observed the 'current trends' towards 'a thriving electronic marketplace in which prevailing patterns of consumer detriment — the compounded disadvantages of low-income groups — are being replicated as new communication and information services come on stream'. William Melody (1990, p. 17), in an essay on communications policy, has noted, with some regret, the trend in US public libraries towards the creation of various data bases at the expense of investments towards increasing physical holdings. This has meant that access is limited to those who can afford to pay for 'computer-searches'. Both examples seem to suggest that the rhetoric that 'surrounds' the uses of information technology does not always tally with the reality of today's 'pay per' society. Information as power has led to privatisation of information, accessible to 'closed-use groups' who are privileged by their status, knowledge of computer codes and control of the networking system.

KNOWLEDGE IN THE AGE OF INFORMATION

Information technology as knowledge is qualitatively different from pre-existing social discourses that promoted knowledge generation as a conscious human activity. The logic of 'information' is built into specialised languages, the knowledge of which allows for data manipulation as well as its transmission. Artificial intelligence has increasingly made its presence felt in manufacturing, production, design, and its impact has begun to affect human life processes as well. The use of information technology is predicated on the working knowledge of abstract analytical skills that highlight the imagination rather than non-mental labour. The much-hyped notion of 'interaction' that is celebrated as the basis of emerging technologies, veils the technology-circumscribed nature of this encounter. Unlike human interactivity that leads to understandings framed by emotions and feelings, technological meditation involve abstract processes at the expense of the 'social'. John Hinkson (1990, p. 89) has referred to the emergence of what he has called 'extended social relationships' borne out of this human technology interaction, i.e., 'social relations extended by a technical medium' as typifying the nature of the 'social' in this era. Tim Druckrey's (1991, p. 26) salient warning of the consequences of ignoring developments in the world of information points to the need for a proactive, ethical framework.

> If the consciousness of the future is to be rooted in technology, a serious evaluation of its effects must take place. The challenge will be to evolve an ethic capable of adapting to the profound effects of technoculture. More than an ethical issue, the effects of technology will shape the whole category of the future. The stakes are not in the computerisation of culture but the computerisation of the model of consciousness itself .... How we know, in what form we know will become as essential to thought as what we know.

The challenge for 'information' ethicists will be to evolve a normative framework that keeps the constitutive power of information in check.

New technologies have become this generation's philosophy and reason for progress. Such is its influence and so pervasive its spread that very few attempts have been made to grapple with the multifarious implications of this model for societal and human growth. In fact, given its obvious applications, the 'power' of this technology has rarely been critiqued, let alone contested. Perhaps this is because the 'invisible' nature of information flows is difficult to comprehend. As an intangible entity that has a space-based rather than place-based logic, it is difficult to deal with the real issues that it has generated, i.e., disemployment, use of IT for surveillance, invasion of privacy, transborder data flows, and its impact on economic and cultural sovereignty. Manuel Castells (1989, p. 349) has brought to our attention the invisible nature of these flows and the inability of governments to control diffuse flows of data. Power over space has enabled transnational companies to bypass statutory restrictions related to place-bound realities. The separation of 'space' and 'place' that has been achieved through the use of information technologies has resulted in the growth of 'two disjointed spheres of the human experience. People live in places, power rules through flow'.

TOWARDS A PUBLIC INFORMATION ETHIC

Information technologies have been crucial to the growth of the global economy. Yet their full benefits have been employed by relatively exclusive groups. The vast majority of people have been excluded by the social logic of these technologies. It is the marginalised, social movements, grassroot groups, Non-Government Organizations (NGOs), trade unions and public bodies that have the responsibility to frame 'ethical' standards and to advocate the use of a technology that is controlled by people. Global fora such as the United Nations, let alone other bodies like GATT, IMF and the World Bank, cannot be expected to take a lead in formulating a world-wide movement for the ethical uses of information technology. Local governments, hamstrung by internal problems, their subordinate position in the global economy, and preoccupied by growth-related concerns, will similarly be reticent at embarking on an exercise of this nature. Local forms of democracy make a lot more sense than national forms that tend to be exclusivist on so many counts and incapable of dealing with the problems of the disadvantaged sectors of society.

In former times, any universally applicable 'ethic' was defined by standards that were patently European in origin. This is no longer the case today. For it is widely accepted that an understanding of a 'universal' ethic needs to be built on a dialogue with locally-inflected 'particulars'. In other words, as in the Caribbean or elsewhere, the framing of an ethics of information must necessarily stem from needs that are autonomously defined. There will, of course, be general correspondences and common links between local-specific understandings and universal standards, but there will be disjunctures and discontinuities as well, that evolve from a 'different rationality', non-occidental epistemologies and processes of representation. A new order of ethics will be established only if this balance is maintained as a matter of course.

The dominant discourse on 'information' assigns it a non-problematic, indeed determining value as a commodity, data or idea. More information is deemed to be a good thing and a natural end-state. However, such understandings rarely grapple with related issues such as 'control' or 'access' and quite often are framed within a rhetoric of globalisation that gives insufficient space to local-specific differentials. For instance, in the developing world, interpersonal communication is conditioned by values that promote tradition, family or community over and above the individual. The concept of information as a product or as a general item of consumption, divorced from other 'tradition'-based requirements, is alien to understandings in many parts of the developing world. However, the logic associated with the modern information environment poses a tremendous challenge to other ways of understanding communication that are based on different normative standards. While to some extent creative adaptation between the 'local' and the 'global' will be a means to avoid information 'anomie', the pressures exerted by the social logic of information in the developing world tends invariably to be immediate. Given the skewed nature of international economic relationships, most countries in the developing world are not able to negotiate the nature and pace of information-led change. For example, the advent of 'automation' and 'flexible' manufacturing processes in South Asia has led to drastic decreases in the workforce employed at both factories and open sites. The social logic of information guarantees 'productivity' and 'efficiency', but its diffuse nature disallows a 'contestation' of its 'essentials'. This places the ordinary non-unionised worker at a disadvantage for it has become increasingly difficult to comprehend the nature of information processes within the overall economy, let alone its mediation of power or its inter-linkages with other information-based discourses.

An 'ethical' standard for 'information' must evolve from a consideration of the various points of interface between the individual, the State and the global community that are essential parts of the information continuum. Given the fact that the 'individual' is a primary focus for 'information flows', any ethics of information must give adequate consideration to this fundamental reality, but from within an understanding that privileges the average citizen in community.

This 'ethical' standard, however, needs to be based on fundamentals that are 'different' to those advocated by communication ethicists today. Clifford Christians (1989), for example, proposes that what is needed today is a commitment to a universal normative ethic in which truth-building is an absolute minimum. Antonio Pasquali (1992), in a discussion on the proto-norms of communication ethics has, following Habermas, affirmed the need for new morals of inter-subjectivity as the basis for communication ethics. Both truth-building and inter-subjectivity are normative standards that can be applied to an evaluative assessment of communication as 'representation' or 'mediation'. However, in an information context characterised by multifunctionality, multidimensional flows, virtual reality and technology-based relationships, their standards for evaluation must be located within understandings that emphasise 'diversity', 'movement' and 'non-dualistic' values. An information ethic must ultimately be based on a practical programme that will ensure

a) an information logic that is contextually grounded in the needs of local culture, religion, ways of life and development priorities;

b) an indigenous, people-based regulatory system for helping to determine how the new technologies are applied;

c) a proactive strategy to deal with information use, information misuse and issues related to 'access' and control' that is local in origin; and

d) forms of interactivity that ensure that information iswards what James Carey (1989, p. 11) terms '... the maintenance of society in time, not the act of imparting information but the representation of shared belief.'

An exercise in ethics-building that evolves from the bottom upwards will be able to contest the power of information as 'surveillance', the invasion of privacy, bureaucracy and control over resource allocation exerted by corporate entities and local or national governments. Ultimately, the exercise of information as power affects people at a local level. Rather than 'ethical standards' evolving from the top downwards, which is the accepted way of doing things, a process that privileges the 'local' rather than the 'national' or the quasi-governmental will allow for a realistic, pragmatic basis for negotiating control. Such a framing of 'ethical standards' can be fed into 'national reasonings' on information ethics. Admittedly, there will be a host of particularities and perhaps even discontinuities. However, there will also be common understandings, reciprocal concerns and solidarities on fundamental ethical questions, thus laying the basis for a nation-wide or regional information ethic. Moreover, such an exercise will allow the State to frame standards on equally important issues — transborder data flows, global surveillance, valuation of data, regulation of satellite-based direct broadcast, access to corporate data bases, compatibility of standards and technological equipment, the configuration of computer networks, the right to frequencies, geostationary orbit allocations, support for local research and development in information technology, and democratic policies with respect to 'automation' and 'cybernetics'.

An ethical framework for 'information' needs to start from the recognition that 'information' cannot be treated in isolation from its embeddedness in a total system of relations. This consists of technologies, laws, patents, philosophies, economics, values and ideas. Such an understanding will enable ordinary people to make a link between ideas and technology on the one hand, and the environment of power and control on the other. It will also help expose the myth that attributes the persistence of inequality to 'fate' rather than to domination of a 'technological apparatus'. Such an understanding, as Antonio Faundez (1989, p. 29) has observed, will help correct dominant interpretations that '... explain the discrepancy between ideas and reality', of 'why concepts and concrete reality fail to coincide', and of 'people's failure to understand and change historical reality', by 'maintaining that it is reality that is wrong and not our ideas or system of ideas'.

NOTES

1. The term 'root-metaphor' as used by the cognitive anthropologist, Victor Turner, refers to the key symbolic images used to describe structures and systems of thought in any given society. Root-metaphors are foundational and dynamic, and are the very essence of a society's self-understanding and orientation. Root-metaphors reflect a society's normative standards.
2. In the rapidly expanding vocabulary of 'tech-talk', the convergence of the phone, media and computer industries in one expansive multi-media sector is called 'communicopia'.

REFERENCES

1. Steurman, E, 'Haberman vs Lyotard: Modernity vs Post-Modernity' (pp. 51-66), *New Formations*, No. 7, Spring 1988.
2. Christians, C, 'Fifty Years of Scholarship in Media Ethics' (pp. 19-29), *Journal of Communication*, Vol. 27, No. 4, Autumn 1977.
3. Craig, G, 'Press Photography, Pixel Technology and Questions of Representation' (pp. 1-8), Paper presented at the Australian Communication Association Conference, Melbourne, July 1993.
4. Jameson, F, 'Post-Modernity or the Cultural Logic of Late Capitalism', *Verso*, UK, 1991.
5. Finlay, M, 'Powermatics: A Discursive Critique of New Technology', Routledge and Kegan Paul, London and New York, 1987.
6. Murdock, G, 'Redrawing the Map of the Communications Industries: Concentration and Ownership in the Era of Privatisation' (pp. 1-11), in Ferguson, M (ed), 'Public Communication: The New Imperatives' Future Directions in Media Research', Sage, London, 1990.
7. Golding, P and Murdock, G, 'Unequal Information Access and Exclusion in the New Communications Marketplace' (pp.71-83), in Ferguson, M (ed), 'New Communication Technologies and the Public Interest - Comparative Perspectives on Policy and Research', Sage, London, 1986.
8. Melody, H, 'Communication Policy in the Global Information Economy: Whither the Public Interest' (pp.16-39), in Ferguson, M (ed), *op. cit.*, 1990.
9. Hinkson, J, 'Postmodernism and Structural Change'(pp. 87-101), *Public Culture*, Vol. 2, No. 21, Spring 1990.
10. Druckrey, T, 'Deadly Representation or Apocalypse Now' (pp.16-27), *Ten*. 8, Vol..2, No.2, Autumn 1991.
11. Castells, J, 'The Information City: The Space of Flows', Basil Blackwell, Oxford/Massachusetts, 1989.
12. Cooper, T. W, Christians, C. G, Plude, F.F, and White, R.A, 'Communication Ethics and Global Change', Longman Inc,New York, 1989.
13. Pasquali, A, Working Paper for the Meeting on Protonorms of Communication Ethics from a Latin American Perspective, Sao Paulo, Brazil, 22 August, 1992.
14. Carey,J.W, 'Communications and Culture: Essays on Media and Society', Unwin Hyman, Boston, 1989.
15. Faundez, A, 'Paulo Freire: Learning to Question: A Pedagogy for Liberation', WCC Publications, Geneva, 1989.
16. Habermas, J, 'The Structural Transformation of the Public Sphere: An Inquiry into a Category of Bourgeois Society', The MIT Press, Cambridge, MA, 1989.

NOTES ON CONTRIBUTORS

Aggrey Brown is Professor of Communication and Director of the Caribbean Institute of Mass Communication (CARIMAC) at the University of the West Indies. He received his doctoral degree in political science from Princeton University. Prof. Brown is the author of several studies on Caribbean media and communication issues.

Hilary D.P. Brown is a communications researcher and lecturer (part-time) in Research Methods at CARIMAC, University of the West Indies, where she completed undergraduate studies in Mass Communication with Social Sciences. Her Masters Degree in Communication Studies was done at the University of Michigan. She is now in the final stages of her doctoral studies at Temple University, Philadelphia.

Hopeton S. Dunn is communications analyst and Lecturer at the Caribbean Institute of Mass Communication (CARIMAC), University of the West Indies. A Carreras Scholar and First Class Honours graduate of the UWI, he holds Masters and PhD degrees in Communications Policy from City University, London. He is currently President of the Caribbean Association for Communication Research (CACR).

Cheryl Renee Gooch is Chair of the Department of Communications Media at Alabama State University, USA. She completed undergraduate studies in political science at Howard University and her doctorate in Mass Communication from Florida State University. Her research interests in international and development communication resulted in research and study attachments at the University of Ibadan in Nigeria, and fieldwork in Barbados.

Dorith Grant-Wisdom is a Caribbean economist specializing in issues of global trade in services. She completed undergraduate studies and a diploma in Public Administration at the University of the West Indies and earned her masters and doctoral degrees from Howard University in the United States. She is currently an Adjunct Professor in the Department of Government and Politics at the University of Maryland.

Lynette M. Lashley is Associate Professor of journalism and mass communication at Creighton University, Nebraska, USA. A national of Trinidad and Tobago, Dr Lashley has maintained a keen interest in Caribbean research themes, making frequent research visits to the region. She is a graduate of the University of Wisconsin, and her current research interests include international information flow.

Robert Martin is Professor of Law and Journalism at the University of Western Ontario in Canada. He is also the Secretary-Treasurer of the Commonwealth Association for Education in Journalism and Communication (CAEJC). He specialises in international communication issues and is the author of numerous papers and publications in the areas of international law and communication.

Martin Mordecai is a communications consultant and publisher. He was the Executive Director of the Broadcasting Commission in Jamaica between 1988 and 1993. He is a former Director of Information in the Jamaican Ministry of Foreign Affairs and has held senior diplomatic postings in Washington and Port of Spain. He was also Deputy Permanent Secretary in the Office of the Prime Minister, Jamaica.

Beverley Mullings is a doctoral candidate in the Department of Geography at McGill University, Canada. She is a graduate of the University of the West Indies and received her Masters Degree from the London School of Economics. She has worked as a research fellow at the Open University in the United Kingdom.

Felipe Noguera is a specialist in telecommunications network planning and administration. He is the Secretary General of the Caribbean Association for National Telecommunications Organizations (CANTO), based in Port of Spain, Trinidad. Mr Noguera is also a part-time lecturer in the School of Continuing Studies of the University of the West Indies, St Augustine Campus in Trinidad.

Pradip N. Thomas is Coordinator of Studies and Publications at the World Association for Christian Communication (WACC) in London. He completed his doctoral studies at the Centre for Mass Communication Research, University of Leicester in the U.K. Before joining WACC, he was an Associate Professor in the Department of Communication, Tamilnadu Theological Seminary at Madurai in India.